Nonideal Theory and Content Externalism

Studies in Feminist Philosophy is designed to showcase cutting-edge monographs and collections that display the full range of feminist approaches to philosophy, that push feminist thought in important new directions, and that display the outstanding quality of feminist philosophical thought.

STUDIES IN FEMINIST PHILOSOPHY

Linda Martín Alcoff, Hunter College and the CUNY Graduate Center

Elizabeth Barnes, University of Virginia

Lorraine Code, York University, Toronto

Penelope Deutscher, Northwestern University

Ann Garry, California State University, Los Angeles

Sally Haslanger, Massachusetts Institute of Technology

Alison Jaggar, University of Colorado, Boulder

Serene Khader, Brooklyn College and CUNY Graduate Center

Helen Longino, Stanford University

Catriona Mackenzie, Macquarie University

Mari Mikkola, Humboldt University, Berlin

Sally Scholz, Villanova University

Laurie Shrage, Florida International University

Lisa Tessman, Binghamton University

Nancy Tuana, Pennsylvania State University

Published in the Series:

Ecological Thinking: The Politics of Epistemic Location
Lorraine Code

Self Transformations: Foucault, Ethics, and Normalized Bodies
Cressida J. Heyes

Family Bonds: Genealogies of Race and Gender
Ellen K. Feder

Moral Understandings: A Feminist Study in Ethics, Second Edition
Margaret Urban Walker

The Moral Skeptic
Anita M. Superson

"You've Changed": Sex Reassignment and Personal Identity
Edited by Laurie J. Shrage

Dancing with Iris: The Philosophy of Iris Marion Young
Edited by Ann Ferguson and Mechthild Nagel

Philosophy of Science after Feminism
Janet A. Kourany

Shifting Ground: Knowledge and Reality, Transgression and Trustworthiness
Naomi Scheman

The Metaphysics of Gender
Charlotte Witt

Unpopular Privacy: What Must We Hide?
Anita L. Allen

Adaptive Preferences and Women's Empowerment
Serene Khader

Minimizing Marriage: Marriage, Morality, and the Law
Elizabeth Brake

Out from the Shadows: Analytic Feminist Contributions to Traditional Philosophy
Edited by Sharon L. Crasnow and Anita M. Superson

The Epistemology of Resistance: Gender and Racial Oppression, Epistemic Injustice, and Resistant Imaginations
José Medina

Simone de Beauvoir and the Politics of Ambiguity
Sonia Kruks

Identities and Freedom: Feminist Theory between Power and Connection
Allison Weir

Vulnerability: New Essays in Ethics and Feminist Philosophy
Edited by Catriona Mackenzie, Wendy Rogers, and Susan Dodds

Sovereign Masculinity: Gender Lessons from the War on Terror
Bonnie Mann

Autonomy, Oppression, and Gender
Edited by Andrea Veltman and Mark Piper

Our Faithfulness to the Past: Essays on the Ethics and Politics of Memory
Sue Campbell
Edited by Christine M. Koggel and Rockney Jacobsen

The Physiology of Sexist and Racist Oppression
Shannon Sullivan

Disorientation and Moral Life
Ami Harbin

The Wrong of Injustice: Dehumanization and Its Role in Feminist Philosophy
Mari Mikkola

Beyond Speech: Pornography and Analytic Feminist Philosophy
Mari Mikkola

Differences: Between Beauvoir and Irigaray
Edited by Emily Anne Parker and Anne van Leeuwen

Categories We Live By
Ásta Kristjana Sveinsdóttir

Equal Citizenship and Public Reason
Christie Hartley and Lori Watson

Decolonizing Universalism: A Transnational Feminist Ethic
Serene J. Khader

Women's Activism, Feminism, and Social Justice
Margaret A. McLaren

Being Born: Birth and Philosophy
Alison Stone

*Theories of the Flesh: Latinx and Latin American
Feminisms, Transformation, and Resistance*
Edited by Andrea J. Pitts, Mariana Ortega, and
José Medina

Elemental Difference and the Climate of the Body
Emily Anne Parker

*Racial Climates, Ecological Indifference: An
Ecointersectional Approach*
Nancy Tuana

On Taking Offence
Emily McTernan

Nonideal Theory and Content Externalism
Jeff Engelhardt

Nonideal Theory and Content Externalism

JEFF ENGELHARDT

OXFORD
UNIVERSITY PRESS

Oxford University Press is a department of the University of Oxford. It furthers
the University's objective of excellence in research, scholarship, and education
by publishing worldwide. Oxford is a registered trade mark of Oxford University
Press in the UK and certain other countries.

Published in the United States of America by Oxford University Press
198 Madison Avenue, New York, NY 10016, United States of America.

© Oxford University Press 2024

All rights reserved. No part of this publication may be reproduced, stored in
a retrieval system, or transmitted, in any form or by any means, without the
prior permission in writing of Oxford University Press, or as expressly permitted
by law, by license, or under terms agreed with the appropriate reproduction
rights organization. Inquiries concerning reproduction outside the scope of the
above should be sent to the Rights Department, Oxford University Press, at the
address above.

You must not circulate this work in any other form
and you must impose this same condition on any acquirer.

CIP data is on file at the Library of Congress

ISBN 978–0–19–775420–7 (pbk.)
ISBN 978–0–19–775419–1 (hbk.)

DOI: 10.1093/oso/9780197754191.001.0001

Paperback printed by Marquis Book Printing, Canada

Contents

Acknowledgments	ix
1. De-idealization, mind, and language	1
0. Introduction	1
1. De-idealization	2
1.1 De-idealization and systemic oppression	5
1.2 Identifying idealizing assumptions	9
1.3 De-idealization and nonideal theory	12
2. Objections, replies, and clarifications	15
2.1 Acceptable idealizations	16
2.1.1 Simplifications	17
2.1.2 Exemplars	20
2.2 Is idealization *antithetical* to the proper goal of the enterprise?	22
2.3 The distinction between idealized and de-idealized theories	24
3. Conclusion	31
2. De-idealizing objective type externalism	32
0. Introduction	32
1. Content externalism	33
1.1 Natural kind externalism	35
1.2 Objective type externalism	38
1.3 Revising the three phases of determination and discovery	42
1.4 Three explanatory goals	54
2. Oppression and the determination of type-terms	57
2.1 Oppression systematically influences the development of social kind terms	60
2.1.1 Political and economic terms	62
2.1.2 Gender terms	65
2.1.3 Race terms	67
2.2 Oppression systematically influences research into social kinds	71
2.2.1 "Intelligent"	71
2.2.2 Race and gender terms 1: Sexual ambiguity	74
2.2.3 Race and gender terms 2: Sentimentalism	79
2.2.4 Manifest and operative concepts, dubious research	82
2.3 Oppression systematically influences responses to empirical research	84

viii CONTENTS

3. The de-idealized theory improves upon its predecessor — 91
   3.1 Ideal and nonideal phases — 92
   3.2 The de-idealized theory is superior — 96
4. Conclusion — 99

3. De-idealizing social externalism — 101
  0. Introduction — 101
  1. Social externalism — 102
    1.1 Motivating social externalism — 102
    1.2 The division of linguistic labor — 105
    1.3 Cognitive value, conventional linguistic meaning, terms, and concepts — 112
    1.4 Social externalism's explanatory goals — 113
  2. Oppression and the division of linguistic labor — 115
    2.1 Tools — 117
      2.1.1 S-rules, g-rules, and exercitives — 117
      2.1.2 Exercitives and patterns of semantic deference — 120
    2.2 Corrections — 126
    2.3 Ranks — 139
    2.4 Enforcement — 147
      2.4.1 Enforcing semantic deference: Legal terms — 147
      2.4.2 Enforcing semantic deference: Dominant terms — 152
  3. The de-idealized theory improves upon its predecessor — 159
    3.1 Ideal and nonideal dialectics — 160
    3.2 The de-idealized theory is superior — 163
  4. Conclusion — 164

4. Applications — 166
  0. Introduction — 166
  1. Epistemic injustice — 168
  2. Externalism and conceptual engineering — 174
    2.1 Is externalist conceptual engineering possible? — 174
    2.2 Engineering meaning-making *processes* — 177
      2.2.1 Can and should we engineer our meaning-making processes? If so, how? — 178
      2.2.2 What would ideal meaning-making processes be like? — 187
      2.2.3 How should we determine who determines meanings? — 191
  3. Conclusion — 195

Bibliography — 197
Index — 205

Acknowledgments

A lot of people share credit for whatever is good about this book; the shortcomings are mine alone. I don't think I would have thought at all about writing a book had Chauncey Maher not told me to think about it. Chauncey also listened to me for dozens of hours as I worked through ideas, arguments, wrong turns, dead ends, and matters of style. He's a good friend; I'm grateful. Susan Feldman, Cheshire Calhoun, and Charles Mills were supportive of the initial idea for this book, and that went a long way toward motivating me to actually write it. Alex Davies read a complete early draft and offered extensive notes that helped shape the book's overall framing and many of its details. Esa Diaz-León read two complete drafts and offered very helpful, insightful comments that helped me deepen, strengthen, and extend the central idea. Anonymous reviewers for Oxford University Press offered detailed criticisms on a first draft that prompted me to be much clearer in explication and more rigorous in argumentation, to expand in some places, to contract in others, and to cut some things entirely. Molly Moran and I worked closely together on a paper that helped reshape the ideas in the first chapter; Anthony Eagle and two anonymous reviewers for the *Australasian Journal of Philosophy* gave detailed, *very* helpful feedback on that paper. This book benefited greatly from all those who contributed to the paper. Cheshire Calhoun and Lucy Randall were enormously helpful while I worked through several drafts, and they were patient with me throughout the review process.

As I worked on the book, I had helpful conversations with Amy McKiernan, Jim Sias, Elspeth Campbell, Ari Watson, Quill Kukla, Sarah Campbell, Patrick Mayer, James Marks, Tesseract Miller, Madeleine Engelhardt, Amber Mowery, Patricia Palao, Peter Schadler, Renee Boman, Annalisa Masini, Leonora Masini, Josh Stump, Mark Schersten, Serene Khader, Rich Lewis, Ammon Allred, Rebecca Warner, Korey Paul, Frank Intessimoni, Vijay Caplon, Justin Weinberg, Elizabeth Schechter, Peter Costello, Lynne Tirrell, Matt Teichman, Ann Helfrich, Cindy Qin, and many others. James Marks deserves special thanks for preparing the index. Amber Mowery and Madeleine Engelhardt provided exceptional emotional support. Overall, I had help from too many people to name; I apologize to anyone I failed to mention here.

1

De-idealization, mind, and language

0. Introduction

Over the past few decades, philosophers working on mind and language have engaged more and more with scholarly work on oppression. This engagement can be usefully divided into two kinds. One kind uses traditional philosophical tools and theories to help us understand aspects of oppressive systems. For instance, there's good work applying philosophical tools to race and gender terms (Haslanger 2012; Saul 2006; Bettcher 2012; Diaz-Leon 2016), implicit biases (Gendler 2008a, 2008b; Brownstein & Saul 2016), propaganda (Stanley 2015; Quaranto & Stanley 2021), and oppressive speech (McGowan 2004, 2009, 2019).

A second kind uses insights from literature on oppression to challenge and modify traditional philosophical tools and theories. For instance, much scholarship in feminist theory, critical race theory, postcolonial theory, disability theory, queer theory, and so on, makes the case that many (if not all) Western societies are structured in ways that systematically give their members differential advantages and disadvantages according to factors like race, gender, and ability status. A number of philosophers have shown that this point challenges an assumption found in many theories of mind and language: the assumption that speakers and thinkers are socially equal—or something close to equal, so that theorizing about mind and language doesn't have to pay attention to differences in race, gender, ability status, and so on. Lýnne Tirrell shows that influential work on language games assumes that the rules of our language games treat all participants equally. But in fact, oppressive social structures make it so that members of oppressed groups tend to be granted fewer and lesser powers (Tirrell 2018a, 9). Jennifer McWeeny makes the case that prominent theories of consciousness developed by Immanuel Kant, John Locke, Jean-Paul Sartre, and others make a similar assumption, while Simone de Beauvoir, Frantz Fanon, and others have shown that structures of consciousness are shaped by gender, race, and status as colonizer or colonized (McWeeny 2016, 2017, 2021). Jessica Keiser has recently

Nonideal Theory and Content Externalism. Jeff Engelhardt, Oxford University Press. © Oxford University Press 2024.
DOI: 10.1093/oso/9780197754191.003.0001

argued that David Lewis's account of linguistic convention assumes that speakers' motivations to communicate outweigh any competing interests they may have, so that all speakers in a community want everyone to converge on the same language. But, Keiser argues, systemic oppression makes it so that our interests diverge along the lines of oppressive social hierarchies, and so Keiser develops a modified version of Lewis's account (Keiser 2023).

This book aims to be a contribution of the second kind; this chapter aims to articulate a particular sort of project that makes contributions of this kind (§1) and to defend such projects from general objections (§2). Along the way, I'll give several examples of recent projects of the relevant sort in philosophy of mind and language. Adapting terminology used by Charles Mills, I say that these projects are "de-idealizations": the theories they challenge *idealize* our social world, so the modified theories de-idealize the originals. In brief, I'll say that because de-idealizations correct false, idealizing assumptions in traditional theories, they improve upon the originals by providing more accurate explanations. And since idealizing assumptions often serve to obscure oppression and its effects, we should (i) use de-idealized theories when trying to understand oppression, as in work of the first kind above, and we should (ii) consider it an urgent matter to de-idealize any other influential theories that make idealizing assumptions.

After clarifying and defending de-idealizations, the rest of the book de-idealizes content externalism, an influential, perhaps dominant, theory in philosophy of mind and language (see, e.g., Pinder 2021, 142). Chapters 2 and 3 de-idealize two prominent versions of the theory. These chapters are meant to contribute to discussions of externalism and oppression, but they're also meant to be examples of de-idealization in mind and language that can guide other such projects. Chapter 4 sketches how de-idealizing content externalism might bear on discussions of epistemic injustice and conceptual engineering.

1. De-idealization

To de-idealize a theory is to replace its model of society as free of oppression with a model that represents systemic oppression and its effects. For any society that is plagued by systemic oppression, theories that model that society as free of oppression will presumably be inaccurate. Indeed, insofar as oppression-free social models are *systematically* inaccurate, and insofar as a theory's social model partly determines the theory's descriptions, explanations, and predictions, we should expect that theories with oppression-free social models will be systematically inaccurate. The aim of de-idealizing a theory is to correct these inaccuracies in description, explanation, and prediction by replacing the theory's inaccurate social model with one that represents systemic oppression and its effects.

We can take the examples sketched in the introduction as illustrations.[1]

De-idealized language games. Lynne Tirrell de-idealized influential work on language games by Wilfrid Sellars and Robert Brandom (Tirrell 2018a). Sellars and Brandom took linguistic interactions to be rule-governed 'games,' and they sought to articulate the rules that determine speakers' powers, permissions, commitments, and entitlements. Sellars assumed that when speakers join language games, all are granted the same conversational permissions and powers: Systemic oppression doesn't influence what one can or may do in a conversation; rather, we all enter language games as "peers with discursive authority" (ibid. 1; see also ibid. 7; Tirrell 2018b, 125). Similarly, Brandom assumes that systemic oppression doesn't influence the rules that determine speakers' commitments and entitlements. He assumes, for instance, that a speaker's race, gender, class, and so on, don't influence whether others will treat her assertions as entitled or not (Tirrell 2018a, 24). But Tirrell shows that, in fact, systemic oppression systematically influences the rules that determine speakers' powers, permissions, commitments, and entitlements (ibid. 9, 16–17, 22–28; Tirrell 2018b, 125). Oppression makes it so that members of oppressed groups have systematically fewer and weaker conversational permissions and powers, and it makes it so that assertions made by members of oppressed groups are systematically more likely to be treated as un-entitled or open to challenge. Thus, the theories developed by Sellars and Brandom are systematically inaccurate: they misdescribe the rules of our language games; they fail to predict how powers, permissions, and so on, are distributed among speakers; and, they have no explanation for why distributions of conversational powers, permissions, and so on, track oppressive hierarchies. Each of these inaccuracies appears everywhere that systemic oppression has influenced language games, and since that influence is systematic, the inaccuracies are systematic too. Since Sellars's and Brandom's theories are systematically inaccurate thanks to their idealized social models, Tirrell replaces those models with models

---

[1] I don't say that these authors used the term "de-idealization," however. They didn't.

that represent systemic oppression—in my terms, Tirrell de-idealizes the Sellarsian-Brandomian theory. She develops an account of language games that accounts for the unequal distribution of powers and permissions, commitments and entitlements.

De-idealized phenomenology. Jennifer McWeeny makes the case that a number of theorists have challenged—and in my view, de-idealized— traditional theories of consciousness found in Locke, William James, Kant, Sartre, and Judith Butler (McWeeny 2021, 175; 2017, 257). In one way or another, each of these authors assumes that systemic oppression doesn't systematically influence the structures of human consciousness. But McWeeny says that these assumptions have been challenged and replaced by W. E. B. Du Bois, Simone de Beauvoir, Frantz Fanon, Deborah K. King, and Maria Lugones (ibid. 175; see McWeeny 2016). According to the latter, one's positioning along hierarchies of gender, race, and class (among others) plays a role in determining the structure of one's consciousness. Human structures of consciousness, then, are systematically influenced by systemic oppression. Thus, traditional theories of consciousness are systematically inaccurate: they systematically misdescribe the determinants of structures of consciousness, they systematically fail to predict differences in consciousness along the lines of social positioning, and they have no explanation for why social positioning should influence structures of consciousness. These inaccuracies are thanks to the traditional theories' idealized social models, and so the de-idealizing theories replace them with models that represent systemic oppression and its effects. The resulting theories are systematically more accurate.

De-idealized linguistic conventions. Jessica Keiser has proposed to replace idealizing assumptions in David Lewis's account of linguistic convention. Lewis proposes that groups of people without a common language nonetheless establish linguistic conventions because they all have outweighing motivations to communicate with one another. Thanks to these motivations, no one has a preference for any particular convention that trumps their motivation to communicate with everyone else; thus, most of all, "everyone wants everyone to converge on the same language" (Keiser 2023, 23). But Keiser says this is an idealization (ibid. 5, 25, 28–36). In fact, systemic oppression systematically influences motivations to communicate and preferences for linguistic conventions. For instance, when two groups without a common language converge because one is colonizing the other and its land, the colonizers tend to *enforce* the linguistic conventions of their own language. Colonizers' preference for cultural domination seems to outweigh their motivation to settle on any convention whatsoever (ibid. 35). Lewis's theory, then, systematically misdescribes the motivations that underpin linguistic conventions, its predictions about which conventions will be established are systematically inaccurate for groups shaped by systemic oppression, and it has no explanation for why, for instance, colonized peoples tend to take on the language of their colonizers. These systematic failures are thanks to Lewis's idealized social model, so Keiser's theory replaces it. The resulting theory is systematically more accurate.

1.1 De-idealization and systemic oppression

Given the description of de-idealization above, it may be tempting to generalize as follows: De-idealizations take as input a theory that idealizes in some way that renders the theory systematically inaccurate, and as output, they deliver a theory that corrects that problematic idealization. *One kind* of problematic idealization is to model society as free of oppression, but it's not the only kind, and de-idealizations can correct other kinds of problematic idealizations as well. On this view, we might say that any theory with a problematic idealization is an ideal theory, and the theories that remove and correct a problematic idealization are nonideal.[2]

I don't object to this understanding of de-idealization, but in this book, I'll focus specifically on idealizations that ignore oppression. This is my focus because there are reasons to think that these idealizations appear systematically in contemporary theorizing; thus, if the goal is to identify and correct theories that are systematically inaccurate, it will be more helpful to identify the problematic idealizations that occur systematically rather than to 'zoom out' and miss the details that reveal this systematicity.

In order to appreciate why these idealizations might occur systematically, we need to articulate some broad epistemic conditions that have formed the backdrop to much theorizing over the past few centuries. I'll make the case that these background epistemic conditions make it so that (A) when theorists have adopted assumptions about social behaviors, interactions, motivations, institutions, and so on, those assumptions have tended to treat oppression as either anomalous or nonexistent, and (B) when a theory

---

[2] Some of Jessica Keiser's accounts of ideal and nonideal theory suggest a view like this (Keiser 2023, 4, 90), but others suggest something more like the approach I'll develop here (ibid. 5). See also Engelhardt 2019c and Mühlebach 2022.

is systematically inaccurate thanks to assumptions that ignore oppression, theorists typically won't notice that the inaccuracies are systematic. Thanks to (A), many theories will be systematically inaccurate. Thanks to (B), those in a position to revise the theory won't notice its inaccuracies, or they'll tend to think that the theory's inaccuracies are mere anomalies.

The epistemic background conditions I have in mind were described most clearly by the late philosopher Charles Mills. The basic idea is that contemporary systems of oppression are often interdependent with epistemic systems that obscure systemic oppression. What's important for us is that ignorance of systemic oppression is produced systematically, so that most people, and especially members of privileged groups, tend to think that oppression is either anomalous or nonexistent. If this is so, then we should expect it to hold systematically that members of privileged groups will be ignorant of systemic oppression. Granted that most people who have developed influential theories have been members of privileged groups, then we should expect that most people who have developed influential theories have been ignorant of systemic oppression. Supposing that this ignorance has influenced the relevant theorists' theorizing, then it should be that (A) when those theorists have adopted assumptions about social behaviors, interactions, motivations, institutions, and so on, those assumptions have tended to treat oppression as either anomalous or nonexistent; because these theorists won't know that oppression is systemic, (B) when a theory is systematically inaccurate thanks to assumptions that ignore oppression, the relevant theorists typically won't notice that the inaccuracies are systematic. Thanks to (A), many theories will be systematically inaccurate. Thanks to (B), those in a position to revise the theory won't notice its inaccuracies, or they'll tend to think that the theory's inaccuracies are mere anomalies.

The crucial claim above is that ignorance of systemic oppression is produced systematically, so that most people, and especially members of privileged groups, tend to think that oppression is either anomalous or nonexistent. If this claim is well motivated, then with a few other plausible assumptions noted above, we can infer (A) and (B). Why think that the crucial claim is true? Mills makes the case in at least three places: (1) In *The Racial Contract*, he says that ignorance of systemic racism among Whites is "psychically required" in order to maintain the systems that have enabled the conquest, colonization, and enslavement of people of color over the past few centuries (Mills 1997, 19). If other systems of oppression work similarly, as Mills suggests they do, we may expect that ignorance of systemic oppression is "psychically required" to maintain oppression itself in all its brutality (Mills 2007, 22). (2) Mills expands on the systems that produce ignorance in his work "White Ignorance," and (3) he applies the idea specifically to ethical theorists in "Ideal Theory as Ideology." I'll focus on (2) and (3) in what follows.

The phrase "White ignorance" refers to ignorance of racial oppression that is produced by social structures that are involved in racial oppression and its effects (ibid. 20). The written work "White Ignorance" makes the case that such ignorance of racial oppression is systematic in a few interdependent ways. I'll sketch three of them. First, since White ignorance is produced by *systems* that support racial oppression, then unless White ignorance is merely an accidental byproduct of those systems, we should expect that it is produced systematically—it is not a bug but a *feature* of those systems that they produce White ignorance (ibid. 20–21). We'll see reasons to deny that White ignorance is an accidental byproduct of systems of racial oppression below; if that's right, then we can conclude that White ignorance is produced systematically (see Martin 2021). As noted above, Mills proposes that the same reasoning works for systems of gender oppression, colonialism, and so on.

Second, Mills makes the case by offering diverse examples in which White ignorance is produced or maintained. The idea, I take it, is this: Given that there are systems that produce racial oppression, and given the number and variety of Mills's examples, the best explanation for the examples is that White ignorance is produced systematically. As the examples multiply, it becomes less and less plausible to explain them by coincidence and more plausible to explain them by appeal to systems, and granted that we already have sufficient reason to believe in the relevant systems, appealing to them to explain away widespread coincidence gives us a more parsimonious explanation.

Mills organizes his examples so as to suggest that all or most of a society's sources of knowledge contribute to the production of White ignorance. For instance, he takes it that the concepts developed and shared widely in a society are one source of its knowledge. For many societies, developing and sharing the concept expressed by "social distancing" contributed to knowledge of safety precautions during the COVID-19 pandemic. Concepts are a source of collective knowledge. But in a society beset by systemic racism, they're also a source of ignorance, as when widely shared concepts help obscure racial oppression. Mills takes the concepts expressed by "discovered," "empty," and "civilization" as they relate to conquest and colonization: It has long been common in U.S. public education and popular consciousness to characterize Europeans as having *discovered* various territories, representing the lands as if they had previously been *empty*, and representing the peoples living there as if they didn't count morally because they weren't *civilized*. These concepts serve to obscure the truth that Europeans colonized the lands and committed genocide against their peoples (Mills 2007, 27).

Similarly, Mills takes it that state archives, public memorials, and museums are—like an individual's memory—another source of a society's knowledge. But in societies structured by oppression, these too contribute to systematic ignorance of histories of racial oppression. Mills notes, as an illustration, that official records of racial oppression are routinely destroyed. The Belgian state archives regarding the deaths of millions of Congolese during King Leopold II's regime in Belgian Congo were systematically destroyed, and official records in Tulsa, Oklahoma, regarding the 1921 Tulsa Race Massacre "mysteriously vanished" (ibid. 29, 32).

Mills provides further examples for these sources of knowledge (concepts and 'memory') and others (perception, testimony, motivational group interest). If his examples (in conjunction with others given in the extensive literatures on racial oppression) are so numerous and diverse that they are best explained by appeal to systems that produce ignorance of racial oppression, then we should conclude that, indeed, White ignorance is produced systematically.

Third, some of Mills's examples point directly to the systematic production of White ignorance. For instance, if it was part of the standard school curriculum in the United States to characterize European colonization as discovery, and if that helped obscure systemic oppression, then the school system produced White ignorance. Insofar as the standard curriculum obscured systemic oppression related to colonization, Jim Crow, American Indian boarding schools, and more, it has been a feature of that system—not a bug—to produce ignorance of systemic racial oppression.

If Mills's arguments in "White Ignorance" establish that ignorance of systemic oppression is produced systematically, then we should be able to conclude that (A) when theorists have adopted assumptions about social behaviors, interactions, motivations, institutions, and so on, those assumptions have tended to treat oppression as either anomalous or non-existent, and (B) when a theory is systematically inaccurate thanks to assumptions that ignore oppression, the relevant theorists typically won't notice that the inaccuracies are systematic. In turn, these points give us reason to suppose that many theories will be systematically inaccurate and that those in a position to revise the inaccurate theories won't notice its inaccuracies, or they'll tend to think that the theory's inaccuracies are mere anomalies.

On these grounds, I take it to be useful to focus on idealizations that ignore oppression. These idealizations appear systematically; when they appear in a theory, they tend to make it systematically inaccurate, and when they make a theory systematically inaccurate, the relevant theorists seldom notice, or they dismiss the inaccuracies as non-systematic. In order to improve our theories, it helps to identify *any* de-idealizations that make them systematically inaccurate. But it's especially important that we know how to identify idealizations that obscure oppression. Because they occur systematically, being able to identify them will be especially helpful. Because their distorting effects are seldom noticed by the theorists who adopt them, identifying them is especially needful.

In the next section, I'll say more about how to identify idealizations that obscure oppression, but let me first clarify what I mean when I say that oppression-obscuring idealizations occur systematically. I don't mean that every theory developed in a society with systemic oppression adopts such idealizing assumptions and is consequently systematically inaccurate. To say that oppression-obscuring idealizations are adopted systematically is not to say that theorists adopt them without exception. It's to say that they are adopted very often, and their frequent adoption isn't a coincidence—rather, it's a result of the systems of ignorance described above.

Similarly, my claim about theories being systematically inaccurate is limited to those theories that turn on assumptions about social behavior, motivations, interactions, institutions, and so on. Not all theories so turn, of course, and I have nothing to say here about those theories that don't turn on the relevant assumptions. I've appealed to Mills to motivate the claim that when philosophers of mind or language do adopt assumptions like these, those assumptions are likely to obscure oppression. I take it that the examples of de-idealization projects throughout this book give us prima facie reason to suppose that *whenever* a theory adopts oppression-obscuring assumptions, the theory is likely to be systematically inaccurate.

1.2 Identifying idealizing assumptions

The previous section made the case that we should focus on idealizations that obscure oppression in part because being able to *identify* these idealizations

10   NONIDEAL THEORY AND CONTENT EXTERNALISM

is especially useful. In this section, I draw again on Mills to sketch some common forms that idealizing assumptions take. These can broaden our understanding of idealizing assumptions while also helping us identify their instances 'in the wild.'

In his "Ideal Theory as Ideology," Mills articulates a distinction between *ideal theory* and *nonideal theory* in moral and political philosophy.[3] For our purposes, we can say that ideal theory adopts oppression-obscuring idealizations while nonideal theory avoids them (or at least tries to). Indeed, in articulating what ideal theory is on his distinction, Mills gives us a list of assumptions commonly found in ideal theories, whereby each assumption obscures oppression in one way or another. Although Mills's focus is on ideal theory in ethics and political philosophy, I propose that we can use his list to identify idealizing assumptions more generally. If what we've said so far is right, then we should expect that philosophers adopt ideal theories at least in part thanks to the influences of systematically produced ignorance of oppression, and since that ignorance is produced systematically, we shouldn't expect that it only affects assumptions found in ethical theory and political philosophy. We should expect it to influence any theory that adopts assumptions about social behavior, interactions, and so on.

Here's the list:

[*Idealized social ontology*] Ideal theory tends to represent humans as "the abstract and undifferentiated equal atomic individuals of classical liberalism," thus abstracting away from "relations of structural domination, exploitation, coercion, and oppression" (Mills 2005, 168).

[*Idealized capacities*] Ideal theory represents human agents as having the same "completely unrealistic capacities," thus misrepresenting actual human capacities and abstracting away from how differences in capacities may be influenced by systemic oppression (ibid. 168).

[*Silence on oppression*] Ideal theory won't consider the significance of "actual historic oppression and its legacy in the present, or current ongoing oppression," thus abstracting away from "the ways in which systematic oppression is likely to shape . . . basic social institutions (as well as the humans in those institutions)" (ibid. 167–168).

---

[3] Note that there are other versions of this distinction in the literature; I'm here concerned only with Mills's version.

[*Ideal social institutions*] Ideal theory represents "fundamental social institutions such as the family, the economic structure, the legal system" as they would be in an ideal-as-idealized model, thus abstracting away from "how their actual workings may systematically disadvantage women, the poor, and racial minorities" (ibid. 169).

[*Idealized cognitive sphere*] Ideal theory won't "recognize, let alone theorize" the ways in which oppression influences agents' social cognition, thus abstracting away from "the distinctive role of hegemonic ideologies and group-specific experience in distorting our perceptions and conceptions of the social order" (ibid. 169).

[*Strict compliance*] "Everyone is presumed to act justly and to do his part in upholding just institutions," thus abstracting away from how people actually behave and how oppression influences our behaviors and interactions (ibid. 169).

The list helps suggest some of the variety in assumptions that can obscure oppression, and it puts us in a better position to identify such assumptions elsewhere. Indeed, if we take the first item on the list—*idealized social ontology*—we can see two more de-idealizations in philosophy of mind and language.

De-idealized memory. An idealized social ontology represents humans as abstract, undifferentiated, equal, and atomic, and it thereby obscures relations of structural domination, exploitation, coercion, and oppression. Sue Campbell has made the case that reconstructivist (also known as constructive or generationist) theories of memory assume this sort of social ontology. Reconstructivist accounts say that remembering isn't a matter of simply retrieving a 'recording' from mental storage but an active process in which an individual *constructs* a representation of the past. In dominant reconstructivist theories, models of this active remembering process abstract away from social positioning and relations (Campbell 2003, 17–18; see Koggel 2014, 494–495). They adopt an idealized social ontology, and they would predict that social positioning doesn't affect remembering, or if it does, then the effects are non-systematic. But this is mistaken. Social positioning and relations systematically influence remembering activities, and thus assumptions that idealize social ontology render a theory systematically inaccurate (Campbell 2003, 16–27). Moreover, Christine M. Koggel argues that Campbell's work shows that a theory of memory with an idealized social ontology can't distinguish between adequate and inadequate remembering because it can't ground that distinction in social normativity (see Koggel 2014, 494). Campbell's social and relational account of memory replaces the reconstructivists' idealized ontology and produces a theory that is systematically more accurate.

De-idealized semantics. Jennifer Hornsby has argued that mainstream theories of meaning in philosophy of language assume speakers to be undifferentiated, equal, and atomic: "When semantic theories are constructed," she says, "languages appear to be treated as objects; the institution of language use, in which people participate, is set to one side" (Hornsby 2000, 91). Speakers' social positions and relations are assumed to be irrelevant to theories of meaning because speakers and their knowledge of language are conceptualized as ultimately separable from the social world and explanatorily prior to it (ibid. 94–97). But this, Hornsby says, gets things fundamentally wrong. If it were true, then since an individual and his knowledge of language are independent of and prior to a social world, it would be possible for someone to "achieve the state of mind of someone who knows a language" but without being able to actually say anything to anyone (ibid. 95–96). Hornsby takes this to be implausible on its face. If it's impossible, then an idealized ontology seems to lead a theory to fundamentally misdescribe language users and their knowledge. Furthermore, Hornsby makes the case in several places that these idealizing assumptions prevent a theory from accounting for various systematic sociolinguistic phenomena: silencing (Hornsby 1993; see also Dotson 2011, 237), kinds of 'ineffability' and 'inaudibility' (Hornsby 1995, 134–138), hate speech (Hornsby 2000, 98–100), and changes in meaning (ibid. 100–101). If Hornsby is right, then adopting an idealized social ontology leads to a theory of meaning that fundamentally misdescribes language users and their behaviors while preventing the explanation of systematic sociolinguistic phenomena. Hornsby has developed various alternatives to theories that adopt idealized social ontologies, thus offering several de-idealized approaches to language and meaning (see, e.g., Hornsby 1993, 38–45; 1995, 134; 2000, 91).

1.3 De-idealization and nonideal theory

Above, I drew on Mills's ideal/nonideal distinction in order to help characterize de-idealization and the idealizations it targets. This raises an obvious question about the relations among ideal theory, nonideal theory, and de-idealizations: What are those relations? Answering this can be especially helpful for situating de-idealization projects in the context of current literature on "non-ideal philosophy of language."[4]

I think part of the answer here is intuitive and somewhat obvious: a de-idealization project takes an ideal theory (in Mills's sense) as input and then gives a nonideal theory (in Mills's sense) as output.[5] I said at the start of this section that to de-idealize a theory is to replace its model of society as free of oppression with a model that represents systemic oppression and its effects. A theory that models society as free of oppression is a theory that adopts oppression-obscuring idealizations—an ideal theory. If we replace such a model with one that represents systemic oppression and its effects, we produce a theory that avoids (at least some) such idealizations—a nonideal theory.

We shouldn't infer from this that all nonideal theories are produced by de-idealization projects, and we shouldn't think that all nonideal theories are de-idealized versions of ideal theories. All it takes to be a nonideal theory in Mills's sense is for the theory to avoid idealizing assumptions; if you develop a theory like that without 'starting with' an ideal theory and replacing its assumptions, your theory will be nonideal, but it won't be the result of a de-idealization project.

Moreover, some of the contemporary work that's called "nonideal theory" or "nonideal philosophy of language" doesn't essentially involve developing theories that avoid or replace oppression-obscuring idealizations. For instance, David Beaver and Jason Stanley say that they develop a "non-ideal philosophy of language" in that they challenge "idealizations that filter political speech out from the core data of semantic and pragmatic theorizing in linguistics and philosophy of language" (Beaver & Stanley, 2019, 503). Similarly, in discussing part of a collection titled "Non-Ideal Semantics and Pragmatics," Justin Khoo and Rachel Katharine Sterken say that nonideal

---

[4] Mills typically says "nonideal theory" without the hyphen, while some prominent uses of the phrase "non-ideal philosophy of language" or its variants (uses I'll discuss below) hyphenate it. I follow Mills's use, but I'll faithfully quote those who use the hyphen.

[5] In the examples reviewed above, the project typically involves demonstrating that the ideal theory is systematically inaccurate so as (i) to motivate the de-idealization and (ii) to identify which assumptions need to be replaced in the nonideal theory. So we might also say that typical de-idealizations projects also demonstrate that some theory is in fact an ideal theory. But I don't see that this is a necessary part of a de-idealization, just a useful one. It is necessary and sufficient for being a de-idealization, however, that a project transforms a theory with idealizations that obscure oppression (an ideal theory in Mills's sense) into a theory that avoids such idealizations (a nonideal theory in Mills's sense).

philosophy of language is "applied philosophy of language" in that it applies theories of language to nonideal speech situations (Khoo & Sterken 2021, 3, 5). On the face of it, these works aren't essentially concerned with any theory's idealizing assumptions but with the sorts of data or speech situations to which theories of language are applied.[6] Prima facie, then, one could undertake this sort of nonideal philosophy by applying a theory with oppression-obscuring idealizations to political speech or to nonideal speech situations. This sort of nonideal theory needn't involve de-idealization at all, of course.

I don't think there's anything especially worrisome about the diversity of approaches to nonideal theory. There are also several different versions of the ideal/nonideal distinction, and philosophers should use whichever distinctions and approaches seem most useful to them.[7] As long as we are clear in our own work about our approach to nonideal theory and the ideal/nonideal distinction, the differences among us shouldn't cause confusion.

That said, I would like to urge caution about applying theories of language to political speech or to nonideal speech situations without considering whether the theory so applied is ideal in Mills's sense—without considering whether the theory adopts assumptions that obscure systemic oppression. The danger is that applying an ideal theory to political speech or to nonideal speech situations will obscure features of that speech/situation that are crucial for an adequate understanding of it. Systemic oppression structures much political speech and many nonideal speech situations; when it does, we won't fully understand the relevant speech/situation if the theory we apply to it obscures oppression and its effects. Indeed, if the theory we apply to political speech or a nonideal speech situation obscures systemic oppression and its effects, then we'll both misunderstand the phenomena under study and reinforce the appearance that oppression is either nonexistent or anomalous—that is, we'll reinforce ideal theory.

Consider gaslighting as an example of a nonideal speech situation. In paradigmatic examples of gaslighting, a man in a heterosexual romantic relationship manipulates his partner and the environment in ways that undermine her credibility, her own perceptions, and, ultimately, her epistemic standing. On Kate Abramson's influential account, a gasligher tries "(consciously

---

[6] Khoo and Sterken do note that applying our theories to nonideal speech situations may in the end "involve interrogating our theoretical tools, or supplementing our theories with resources from neighboring fields" (Khoo & Sterken 2021, 5).

[7] See Cappelen and Dever (2021) for a survey of ideal/nonideal distinctions and a critique of using them in philosophy of language. See Engelhardt and Moran (in press) for a reply that focuses on Mills's distinction.

or not) to induce in someone the sense that her reactions, perceptions, memories and/or beliefs are not just mistaken, but utterly without grounds— paradigmatically, so unfounded as to qualify as crazy" (Abramson 2014, 2). Suppose we want to understand a gaslighting speech situation by considering the participants' conversational powers, permissions, commitments, and entitlements. Recall that, above, we reviewed Lynne Tirrell's de-idealization of the Sellarsian-Brandomian account of the rules that determine conversational powers, permissions, and so on. Suppose we apply the idealized theory to gaslighting. It assumes that speakers enter a speech situation with the same permissions and powers. Thus, if we apply the theory to gaslighting without considering whether it's idealized, we'll describe the situation as though all participants have the same permissions and powers. In particular, we won't describe the situation as one in which systemic gender-based oppression has made it so that "men tend to have greater [conversational] powers, women fewer, and the powers women do have tend to support men's enhanced status" (Tirrell 2018a, 9). The influences of oppression captured by Tirrell's de-idealized theory won't enter the analysis. But systemic power differences like those Tirrell describes are central to nearly every account of gaslighting in the literature (see, e.g., Abramson 2014, 19; Ruiz 2014, 201; Stark 2019, 230; Adkins 2019, 84; Pohlhaus 2020; Engelhardt 2023). If any of these accounts is on the right track, then applying the idealized account of conversational permissions, powers, and so on, to gaslighting speech situations will obscure crucial features of the phenomenon, and it will put us in no position to understand gaslighting.

I suggest, then, that we must be careful with nonideal theory; while we should support efforts to bring political speech and nonideal speech situations into view for 'mainstream' philosophy of language, we should be careful not to do it in a way that reinforces (Millsian) ideal theory and inhibits our understanding. De-idealizing the theories we use should help us avoid these pitfalls.

2. Objections, replies, and clarifications

Why should we undertake any de-idealizations? I hope I've made clear at least two reasons: (1) to correct distortions in the idealized theory and (2) to reveal oppression, its mechanisms, or its effects that are obscured by the idealized theory. In many of the examples reviewed above, there are good reasons to think that both of these aims are achieved. If (1) and (2) are worth achieving for some theory, then de-idealizing that theory is motivated by the promise of those achievements.

This isn't to say that every de-idealization will achieve (1) and (2). If a theory has no model of society or if the theory's model isn't idealized, then there won't be any of the relevant distortions to correct, and (1) won't be achievable for any attempted de-idealization. Or perhaps it could happen that a theory has an idealized model of society, but this model plays no role in achieving the theory's goals: no role in explanation, prediction, and so on. The model is explanatorily epiphenomenal. Presumably, the idealized model in such a theory wouldn't obscure oppression or its effects, and consequently, a de-idealization of the theory wouldn't reveal what the original theory obscured. For such a theory, (2) would be achievable only vacuously.

Moreover, for any given theory, there might be disagreement about whether (1) and (2) are worth achieving. Such disagreement could arise from several places. In this section canvassing objections to de-idealizations, I'll try to sketch some of the more reasonable arguments that (1) and (2) might not be worth achieving for a theory; afterward, I'll consider a recent argument to the effect that there is no useful distinction between ideal and nonideal philosophy of language. In my replies, I don't claim that every de-idealization in mind/language will be fruitful or worthwhile. I don't make a general commitment to de-idealizations as the best way to move forward for every theory in mind or language. Rather, I propose two loose guidelines for deciding whether it will be fruitful to de-idealize a theory. First, if the theory's idealized social model renders it systematically inaccurate in its predictions or explanations, then achieving (1) should be fruitful. It will correct systematic inaccuracies in the theory. Second, if the theory is or has been used to help understand oppression, its mechanisms, or its effects, then achieving (2) should be fruitful for those uses. Indeed, the idealized theory will be self-sabotaging for such uses. De-idealizing the theory will make it usable for those purposes.

2.1 Acceptable idealizations

I've characterized de-idealizations as replacing a theory's idealized model of society with a model that acknowledges oppression and its effects. I've said that the de-idealized theory typically improves its idealized predecessor, and

I've sometimes said that de-idealization *corrects* the original theory's model of society. One might take these claims to be justified thanks to a more general claim to the effect that *any* inaccuracy or simplification in a theory's model of society is detrimental, and thus replacing the theory's social model with something more accurate would improve the theory, all things considered. But this is implausible. As Mills himself acknowledges, some idealizations *improve* a theory. Replacing idealizations like these would thus run the risk of producing worse theories, not better. And even if a de-idealized theory isn't worse than its predecessor, these considerations raise doubts about what makes de-idealizations better than the theories they replace. Why should we think that the idealizations that get replaced in de-idealizations are in fact detrimental to the theory, not helpful (or at least neutral)?

In developing his criticisms of ideal theory in moral and political philosophy, Mills distinguishes between several senses of "ideal." These enable him then to differentiate between idealizations that improve a theory and those that don't. I'll note two uses of "ideal" and use them to distinguish between idealizations that can be fruitfully replaced and those that probably can't be. The de-idealizations described above and those to follow in the next chapters replace idealizations of the former sort.

2.1.1 Simplifications

A typical model is a simplification of what it's modeling. The model's simplifications help make salient the most important features and functions of the phenomena we're using the model to understand or explain. If you use pieces of paper to make scale models of your furniture and then position them on an outline of your apartment at the same scale, you can use it to figure out whether the love seat will fit next to the couch, whether there's room for the couch you're thinking of buying, whether moving your bed will block the doorway, and so on. These models of the furniture and apartment will be inaccurate in many ways. The paper couch isn't soft like the real couch. None of the colors is right. The paper models represent the couch as being the same height as the bookshelf, even though the bookshelf is at least twice as tall. And so on. But these inaccuracies are harmless because the model's distortions are irrelevant to what the model's being used to understand. The model is meant to help you think about the spatial relations of the furniture relative to the floor plan. Textures, colors, and heights are irrelevant to those spatial relations, so the model's inaccuracies with regard to those features are acceptable simplifications. As long as the model gets things right

18   NONIDEAL THEORY AND CONTENT EXTERNALISM

with regard to the features relevant to its purposes, adding accurate details won't improve the model or our understanding. For instance, to 'de-idealize' the paper model by adding all the right colors will not produce a model that improves upon its predecessor. The model with accurate colors will make the same predictions as the original: if one predicts that the couch won't fit next to the love seat, so will the other; if one says there's no room for the new couch, so will the other.

A model of society can likewise have acceptable simplifications. As we'll see in the next chapters, content externalism models society in order to explain how words come to have the meanings they do. The model represents individual speakers as having differential expertise relevant to different words, and it represents language communities such that speakers with less expertise defer to those with more expertise about the meanings of various words. For instance, it says that people who don't know the difference between beech trees and elm trees tend to defer to botanists about the meanings of the terms "beech" and "elm." The model doesn't represent different individual speakers as having different heights, different salaries, or different sleep habits. Since different speakers often do have different heights, salaries, and sleep habits, the model is inaccurate. These inaccuracies are presumably harmless because the model's distortions are irrelevant to what it's being used to understand. The model is meant to tell us how speakers depend on one another with regard to the meanings of various words. Since speakers' heights, salaries, and sleep schedules are (presumably) irrelevant to this, the models' inaccuracies are acceptable simplifications. As long as the model is accurate for the features relevant to its purposes, adding accurate details won't improve the model or our understanding. To 'de-idealize' content externalism by adding the heights of every speaker in a language community will not produce a model that improves upon its predecessor. The model with accurate heights will make the same predictions and give the same explanations as the original.

If oppression and its effects are also irrelevant to what content externalism or any other theory of mind/language seeks to explain, then it would be acceptable for the theory to adopt idealized social models; the models' idealizations would be acceptable simplifications. If a de-idealization of a theory is to be an improvement, then it must be that oppression and its effects are relevant to what the theory seeks to predict or explain.

But even if oppression and its effects are relevant to the theory's explananda, it still may be acceptable for the theory to abstract away from oppression in its social models. That's because the oppression-free model could be *close enough*. If the paper model of the couch is rectangular but the actual couch is oval, it probably won't matter much for figuring out what furniture will fit where. The model is inaccurate, but rectangles are easier to cut with ordinary scissors, and the inaccuracy won't affect its uses much. As Mills points out, if we model a very smooth, Teflon-coated plane suspended in a vacuum as an ideal frictionless plane, then our calculations will be easier and not so very inaccurate (Mills 2005, 167). In these cases, although the models are inaccurate in ways that are relevant to the explanations and predictions that they're used to derive, these inaccuracies are still often acceptable. The inaccuracies make it easier to derive predictions or to understand the explanations the model provides; these benefits make the theory easier to use at little cost in accuracy.

Similarly, the idealized social model in a theory of mind or language may be close enough. Understanding how systemic oppression is relevant to consciousness, language games, or the meanings of terms is difficult and time consuming. It's certainly more difficult and time consuming than cutting (or otherwise acquiring) oval pieces of paper. Adopting an idealized model of society is much easier, or it would be so for theorists broadly unfamiliar with White supremacy, patriarchy, colonialism, and so on, and the extensive, complicated literatures on each. It may be, then, that the inaccuracies introduced by an idealized model of society are acceptable given the costs of making the models more accurate and the extent of the inaccuracies. If oppression is relevant to a theory's explananda, but de-idealizing the theory doesn't affect its accuracy much, then still the theory's idealized models may be acceptable, and the de-idealizations may not be very helpful.

It's not clear just how inaccurate an idealized model would have to be in order for its idealizations to be unacceptable, but Mills's remarks on the ideal frictionless plane are suggestive. While we might accept that the frictionless plane is an acceptable model of a very smooth, Teflon-coated plane suspended in a vacuum, it would be absurd to accept it as a model of a plane that is covered in Velcro or a plane that's pitted, cracked, and abraded. With planes like these, Mills says, in order to model the actual workings of the plane, we'll need to start with an actual investigation of the plane's properties, which cannot be conceptualized "in terms of a minor deviation from the ideal" (ibid. 167). We might put the point this way: if the model is *systematically* inaccurate in its representation of relevant features, then its inaccuracies are not minor deviations, and we need to undertake an actual investigation of what we're trying to model. If this is right, then a theory's idealized social models will be unacceptable if (i) oppression is relevant to the theory's explananda and (ii) the theory's idealized models are systematically inaccurate with regard to oppression and its effects. If (i) and (ii) hold, then deidealizing such a theory should produce a theory that is systematically more accurate than the idealized theory. The chapters to come will show that systemic oppression is relevant to content externalism's explananda, such that the theory's idealized social models make it systematically inaccurate.

2.1.2 Exemplars

Some models are meant to be idealized in that they are exemplars of the kind they model. They model what members of the kind *should* be like. Phrases like "model student" and "model citizen" are typically used to refer to an exemplary student or citizen, not an accurate representation of all (or most or even many) members of the kind *student* or the kind *citizen*. Accounts of ideal cities, states, or societies, as in *The Republic*, produce models like this. The model citizen represents what citizens (allegedly) should be, not what they are. Many citizens will be unlike the model citizen. A description of an ideal society represents what cities ought to be, not what they are. So if we use the model citizen or society as a tool for understanding or predicting the behaviors of other citizens or societies, we are likely to be misled. The more significant the differences between the model society and the society we're trying to understand or predict, the less useful the model will be.

But when we appeal to exemplars like this, we're not always trying to understand or predict the behaviors of others. We're often concerned instead with how things should be or how they would be if all were optimized. Exemplars tell us what citizens or students should do, not what they will do. They tell us how a just society would be arranged, not how any particular society is arranged. The inaccuracy—the difference between the model and ordinary citizens or societies—is acceptable because we're not using the model to get an accurate prediction or explanation of what ordinary citizens or societies are like. The model isn't supposed to be accurate in predicting what an ordinary citizen or society would do. It's supposed to help us understand what citizenship or justice or studiousness calls for in various situations.

When the model is an exemplar, its inaccuracies may be harmless because they're irrelevant to what it's being used to understand. To 'de-idealize' a model of the exemplary citizen or state by adding features that characterize the typical citizen or state will not produce a model that improves upon its predecessor *with regard to the model's specific explanatory goals.* The model with more typical features will be no better than its predecessor—and likely worse—at telling us what an exemplary citizen would do or how a just society would be arranged. When the idealized model is an exemplar, de-idealizing the model won't improve the theory.

Could the idealized models found in theories of language and mind be models like these, exemplars, so that their inaccuracies don't undermine their uses?

In the de-idealization projects sketched above, it's implausible that the idealized theories were deploying their social models as exemplars. Take Sellars's assumption that all entries into language games are neutral. In the social model he deployed in developing his account of language entrances, he abstracted away from oppression and its effects. His model thus fails to represent the ways that oppression systematically gives us unequal powers upon language entrance (Tirrell 2018a, 16–17; see Tirrell 2018b, 125). But if Sellars's model is meant to be an exemplar, then this isn't in fact a failure. Rather, it would be that his model isn't meant to tell us what our actual language games are like. It would be meant to tell us how language games *should be* in the way that a model of an exemplary citizen tells us how citizens should be. Or, in the way that *The Republic* tells us about justice partly by describing an ideal society, Sellars's model of language games might appeal to an ideal language game in order to tell us about, perhaps, rule-governed linguistic activities?

It's difficult to find a plausible way to end that sentence. Rather, it seems clear that Sellars, like Wittgenstein and Brandom, intended to represent the essential features of our actual language games. They were trying to model the underpinnings of our actual linguistic activities. If so, then the social models they deployed weren't meant to be exemplars. They were meant to be used for accurately representing the social features of language games. This isn't to foreclose the possibility that their models abstracted away from oppression as *simplifications*, as discussed above. If their social models leave out oppression for the sake of simplicity, then this omission is to be justified by deciding (i) whether oppression is relevant to the theory's explananda and (ii) whether the model is systematically inaccurate regarding oppression. Maybe Sellars's social model for language games does make acceptable simplifications. (I think Tirrell shows otherwise.) But that's not what's at issue here. Here, we're considering whether the Sellarsian model's omissions with regard to oppression are acceptable because the model is meant to be

22 NONIDEAL THEORY AND CONTENT EXTERNALISM

an exemplar. And *that* is implausible on its face. If one says it is meant to be an exemplar, we should like to know what purpose the exemplary language game is meant to serve. Is it meant to tell us how language games *should* be? Is it meant to tell us something about justice or citizenship or maybe sportsmanship in the game of giving and asking for reasons? I don't see that there are plausible answers here.

The same holds for the other idealized social models discussed in the review of de-idealizations above. It's implausible on its face that those models are meant to be exemplars. The theories at issue in each case aim to tell us about our actual speech acts, consciousness, memory, and so on. None is trying to tell us how speech acts, memory, or consciousness *should be*, and none is trying to tell us something about the values that speech acts, consciousness, or memory ought to realize. Each model is meant to be more or less accurate (with simplifications, of course). So none of their inaccuracies with regard to oppression should be regarded as acceptable on grounds that the theory's model isn't meant to be an accurate model of society.

These same points apply to content externalism. If its oppression-free model of society were meant to be an exemplar and not a simplified representation of actual language communities, then the theory would not tell us how words *actually* come to have meanings, and it would not be meant to. Inaccuracies in its model of society would or could be acceptable, then, because the model and the theory aren't meant to give accurate representations of any actual language communities. Rather, the theory would purport to tell us what our terms *ought* to mean or refer to. I take it that this is implausible on its face. We should take the model(s) of society that feature(s) in content externalism to be simplified representations, not exemplars. Accordingly, if (i) it is (they are) systematically inaccurate with regard to oppression and (ii) oppression is relevant to its (their) explananda, then its (their) idealizations are unacceptable. If its (their) idealizations are unacceptable, then de-idealizing the varieties of content externalism should produce improved theories.

2.2 Is idealization *antithetical* to the proper goal of the enterprise?

In "Ideal Theory as Ideology," Mills argues that idealizations in moral and political philosophy are "*antithetical* to the proper goal of theoretical ethics as an enterprise" (Mills 2005, 170, original emphasis). Are there any reasons to think the same is true of idealizations in philosophy of mind or language?

Mills makes his case by first characterizing ideal theory and then adopting an "uncontroversial premise" about the ultimate point of ethics: it is "to guide our actions and make ourselves better people and the world a better place" (ibid. 170). He proposes that ideal theory as characterized is in many respects antithetical to that ultimate point.

Mills takes it that what's distinctive of ideal theory in moral and political philosophy is not merely that it idealizes (in the sense of adopting simplified models and/or exemplars) but that it relies on idealization "to the exclusion, or at least marginalization, of the actual" (ibid. 168). Consequently, ideal theory in moral and political philosophy tends either to represent the actual as a simple deviation from the ideal or to claim that "starting from the ideal is at least the best way of realizing it" (ibid. 168). I take it that in the former case, one takes the idealized society to be a model with acceptable simplifications; in the latter case, meanwhile, the idealized society is taken to be an exemplar, and it's claimed that theorizing that begins with analyzing exemplars is the best way to bring an actual state, society, community into correspondence with the exemplary state, society, community. Both approaches model society as free of oppression. They adopt the idealized social ontology, idealized institutions, and idealized 'cognitive sphere' criticized by the de-idealizations described above.

But if ideal theory excludes or marginalizes the actual, then it shall never consider the realities that are crucial to comprehending the actual workings of injustice; it will never consider the things that keep our actual society from realizing the ideal model. It's plausible that this is indeed antithetical to the goal of making our actual society more like the ideal.

This reasoning doesn't go through for philosophy of mind and language. Any version of the uncontroversial premise adapted for mind and language would be uncontroversially false. While we might use what we learn from doing philosophy of mind and language to make the world a better place, it's not the point of the endeavor in anything like the way it is for ethics. The goal(s) of philosophy of mind/language is (are) more plausibly to understand how language and minds work, the nature of meaning, and so on.

Relatedly, as I said above, it's implausible that the social models adopted in philosophy of mind and language are meant to be exemplars. So while it may be plausible that there are traditions in philosophy of mind and language that exclude or marginalize the actualities of systemic oppression, it remains

24 NONIDEAL THEORY AND CONTENT EXTERNALISM

implausible that theories in this tradition 'start from' exemplars. Rather, the theories of mind or language that exclude or marginalize systemic oppression are still purporting to describe actuality, not an ideal society. Plausibly, then, neither of the premises in Mills's argument against ideal theory in ethics has a true counterpart that applies to ideal theory in the philosophies of mind or language. An argument that carries Mills's points over from ethical theory to philosophy of mind or language would seem to be a nonstarter. We don't have reason to think that idealizations are *antithetical* to the enterprise of philosophy of mind or language.

But this isn't to say of course that de-idealizations aren't helpful. Insofar as the goal for philosophy of mind and language is to understand how minds and language work, and insofar as idealizations systematically mislead us about oppression's influences on minds and language, idealizations will systematically undermine our attempts to achieve the goal(s) of theorizing about minds and language. De-idealizations will correct the systematic distortions in our understanding.

Moreover, the points above don't establish that idealizations aren't antithetical to the goals of *individual theories* in philosophy of mind or language. While it may be true that the goal of *the enterprise* isn't to make the world a better place, individual theories might take that or a related goal. If a theory adopts the goal of understanding or articulating oppression, then abstracting away from actual oppression in its social model(s) would plausibly be antithetical to its goals. As we'll see in the next chapter, Sally Haslanger has developed a distinctive account of content externalism partly in order to reveal oppression. If the view is distorted by idealizations, then the theory will obscure what it aims to reveal. The theory's idealizations will prevent it from achieving its goal. If a theory of mind or language seeks to articulate oppression while deploying an idealized social model, then its idealizations may very well be antithetical to the enterprise in which the theory participates.

2.3 The distinction between idealized and de-idealized theories

Herman Cappelen and Josh Dever have recently argued that the distinction between ideal and nonideal theory in philosophy of language is "useless." One might suspect that their arguments also apply to the distinction between idealized and de-idealized theories. If so, then it would raise doubts about my claim that successful de-idealizations improve upon the theories they replace. I'll review Cappelen and Dever's argument and consider the extent to which it challenges the utility of de-idealizations.

Cappelen and Dever make their case by considering several possible articulations of the ideal/nonideal distinction and arguing that none "can provide frameworks to help us pick out interesting subsets of work in philosophy of language" (Cappelen & Dever 2021, 91). This shows, in their view, that attempts to make a distinction between ideal and nonideal philosophy of language "don't find a distinctive failing in philosophy of language to latch onto" (ibid. 92). Expanding on the absence of this distinctive failing, they say that "there is no evidence of any *systematic patterns* in what topics are underexplored [in philosophy of language]" (ibid., original emphasis). As Cappelen and Dever understand it, the distinction between ideal and nonideal philosophy of language would be useful only if there were systematic patterns in the topics that are underexplored in philosophy of language and the ideal/nonideal distinction 'latched onto' the systematic failure to explore some topic(s). But since there is no such systematic failure, the distinction has nothing to latch onto, or in any case, several versions of the distinction that they consider don't point to any such systematic failure. In their view, then, the distinction fails to meet a necessary condition for its usefulness, so it is useless.

Can the same argument be levied against the distinction between ideal and de-idealized theories of language? No. If we try to apply the argument to de-idealization without altering the argument at all, it's a nonstarter. It's not plausibly a necessary condition for the utility of the ideal/de-idealized distinction that it latch onto a systematic failure to explore any *topics*. The distinction has nothing to do with the topics explored in philosophy of language as a subfield. So if we formulate the argument as follows, the first premise is unsupported:

[P1] The idealized/de-idealized distinction is useful in philosophy of language only if the topics on the de-idealized side have been systematically underexplored.

[P2] It's not true that the topics on the de-idealized side of the distinction have been systematically underexplored.

Thus:

[C] The idealized/de-idealized distinction is not useful in philosophy of language.

26 NONIDEAL THEORY AND CONTENT EXTERNALISM

If we revise the argument so that the first premise is more plausible and then we revise the second premise accordingly, P2 comes out false.

[P1*] The idealized/de-idealized distinction is useful in philosophy of language only if the theories on the idealized side are systematically inaccurate and the theories on the de-idealized side correct these inaccuracies.

[P2*] It's not true that the theories on the idealized side are systematically inaccurate and the theories on the de-idealized side correct these inaccuracies.

Thus:

[C] The idealized/de-idealized distinction is not useful in philosophy of language.

Cappelen and Dever motivate their necessary condition by supposing that a useful distinction would provide frameworks to help us pick out interesting subsets of work in philosophy of language. P1* can be motivated in the same way. I take it that if the idealized/de-idealized distinction helps us pick out theories that are systematically inaccurate in their explanations/predictions on one hand and those that correct these inaccuracies on the other, then it helps us pick out interesting subsets of work. Given their motivations, then, Cappelen and Dever should accept that P1* is just as well motivated as P1. There may be other necessary conditions for a distinction's usefulness, but among those conditions that would be relevant to the idealized/de-idealized distinction, I take this to be the closest in spirit to what Cappelen and Dever propose for the ideal/nonideal distinction.

In this argument, in order to reach the conclusion that the distinction is useless, the second premise has to claim that it is not true that idealized theories are systematically inaccurate and that de-idealized theories correct those systematic inaccuracies. But this is false. What it is to be an idealized theory is to be a theory with a social model that ignores and/or obscures systemic oppression. Since systemic oppression is systemic, social models that ignore or obscure it are systematically inaccurate. What it is to de-idealize a theory—and thus to produce a de-idealized theory—is to correct the systematic inaccuracies regarding oppression in an idealized theory. So the de-idealized theories correct the systematic inaccuracies of the idealized theories. P2* is false.

Perhaps there are other plausible necessary conditions for the usefulness of the idealized/de-idealized distinction that would improve this argument.

I don't see that any are worth exploring in detail, though. What motivates the distinction is, as discussed above, that the idealized theories are systematically inaccurate, and in some cases their idealizations undermine the theory's goals. The de-idealized theories, however, correct these inaccuracies and produce theories that better serve the theory's goals.

Finally, it's worth noting that the Cappelen/Dever argument fails to show that Charles Mills's version of the ideal/nonideal distinction—the version to which I appeal above—is useless for philosophy of language. One might think that the idealized/de-idealized distinction stands and falls with Mills's distinction, so if the argument against Mills's distinction succeeds, then the idealized/de-idealized distinction is useless in philosophy of language too. I don't think this is true, but I also think it's immaterial. For Cappelen and Dever fail to show that Mills's version of the distinction is useless for philosophy of language. I'll review their argument and then make my case that it fails. I'll say that they concede the crucial premises for an argument that establishes the usefulness of the Millsian distinction in philosophy of language.

Cappelen and Dever make their case against the utility of Mills's distinction by raising considerations very similar to those noted above in the discussion of whether ideal theory in mind and language is *antithetical* to the goals of the enterprise. As we saw above, Mills's argument starts with the "uncontroversial premise" that the ultimate point of ethics is to help us make ourselves and the world a better place. When dominant structures in our world perpetuate injustice rather than produce it, starting from an ideal model of society—an exemplar—will prevent us from understanding what we need to change in order to realize the ideal. So adopting models as exemplars in ethics is plausibly antithetical to the goals of the enterprise. But as we pointed out above, this reasoning doesn't go through for philosophy of language. There's no plausible analog for the uncontroversial premise that holds for philosophy of language, and theories of language don't adopt ideal models of society in the sense of *exemplars*.

Cappelen and Dever agree. Here's how they propose to adapt Mills's argument for application to philosophy of language:

> If we start from what is presumably the uncontroversial premise that the ultimate point of philosophy of language and communication is to guide our speech and make ourselves better speakers, then the ideal-idealized philosophy of language [the kind that adopts models as exemplars] will

not only be unhelpful, but will in certain respects be deeply antithetical to the proper goal of philosophy of language as an enterprise. In modeling human speech on ideal-as-idealized-models and in never exploring how deeply different this is from ideal-as-descriptive-models, we are abstracting away from realities crucial to our comprehension of the actual workings of speech and communication and thereby guaranteeing that the ideal-as-idealized-model will never be achieved. (ibid. 98)

And here's what they say about this adapted argument:

This type of reasoning is deeply flawed. First, the goal of philosophy of language is not to make us better speakers or communicators. That much is, we take it, common ground here. Second, as we have seen, philosophers of language have not presented ideal-idealized models of how language *ought* to be. They've tried to describe how languages actually are and how speakers actually behave. In so doing they by necessity abstract from certain feature[s] of real speakers, but that's essential to all theorizing (as Mills recognizes). Russell doesn't say that descriptions *ought* to be quantifiers. He says that they are. Kripke doesn't claim that names ought to be rigid designators. He claims that they are. Grice doesn't claim that people ought to follow the cooperative principle. He claims that some people sometimes do (and that if you want to exchange information, the maxims of conversation are useful). So . . . the objection to ideal-idealized models doesn't work when applied to philosophy of language. (Ibid. 99)

Here, Cappelen and Dever reject the same two claims that we did above. Philosophy of language doesn't have the same goals as ethical theory, and it doesn't adopt models as exemplars. So the argument that ideal theory in philosophy of language is *antithetical* to the enterprise is unconvincing.

As we saw above, however, that doesn't show that the distinction is *useless* for philosophy of language. Instead, the distinction would be quite useful if it nonetheless points to a way in which dominant theorizing undercuts our attempts to realize the goals of philosophy of language. Where the goal is, as Cappelen and Dever say, to describe how languages actually are and how speakers actually behave, then this goal would be undercut if there's something about dominant theorizing that systematically inhibits our ability to describe languages and speakers accurately.

If dominant theorizing in philosophy of language were making use of models as *exemplars*, then that would indeed undercut the goal, but this isn't the only way the goal may be undercut, and I don't see any reason to insist that this is what Mills's version of "ideal theory" refers to in philosophy of language. When Mills outlines the common features of ideal theories, he's concerned with the ways that they model society as free of oppression—the idealized social ontology, idealized institutions, idealized cognitive sphere, and so on. These can show up in a model that's meant to be descriptive just as they can show up in a model that's meant to be prescriptive or an exemplar. And when they show up in a model that's meant to be accurate (but of course simplified) to what our society is like, they can be systematically misleading. If the society being modeled has various oppressions that systematically affect its social ontology, institutions, and cognitive sphere, for instance, then the idealized model will be systematically inaccurate. If we nonetheless take the model to be accurate (though of course simplified), then we will be systematically misled about our society. We will treat oppression as a minor deviation from the norm, when it is in fact a feature of the social system we're trying to understand. Moreover, if we make this mistake when we're trying to describe how languages actually are and how speakers actually behave, then we're liable to be misled also about how languages actually are and how speakers actually behave. So I propose that we take "ideal theory" in philosophy of language to refer to theorizing that adopts models of society that idealize the society's ontology, institutions, and so on. If dominant theorizing in philosophy of language adopts idealized models, then these models might undercut attempts to realize the goals of the enterprise. If they do, then the ideal/nonideal distinction would be quite useful in philosophy of language.

Does dominant theorizing in philosophy of language adopt idealized models? The examples of de-idealization above suggest, at least, that such models are widespread in philosophy of language. Moreover, Cappelen and Dever seem to concede that the answer is "yes." In responding to an objection, they concede that in philosophy of language, "there's important data that some theorists have overlooked and that the reason they have overlooked it is because the majority of the theorists have certain socio-cultural biases" (ibid. 99–100). In the objection they consider, the overlooked data involve non-Western speakers, but the point they concede is general: when a majority of theorists has the same or similar sociocultural biases, it can happen that this majority will overlook important data. Cappelen and Dever say this "happens all the time" (ibid. 100). Mills suggests that for the middle- to upper-class White males who constitute the majority in philosophy, their sociocultural biases tend to make them overlook that oppression is systemic and that it systematically affects social ontology, institutions, and so on (Mills 2005, 172). Cappelen and Dever seem to be conceding that it happens all the time that White, middle- to upper-class male theorists overlook oppression and its effects when those are nonetheless important to their theorizing. But if this happens in philosophy of language, then dominant theorizing in philosophy of language adopts idealized models.[8]

Do idealized models undercut attempts to realize the goals of philosophy of language? Again, the examples of de-idealization above should show us

---

[8] Cappelen and Dever seem unconcerned that granting this point undercuts their earlier claim that "ideal theory" fails to pick out a distinctive failing in philosophy of language because there aren't any systematic patterns in the topics it fails to explore (Cappelen & Dever 2021, 92). But if dominant theorists systematically overlook oppression and its effects, that would be a systematic pattern in the topics they fail to explore, and if these data are important, that would be a distinctive failing. It may be that they aren't concerned because the paper includes threads of a seemingly very different argument against the ideal/nonideal distinction that could concede these points. This argument, however, is neither fully fleshed out nor compelling, so I'm discussing it only in a footnote. The argument goes like this: The ideal/nonideal distinction is useless because "a lot of what people aim to capture with the ideal/nonideal distinction is unimportant or incoherent, and we suggest that the remaining sensible parts reduce to" the claim that some topic or other is simply underexplored (ibid. 94). In the case of overlooked data about oppression and its effects, then, perhaps Cappelen and Dever would say simply that although this use of the ideal/nonideal distinction is "sensible," it reduces to the simple claim that oppression and its effects have simply been underexplored. Indeed, they say that the claim that "in any field, there will always be topics that are under-explored" is "perfectly placed to account for" the fact that dominant theorizing has overlooked oppression and its effects (ibid. 92, 99). This argument fails for at least two reasons. First, the mere observation that there will always be topics that are underexplored does not perfectly account for idealizations, even by Cappelen and Dever's own lights. As noted in the main text, they concede that oversights in philosophy of language are accounted for by theorists' biases, not by the mere fact that there will always be underexplored topics. This is important because when the vast majority of theorists have similar biases, some topics are *systematically* underexplored. Simply noting that there will always be underexplored topics won't explain why some underexploration is systematic. Since the issue is whether there are systematic oversights in philosophy of language, their concession about theorists' biases undercuts their attempt to dismiss the existence of underexplored topics as trivial. Second, even if their argument here did go through, it wouldn't establish that the ideal/nonideal distinction is useless. If it's true that "the remaining sensible parts" of the ideal/nonideal distinction in philosophy of language "reduce to" the claim that some topics are underexplored, that wouldn't show that the distinction is useless. The distinction would still be useful for picking out the "remaining sensible parts." If Cappelen and Dever then introduce another way of picking out those same "sensible parts," then we have two ways of picking out those remaining sensible parts. This doesn't make it so that either way is useless. It makes it so that, now, there's something else—Cappelen's and Dever's claim—that has the same use as the ideal/nonideal distinction. The distinction remains useful. Moreover, it's plausible that the ideal/nonideal distinction serves this use much better than the general claim to which Cappelen and Dever appeal does. As we saw, the ideal/nonideal distinction points out topics that are systematically underexplored; it gives us a way to identify systematically underexplored topics by noting and correcting researchers' biases. The general claim offers no such aid; it simply asserts that there exist underexplored topics, giving us no clues as to what these topics are or which among them are underexplored by coincidence and which are underexplored thanks to features of the systems that shape our inquiry.

that in many cases, they do. If Sellars's goal was to accurately describe actual languages and how speakers actually behave, then Lynne Tirrell shows that he undercut his own attempts to realize this goal by adopting an idealized social ontology. His assumption that all language entrance transitions are neutral undercut his ability to accurately describe language games and instead made his account systematically inaccurate. If David Lewis's goal was to accurately describe actual human conventions and how we arrived at them, then Jessica Keiser shows that his idealizations undercut his attempts. And so on.

Thus, although Mills's argument against ideal theory in ethics doesn't transfer straightforwardly to philosophy of language, we nonetheless have good reason to find the ideal/nonideal distinction useful in philosophy of language. If we take "ideal theory" to refer to theories that adopt idealized social models, then ideal theory would seem to be widespread in philosophy of language, and it would in many cases undercut our attempts to realize the goals of philosophy of language as an enterprise. "Ideal theory" picks out a systematic pattern of oversights in theorizing about language, and the ideal/nonideal distinction gives us a framework that helps us pick out interesting subsets of work. On the "nonideal" side, it picks out those works that help correct the works that undercut attempts to accurately describe language and language users. On the "ideal" side, it picks out works that adopt idealized models and may (but also may not) thereby undercut our attempts to describe language and its use.

3. Conclusion

My aim in this chapter was to introduce, clarify, and motivate de-idealization as a kind of philosophical project generally and de-idealizations in philosophy of mind and language more specifically. I gave examples of de-idealizations in philosophy of mind and language and responded to objections. In the next chapter, I'll introduce and motivate content externalism before developing the de-idealization of one prominent version of the theory.

2

De-idealizing objective type externalism

0. Introduction

This chapter motivates and develops a de-idealization of one influential version of content externalism—namely, objective type externalism. After introducing content externalism and terminology important for understanding it, I'll characterize objective type externalism in more detail and argue that systemic oppression is relevant to its central explananda. In the previous chapter, we saw that if oppression is relevant to an idealized theory's explananda, then since idealized models are systematically inaccurate with regard to oppression, such theories will be systematically inaccurate, and their idealizations will be unacceptable. Using some terminology that will be explained below, we'll see that oppression systematically influences both (i) the meanings, extensions, and contents of our social kind terms and (ii) the processes that, according to objective type externalism, determine those meanings, extensions, and contents. By idealizing or simplifying away from oppression and its effects, the idealized version of objective type externalism fails to recognize systematic features of the meaning-determining processes it posits, and it fails to recognize systematic influences on the meanings, extensions, and contents it aims to explain. By incorporating these features and influences into its account, the de-idealized theory gives us an account of social kind terms' extensions and how they're determined that is systematically more accurate than the idealized theory. In addition, it reveals effects of oppression that are obscured by the idealized theory.

In Section 1, I'll introduce content externalism, objective type externalism, and the theory of which the latter is an extension, natural kind externalism. At the end of the section, I'll say that objective type externalism has three explanatory goals when applied to social kind terms, and it satisfies these goals by appealing to three stages in the determination and discovery of terms' extensions. In the idealized account of objective type externalism, no stage is systematically influenced by oppression or its effects. But Section 2 argues that for social kind terms, in fact each stage is systematically influenced by

Nonideal Theory and Content Externalism. Jeff Engelhardt, Oxford University Press. © Oxford University Press 2024.
DOI: 10.1093/oso/9780197754191.003.0002

oppression. Section 3 outlines changes to the view so that the de-idealized version can account for oppression's influences at each stage; this makes it so the de-idealized theory can better serve objective type externalism's three explanatory goals. Thus, the de-idealized theory is an improvement over its idealized predecessor.

1. Content externalism

Content externalism is the view that the contents of at least some thoughts or the meanings of at least some words aren't fully determined by what's going on inside the body or brain of the relevant thinker or speaker.[1] Many people think that if Ghassan says, "Elm trees bend in the spring wind," then the meaning of Ghassan's utterance of "elm trees" is determined by what's going on 'inside' Ghassan. Something about his brain or central nervous system makes his words refer to specific parts of the world and mean the things they do. Indeed, the common thought is that *nothing more than* something about Ghassan's brain or central nervous system makes his utterance of "elm trees" refer to and mean what it does. Ghassan's physical body fully determines the meaning and reference of all his words. Content externalism denies this.

Similarly, it's common to think that concepts are fully determined by thinkers' bodies. When Ghassan says "elm trees," his words express a concept. Call it ELM.[2] Many people would find it intuitive to think that something about Ghassan's body fully determines what ELM is about, what it represents and which parts of the world it picks out. Generalizing, the intuition here is that for every concept, the concept's content is fully determined by the thinker's body. Content externalism denies this too.

Because content externalism denies these common claims, it should say what *does* do the determining. For those cases in which a term's meaning or a concept's content isn't determined by the speaker's or thinker's body, what does determine that meaning or content?

Note that content externalism says only that *at least some* terms or concepts don't have their meanings/contents determined by the speaker's or

---

[1] This is a common formulation of the externalist thesis, and it's acceptable for our purposes, but note that there is controversy over whether we can take 'skull or skin' to be the boundary between *internal* and *external*. See, for example, Farkas (2003).

[2] I'll use small caps to indicate when I'm referring to concepts. I'll use double quotation marks to indicate when I'm referring to words. Thus, when Chitra says the word "tree," she expresses the concept TREE, and both her word and concept refer to trees.

thinker's body. So the explanation it owes us doesn't have to hold for all terms and/or concepts, just for some. Or, similarly, a content externalist could say that terms/concepts of one kind have their meanings/contents determined in way Alpha, while terms/concepts of another kind are determined in way Beta, and so on. That is, one could identify several different externalist ways for determining meanings/contents.

I'll focus on two. One says, loosely, that some meanings/contents are determined by the things in the world to which they refer. The word "water," for example, is supposed to have had its reference fixed by people pointing at samples of water and saying the word. That fixed the word so it picks out not only the stuff once pointed to but to all stuff of the same *kind*. Whatever that kind is, it's that stuff itself that determines what the word "water" refers to. We learned after the term had its reference fixed this way that the kind includes all and only stuff composed of H_2O. That kind, then, determined the meaning and reference of "water"; the speakers before that discovery couldn't have done it, it seems, because they didn't know about that kind, H_2O. Usually, the kinds of terms/concepts that are said to have their meanings/contents determined this way are called "natural kind terms." They refer to and have their meanings determined by kinds that are objective or part of the nature of things. Accordingly, I'll call this "natural kind externalism."

Natural kind externalism is often associated with 20th-century philosopher Hilary Putnam and his Twin Earth thought experiment. I'll review the thought experiment in the next section. But before getting to those details, it is helpful to contrast this view with another way in which Putnam says terms may have their meanings determined. On this account, some meanings/contents are determined by facts about the linguistic community to which the speaker/thinker belongs. In particular, Putnam says there is a "division of linguistic labor" that is much like the more familiar division of labor: while a great many use the products of the divided labor, select members of the community make those products usable, and the rest of us depend on them for those products. Using "extension" for the set of things that a term picks out, Putnam says,

> Whenever a term is subject to the division of linguistic labor, the "average" speaker who acquires it does not acquire anything that fixes its extension. In particular, his individual psychological state certainly does not fix its extension; it is only the sociolinguistic state of the collective linguistic body to which the speaker belongs that fixes the extension. (Putnam 1975, 146)

John Hawthorne and Juhani Yli-Vakkuri illustrate Putnam's point with the terms "topside" and "sirloin" (Yli-Vakkuri & Hawthorne 2018, 7–8). Many competent speakers of English are (like I am) unable to tell the differences between topside and sirloin, but when they talk and think about topside and sirloin, they refer to different things because they think and talk about whatever the experts in their community are referring to with the terms "topside" and "sirloin." Those of us who can't tell the difference defer to the experts who can. The meaning of "topside" when I say it isn't fully determined by my brain or body, and neither is the content of my concept TOPSIDE; they're determined by "the sociolinguistic state of the collective linguistic body" to which I belong. Prima facie, they're determined by those who can tell the difference between topside and other cuts of meat—butchers and chefs, for example—and by our collective linguistic body's practices of deferring to these experts when it comes to the term "topside." Call this "social externalism." I'll focus on social externalism in Chapter 3.

In order to avoid the tedious repetition of constructions like "terms/concepts" and "meanings/extensions/contents," I'll talk primarily of terms and their extensions or referents, except where the difference between terms and concepts matters to the relevant reasoning. If we take it that the relevant terms mean what they do because of what they refer to, and that the relevant concepts have the contents they do because of their extensions, then there should be few cases, if any, in which the arguments that follow can't be translated from the language of terms and extensions into the language of meanings, concepts, and contents (see Yli-Vakkuri & Hawthorne 2018, 1–5, 18).

1.1 Natural kind externalism

There are two famous arguments for content externalism. Each relies heavily on a thought experiment, and it's common to refer to each argument by naming its associated thought experiment. Hilary Putnam's 1975 Twin Earth thought experiment is the most famous argument for natural kind externalism, and Tyler Burge's 1979 'tharthritis' thought experiment is often taken as being the most famous argument for social externalism.[3] I'll discuss the

---

[3] But see Yli-Vakkuri and Hawthorne (2018), who point out that Putnam also argued for social externalism and who offer a more recent and more ambitious argument for a conclusion that supports content externalism.

36 NONIDEAL THEORY AND CONTENT EXTERNALISM

Twin Earth experiment and argument here, and I'll review the tharthritis thought experiment in the next chapter.[4]

On one traditional interpretation, the Twin Earth thought experiment aims to establish that some thought contents are partly determined by a thinker's natural environment outside their body. If some contents are partly determined by one's natural environment, then some contents aren't fully determined by what's going on inside the thinker's body. Since content externalism is the view that the contents of at least some thoughts or the meanings of at least some words aren't fully determined by what's going on inside the body or brain of the relevant thinker or speaker, the thought experiment would establish content externalism.

In order to show that some thought contents are partly determined by a thinker's environment, the Twin Earth thought experiment aims to show that for the relevant thought contents, a speaker can't have a thought with that content unless her environment contains the right objects, facts, properties, and so on. For instance, the experiment suggests that it's impossible to have a thought with the content of our concept WATER unless one's external environment contains the right stuff, H_2O.[5] If it's true that one can't have the concept WATER unless one's environment contains H_2O, then, prima facie, the presence of H_2O in one's environment plays a role in making it the case that one has the relevant content whenever one does, in fact, have the concept WATER.[6] That is, the stuff in the environment, H_2O, partly determines the contents of thoughts that involve the concept WATER. If this is true of WATER or other contents, then some thought contents are partly determined by a thinker's natural environment outside their body.

Putnam argues for the point by drawing on our intuitions about two people, Oscar and Twin Oscar, who live on different planets: Earth before 1750 and Twin Earth (before Twin 1750), respectively. The two planets are almost exactly alike, and Oscar and Twin Oscar are meant to be molecule-for-molecule duplicates. Indeed, for every person on Earth before 1750, there

---

[4] I don't offer these arguments in an attempt to convince you that content externalism is true. I'm just showing you why some take it seriously and using the arguments to help clarify some versions of the view. The arguments I'll offer—regarding de-idealization—are directed at those who already take content externalism seriously.

[5] This is how the point is expressed in Rowlands et al. (2020, §3). I have doubts about this way of putting it, but they won't matter for our purposes here.

[6] The fact that we do have H_2O in our bodies wouldn't undermine the point—it's the water outside our bodies that enables us to think about H_2O. However, if you think this fact does undermine the conclusion, you can replace H_2O in the thought experiment with another 'natural kind,' as discussed below, that doesn't occur in human bodies.

is a duplicate on Twin Earth; if a person speaks English on Earth, her duplicate on Twin Earth speaks a language that sounds exactly like English, she will say things that sound the same, and her brain activity will be the same. The one difference between the two planets is that wherever there is H_2O on Earth, there is a substance that looks, tastes, and smells just like water to Twin Earthians, is called "water" in Twin English, and plays in Twin Earth life the same role that water plays in Earth life—but this substance is not H_2O. It has a different chemical composition—call it XYZ—but since it is before 1750 on Earth and Twin Earth, neither chemical composition has yet been discovered. Oscar on Earth doesn't know he drinks and bathes in H_2O, and his twin on Twin Earth doesn't know he drinks and bathes in XYZ. Each would utter a word that sounds like the English word "water" to refer to the stuff in his respective world, and since they're molecule-for-molecule duplicates (except that one has H_2O where the other has XYZ), whatever is going on in Oscar's body when he says "water" is type-identical to whatever is happening in Twin Oscar's body when he makes the same sound.

In this situation, on the one hand, when Oscar says "water," he is presumably referring to H_2O. That's the stuff he drinks, bathes in, sees when he visits the ocean, and so on. On the other hand, when Twin Oscar says "water," he is also referring to the stuff he drinks, bathes in, and sees when he visits the ocean. But if so, then Twin Oscar isn't referring to H_2O; he's referring to XYZ. The extension of Oscar's term differs from that of his twin's term. Similarly, it would seem that when Oscar thinks about the stuff in his environment, he's thinking about H_2O, while Twin Oscar is thinking about XYZ.

On one common interpretation of Putnam's argument, he assumes that for *natural kind terms,* they can't differ in their extensions unless they differ in their meanings—ergo, Oscar's and Twin Oscar's utterances of "water" have different meanings (Putnam 1975, 219–227).[7] Natural kind terms are terms that refer (or purport to refer) to natural kinds—kinds of thing that are distinguished from one another by nature itself, not merely by our conventions, interests, perceptual capacities, and so on. "Electron," "hydrogen," "water," and "*Tyrannosaurusrex*" are plausibly natural kind terms, while "national border," "blog," and "companion animal" presumably are not. If that's true, and if "water" out of each twin's mouth is a natural kind term, then the only way for the two terms to differ in extension is if they have

---

[7] See Yli-Vakkuri and Hawthorne (2018, 8) for one account of this interpretation, but also see their discussion of complexities that this interpretation plausibly overlooks (ibid. 8n12).

different meanings. Since the terms do have different extensions, they must have different meanings. If their terms have different meanings, then since meanings correspond to conceptual contents, their conceptual contents must differ too.

If this is right, then when Oscar and his twin think about the stuff they drink and bathe in, they are having thoughts with different contents, even though what's going on in their bodies is the same. The content of Oscar's thought is such that it picks out water—its extension contains all and only H_2O. This is our Earth concept WATER. The content of Twin Oscar's thought doesn't pick out H_2O but XYZ. This is a Twin Earth concept that's expressed by a Twin English word that sounds just like our word "water." Say that this concept is TWATER. Although what's going on inside Oscar's body is the same as what's going on inside Twin Oscar when they make sounds like "water," their terms nonetheless have different meanings, and their concepts have different contents. The meaning of "water" out of their mouths, then, is not fully determined by what's going on inside their bodies, or else their words would have the same meaning. Similarly for the contents of their concepts. Presumably, this extends at least to other natural kind terms and their correlated concepts. The externalist claim is justified: the contents of at least some thoughts and the meanings of at least some words aren't fully determined by what's going on inside the body or brain of the relevant thinker or speaker.

1.2 Objective type externalism

As motivated by the Twin Earth thought experiment, natural kind externalism seems (i) to be limited to natural kind terms/concepts and (ii) to require differences in natural environment to underwrite differences in meaning/content. Here, we'll see that Sally Haslanger has extended the view to apply also to social kind terms/concepts; I'll follow her in calling the resulting view "objective type externalism."

Haslanger makes the case that what's true of natural kind terms and their reference to natural kinds is true for all "type-terms":

> Type-terms (such as general nouns) pick out a type, whether or not we can state the essence of the type, by virtue of the fact that their meaning is determined by a selection of paradigms together with an implicit extension

of one's reference to things of the same type as the paradigms. (Haslanger 2008, 63)[8]

She offers a vivid illustration. Imagine a meeting between the R&D and marketing departments at a toy company. Members of the former present a sample of a stretchy, squishy, fungible substance, and the marketing director dubs the substance "Floam." Thereafter, "'Floam' refers to a whole kind of stuff, some of which has not yet been produced, and the ingredients of which are totally mysterious" (ibid.). In this example, the stuff Floam doesn't seem to be a natural kind.[9] And yet the characteristic points of natural kind externalism still seem to hold. When members of the marketing department say "Floam," they refer to the stuff presented to them by R&D, even if the speakers don't know what Floam is made of, and even if they can't tell Floam from flubber, glorp, or glurch. The extension of their term (and its associated concept) doesn't seem to be fully determined by what's going on in their bodies. Rather, the extension is determined by "a selection of paradigms together with an implicit extension of one's reference to things of the same type as the paradigms."

Indeed, we can use this case in a Twin Earth–style thought experiment. Suppose that on Twin Earth, there are molecule-for-molecule duplicates of the aforementioned R&D and marketing teams. They have a meeting during which the utterances they produce would sound to us exactly like the utterances produced during the Earthian meeting that Haslanger describes. The twin R&D team produces a substance, and the twin marketing director dubs it "Floam." But on Twin Earth, the stuff they dub "Floam" isn't the same stuff dubbed "Floam" on Earth. Instead, it's the stuff that middle school science teachers on Earth call "glurch" or "slime": a mix of mostly Borax and glue. When speakers on Twin Earth say "Floam," they refer to a different substance. Since Twin Earthians are physical duplicates of the Earthian speakers, the difference in the extension of their term can't be explained by

---

[8] It's important to note that in this part of the paper, Haslanger proposes to identify the meaning of our ordinary term "race" or the concept it expresses. This is important to note because there are other places in which Haslanger appeals to content externalism regarding race and gender terms, but she explicitly denies that her aim is to identify the meaning or extension of the ordinary terms. See, for instance, Haslanger (2000, 34): "My priority in this inquiry is not to capture what we do mean, but how we might usefully revise what we mean for certain theoretical and political purposes."

[9] Floam doesn't *seem to be* a natural kind on grounds that it doesn't occur naturally. It doesn't seem to be distinguished from other stuffs 'by nature itself,' as I said above. But if we take "natural" in "natural kind" to pick out those kinds that have an underlying unifying essence, then Floam plausibly is a natural kind. Thanks to an anonymous reviewer for suggesting that this point be made explicit.

any difference in their bodies. The extension of their term isn't fully determined by what's going on in the body or brain. Instead, it would seem to be explained by the stuff in their environment. And this would seem to be true even if the term at issue isn't a natural kind term.

"'Floam,'" Haslanger says, "refers to the most unified objective type of which the sample is a paradigm instance" (ibid.). Why does "Floam" refer to this type? It's thanks to "the phenomenon of reference magnetism" (ibid.). There are different accounts of what this is and how it works, but the basic idea is that "the most unified objective types" in the world somehow 'attract' reference like a magnet. And it is by this attraction that some most objective kind (presumably the stuff *Floam*) thereby determines the extension of the word "Floam." Thus, although the sample of Floam is a member of many different kinds of thing—squishy things, toys, artificial things, and so on—the word "Floam" doesn't refer to any of these kinds; rather, thanks to reference magnetism, it has its extension determined by the most unified objective type of which the sample of Floam is a member. If this point holds for all type-terms, as Haslanger says, then it holds for a given social kind term provided that there is a unified, objective type to attract its reference.

On the objective type externalist account, we can distinguish three stages or phases in the determination and discovery of a type term's extension. In the first phase, there's a term that roughly or for the most part picks out an objective kind in the world. If Floam is an objective kind, then the uses of "Floam" would seem from the time of the term's first coining to pick out all and only the members of a unified, objective kind. However, the R&D team might later realize that the samples they were producing were in fact of two different substances, say, Floam and flubber. In this case, it may be that there is no one objective kind of which all the term's referents are instances. This often happens with our terms, but it doesn't foreclose the possibility that the term has its extension determined in the way described by natural kind or objective type externalism. "Water" was (and is) used for many things that aren't pure H_2O, but it's one of the natural kind externalist's leading examples. This seems to hold for many social kind terms, including race and gender terms, as well. Natalie Stoljar has made the case, for instance, that there are no features shared by all and only the people to whom the word "woman" refers (Stoljar 1995; see Spelman 1988). But a term can refer to an objective type even if speakers also apply it (the term) to things that aren't members of that type. Speakers might be mistaken, some uses might be figurative, and so on. "Gold" refers to the element with atomic number 79, even if speakers sometimes apply the term mistakenly (to iron pyrite, for example) or figuratively (as in "that joke is gold"). Despite such disparate uses, when a term's paradigmatic applications fall into a most unified, objective kind, then there is an implicit expansion of the term's extension to things of the same type as the paradigms (or some of the paradigms, anyway), even if speakers couldn't identify this type or distinguish it from other similar types. The term is attracted to a reference magnet in the world, and this magnet determines the term's extension, whether the term's users know about the magnet or not.

In the first phase, the term's extension has been determined by the unified, objective type that attracts its reference. In the second phase, we undertake efforts to discover the term's extension. In Haslanger's example, the R&D team would try to identify the essential features of Floam that make it what it is. They might ask, Is it still Floam if you add colorful dye during its production? If the original sample were made with an expensive and rare compound, could samples with the same Floam essence be produced with substitutes for this expensive compound? What makes Floam an *entirely different kind* from other stretchy, squishy substances like putty? And so on. In answering these questions, the researchers will identify the kind to which "Floam" already refers—the kind to which the term's extension has already been extended. In deciding whether it's possible to make Floam with a cheaper substitute for its most expensive ingredient, researchers won't be simply stipulating that "Floam" does or doesn't refer to the substance made from the substitute compound; they'll be *discovering* whether or not the term *already* has the substance made with the cheaper compound in its extension. Just as empirical research revealed that seawater, lake water, and tap water all have the same essence and that the term "water" had all and only instances of this essence in its extension all along, so too will the R&D team discover what "Floam" had in its extension all along.

On Haslanger's view, the same goes for social kind terms, so long as there is some unified, objective type that a given term picks out. The second stage involves discovering what race terms, gender terms, or other social kind terms already have in their extensions. Researchers aim to figure out what, if anything, makes the paradigmatic applications of "woman," "Black," or "poor," applications to the same kind of person. They might ask whether identifying as a woman is necessary and/or sufficient for being a woman. They might ask whether it's necessary and/or sufficient for being a woman that one is systematically subordinated along some dimension and targeted for this subordination thanks to their presumed female role in reproduction (see Haslanger 2000, 39, 42). Maybe they'll ask whether a person's race is determined by their ancestry, their morphological features, community consensus, and so on. In answering these questions, researchers will identify the kinds to which social kind terms already refer. They'll be discovering what each term already has in its extension. If this is discovered for some term, then the discovery will reveal the reference magnet that has been attracting the term's reference all along.

In the third phase, ordinary speakers accept that the empirical results of the second phase tell them what the term does and has always referred to. If the R&D team discovers that the stuff made with the cheaper compound isn't (and never was) the same stuff as the original Floam—if the stuff made with the cheaper compound isn't a member of the kind that attracts the reference of "Floam"—then the marketing team and everyone else at the toy company will accept it. If anyone uses the term "Floam" for the cheaper stuff, they'll regard these uses as erroneous or nonliteral, and they'll take it that their rules or norms for using the term had, ever since the term was coined, made it erroneous to apply "Floam" to the cheaper substance.

So too for social kind terms. If researchers discover that race and gender terms refer to social constructs that position people in oppressive hierarchies according to their presumed sex or ancestry, then ordinary speakers will accept this conclusion. If anyone were to apply "woman" to a person S who isn't targeted for systematic subordination along some dimension thanks to S's being presumed to play a female's biological role in reproduction, then ordinary speakers would regard this use of the term as erroneous or nonliteral. And they would take it that the community's norms or rules for using the term "woman" had made such uses erroneous or nonliteral ever since the term "woman" entered the language—ever since the unified, objective kind had attracted the term's reference.

1.3 Revising the three phases of determination and discovery

In Section 2, I'll make the case that oppression has a systematic influence on each of the stages that objective type externalism credits with determining the extensions of social kind terms. But before we turn to the de-idealization of objective type externalism, we should revise the foregoing account for reasons that have little to do with oppression and social kind terms. For it's implausible that extensions are determined and discovered as described above, *even for natural kind terms*. For many natural kind terms, it's implausible that researchers simply *discovered* the kind to which the term had already referred; for many natural kind terms, it's just false that ordinary speakers accepted the results of empirical research and changed their usage accordingly. Moreover, we'll see reasons to think that Haslanger herself accepts the points raised to cast doubt on the above descriptions. In light of these considerations, we'll give more plausible descriptions of the stages involved in the determination of type-terms' extensions. It'll be these revised stages of objective type externalism that I de-idealize in Section 2.

Why think it's implausible that researchers *discover* the extensions to which natural kind terms *already* refer? Briefly, the reasoning goes like this: Suppose it's true of every natural kind term that its extension is determined and discovered in the way described in the first two stages above. If this were true, then there wouldn't be any natural kind terms T such that (i) all T's paradigmatic applications for hundreds (or thousands) of years pick out instances of the same unified kind, K1, but then (ii) at some point, speakers of the language to which T belongs are introduced to a superficially similar but chemically distinct substance, K2, and they accept that T's extension also includes instances of K2, even after they're aware that K2 is chemically distinct from K1. In a case like this, T should have K1 in its extension and not K2. As a natural kind, K1 should attract T's reference and fix its extension in the hundreds of years before the language community is introduced to K2. When the language community is introduced to K2, then since K1 and K2 have different chemical compositions, the reference-magnetic connection between T and K1 should make it inappropriate to use T to refer to K2. If anyone does use T to refer to K2, then the language community should regard these uses as erroneous or nonliteral—at least once researchers determine that K1 and K2 have different chemical compositions. If both (i) and (ii) are true of a term, however, then this isn't what happens. Instead, speakers of the relevant language accept that T has both K1 and K2 in its extension. Thus, if there are any natural kind terms like this, then it's false that all natural kind terms have their extensions determined and discovered as described above. We'll see that there are natural kind terms like T. This makes it implausible that natural kind terms have their extensions determined by the most objective kinds into which their paradigms fall and then discovered by empirical research into the relevant kinds.

44 NONIDEAL THEORY AND CONTENT EXTERNALISM

Examples like this also make it implausible that ordinary speakers accept the results of empirical research and change their usage accordingly. If this were true, then when speakers learn that K1 and K2 have different chemical compositions, they would start treating uses of T that refer to K2 as erroneous or nonliteral. Indeed, they would carry on as though their linguistic norms had always made such uses erroneous or nonliteral. But, again, this isn't what happens in the relevant cases.

Joseph LaPorte has provided several examples that realize features (i) and (ii) above. I'll review one: the actual history of the Chinese term "yü."[10]

As readers might know, the English word "jade" has in its extension two kinds of precious stone with two different and unrelated microstructures: jadeite ($NaAl(SiO_3)_2$) and nephrite ($Ca_2(Mg,Fe)_5Si_8O_{22}(OH)_2$). One might think this term realizes features (i) and (ii), but that's contentious. Putnam says the term "jade" had an established application to both kinds—we might say the term has had both jadeite and nephrite among its paradigms as long as it's been in use (Putnam 1975, 241; see LaPorte 2004, 94). If so, then there was never a time when the term's paradigms might have been implicitly extended to jadeite only or nephrite only. And so the case of "jade" wouldn't satisfy the first condition: there was never a time when its paradigmatic applications were instances of a single, unified chemical type (say, nephrite).

But the same can't be said about the Chinese word for jade, "yü." In China, nephrite was used and regarded for thousands of years in a way analogous to how Westerners used and regarded gold: as the most precious of material substances, as a currency, as an indicator of the highest excellence, as the material from which the most precious and masterful carvings were made. And, as with gold, it was important to be able to distinguish nephrite from other, less precious materials that resemble it (LaPorte 2004, 95). After thousands of years of working with nephrite, LaPorte says, it wasn't until the end of the 18th century that a shipment of jadeite from Myanmar (then Burma) made its way to China. Before the introduction of jadeite to China, all the paradigms of "yü" were nephrite. The most objective, unified type into which the paradigms of "yü" fell would have been the type that includes all and only nephrite. If the term had had its extension determined by this type, then the term would have referred to nephrite and not jadeite. Accordingly, when

---

[10] Also see his discussions of "reptile," "rodent," "fish," "lizard," and many more (LaPorte 2004, 68–69).

jadeite was introduced, then although speakers might initially have mistaken it for nephrite, and so they might have called it "yü," they would have corrected themselves upon learning that they are two different substances. They should have treated applications of "yü" to jadeite as either erroneous or nonliteral.

That's not what happened. "Yü" now has in its extension both nephrite and jadeite (ibid. 96).

> Significantly, the Chinese have come to accept jadeite as true jade. "Yü" and "jade" both apply clearly to jadeite as well as to nephrite. True jade includes and is limited to nephrite and jadeite. Jadeite has now even surpassed nephrite in use.
>
> The acceptance of jadeite as the real thing is remarkable, in view of the venerable status of yü in Chinese culture. Authorities have marveled at the phenomenon. Thus, Ward and Ward (1996, p. 24):
>
>> For the past two hundred years (and disregarding the 5,000 years that preceded them) jadeite has been the preeminent stone and gem within China. It seems that no one objected to the culture's central substance being supplanted by a totally different material. Perhaps calling both yü eased the transition. (LaPorte 2004, 96)

And this use of "yü" doesn't seem to have been threatened by evidence that the two are different substances. The 1863 discovery that nephrite and jadeite have different chemical compositions came less than a century after the introduction of jadeite in China, and the application of "yü" to both has continued for over a century afterward. Moreover, LaPorte suggests that the Chinese well could have distinguished between the two even before their chemical compositions were discovered. Having worked nephrite by hand for generations, they could tell by its feel that it is a different material. There is some evidence that some at first considered it a cheap imitation of jade, and it wasn't uncommon to mark the distinction with modifiers: they called it "new jade," "Yün-nan jade" (because "it entered China through the province of Yün-nan" (ibid 96)), and "kingfisher jade" (because its color resembles the kingfisher's feathers).

Thus, at the time jadeite was introduced in China, it was true that the paradigms of "yü" were nephrite, and there were grounds for identifying the most objective, unified type to which these paradigms belonged as a type that didn't include jadeite. If the term's extension had been determined by

46   NONIDEAL THEORY AND CONTENT EXTERNALISM

the most objective, unified type into which its paradigms fell, then jadeite would have been excluded from its extension. But speakers didn't carry on as though jadeite was excluded from the term's extension. Prima facie, the term's meaning wasn't *forced* on the language community by the substances in the world or their alleged reference-magnetic powers.[11]

What examples like this show is that language communities play a larger role in determining the extensions of their terms than objective type externalism typically acknowledges. A language community can respond to the results of empirical inquiry in various ways. They can change their usage in the way traditional natural kind externalism predicts they will, but they need not. Unless we want to ignore a term's actual usage, we should take it that a language community's response to relevant empirical research also plays a role in determining the extensions of kind terms. This is true even for terms that have been used to refer to the same natural kind for millennia.

Notice that this suggests further possibilities for how language communities influence the extensions of natural kind terms and other type-terms. If there are competing research results for some term, for instance, then a language community might be influenced by some results and not others. A language community's usage might be influenced by biological accounts of race and gender, for instance, while mostly ignoring social construction accounts. Relatedly, a language community's usage for a term might be influenced by outdated research and not by contravening contemporary research. And, again, a language community might be influenced

---

[11] There are, of course, many ways that one might defend the claim that a term's extension is determined by the most objective type into which its paradigms fall. Maybe "yü" referred to both nephrite and jadeite all along—somehow, the kind that included all and only nephrite and jadeite was the most unified type to which the paradigms of yü belonged. Since the paradigms for thousands of years were all of nephrite, and since jadeite and nephrite have completely different chemical compositions, this response would have to explain why—contrary to what we know—the disjunctive kind *jadeite or nephrite* is the most objective and unified kind into which samples of nephrite fall.

Alternatively, one might say that the extension of "yü" excluded jadeite for thousands of years before its introduction in China, and then the term's extension changed (or, if you prefer, the old term was replaced with a homophone with a different extension). Indeed, one might say that as paradigms of "yü" came to include jadeite, the term's extension shifted from an objective and unified type that excludes jadeite to one that includes it. LaPorte argues against this reply, but we can accept it, given our purposes (LaPorte 2004, 97–98). We can accept it because this reply accepts that the language community could have responded to the introduction of jadeite in several different ways (e.g., calling it "yü" or not) and that *this response*—not the most objective, unified kind in the environment—is what determined the term's extension. Our point here is to establish that language communities play a larger role in determining terms' extensions than natural kind externalism typically acknowledges. This opens up the possibility that if a language community is structured by oppression, then oppression and its effects will influence the determination of the term's extension—a possibility ignored by idealized versions of externalism.

by pseudoscientific results or biased 'research' funded and promulgated by corporations who stand to profit from public ignorance. Or, indeed, ordinary usage might be influenced by forces that have nothing to do with research: ad campaigns, trends in a society's educational system, government policies, demagoguery, and so on.

Moreover, it's not just ordinary, nonexpert speakers who may respond to empirical results in many different ways, linguistically speaking. The same goes for the researchers themselves. Indeed, LaPorte has argued that *in the usual case*, researchers *stipulate* (rather than discover) a natural kind term's extension. Researchers typically aren't 'forced' by their empirical work to identify one kind into which a term's paradigms fall. Instead, they tend to choose a way of proceeding, linguistically, and this choice tends to change the meanings of terms in the language rather than to identify what some term(s) meant all along.

LaPorte makes the case that this is true even for the externalist's leading example, "water." The decision to identify water and H_2O was not forced on us by empirical research, he says; rather, researchers could have opted not to identify water with H_2O. Consequently, accepting that "water" has all and only H_2O in its extension was a choice, not a position forced on us by empirical results. Why think we could have opted not to identify water and H_2O? Here's LaPorte:

> *The majority of what we prescientifically called "water" has more than one microstructural feature that we could have concluded distinguishes the true from the spurious samples believed to be water.* A feature other than being H_2O, perhaps one that overlaps with being H_2O, might have been taken to characterize what was to be called "water," and it would have been no more right or wrong to draw the conclusion that some other feature characterizes what is called "water" than to draw the conclusion that being H_2O does the job. (ibid. 103, original emphasis)

To illustrate his point, LaPorte appeals to deuterium oxide, D_2O, discovered in 1931. Like H_2O, D_2O has an oxygen atom combined with two atoms that have the atomic number 1. But H_2O and D_2O differ in both behavior and underlying structure. Deuterium is an isotope of hydrogen: while most hydrogen on Earth has only a proton in its nucleus, deuterium has a proton *and a neutron*. You can make a hydrogen bomb from deuterium but not from ordinary water. H_2O and D_2O have different melting and boiling points. H_2O

can support sea life; D_2O can't. The two substances can be separated with appropriate scientific treatments (ibid. 107). LaPorte imagines a crew of Earth scientists traveling to a planet where D_2O plays a role much like H_2O plays on Earth. Call it "Deuterium Earth." D_2O fills the oceans and streams on Deuterium Earth, pours from the faucets, and falls from the sky when it rains. The inhabitants of Deuterium Earth drink D_2O, just as we drink H_2O. But the crew from Earth discovers that the goldfish and plants they've brought from Earth can't survive on D_2O, and they don't try to drink it themselves. Chemical testing on the substance reveals the aforementioned differences between D_2O and H_2O.

Prima facie, the chemical and behavioral differences between H_2O and D_2O suffice to exclude the latter from the extension of "water." Indeed, the differences between H_2O and D_2O are more extensive than the differences between H_2O and XYZ in the original Twin Earth thought experiment: H_2O and D_2O are separable, they have different boiling and melting points, and so on. So if the differences between H_2O and XYZ suffice to establish that XYZ isn't and *could not be* in the extension of "water," then the differences between H_2O and D_2O should suffice to establish the same. If such ways of carrying on linguistically are discovered and forced upon us by our discoveries, then the researchers who discovered D_2O should have been forbidden from including D_2O in the extension of "water."

Moreover, suppose it were true before the discovery of D_2O that the extension of "water" had been determined by a reference magnetic attraction to H_2O with hydrogen atoms that have no neutron in their nucleus. Then the term's extension would have excluded D_2O, and any applications of "water" to D_2O would have to be erroneous or nonliteral.

But "D_2O is in fact considered water. Often D_2O is called 'heavy water' and normal water 'light water'" (ibid. 107). Researchers elected to include D_2O in the extension of "water." This isn't to say that *this decision* was forced on researchers, either. LaPorte's position—and the point I'm endorsing here— is that researchers could have responded to the evidence in various ways. They could have included D_2O in the extension of "water" or not, and neither choice would have been more right or wrong than the other. And, as LaPorte says above, the same was true when researchers decided that being H_2O is essential to what we call "water." There are other microstructural features that we could have taken as distinguishing true from spurious samples of water. And, indeed, we could have demarcated true from spurious samples of water in different ways: When researchers later included D_2O in the extension of "water," they counted some samples that don't behave like most H_2O among the samples of true water. Researchers, just like language communities, can respond to the results of empirical research in various ways. These responses are not forced on the researchers by their discoveries, by reference magnetism, or by the meanings/extensions of the terms they use.

What these examples show is that researchers' and language communities' responses to empirical results are not forced on them by empirical discoveries, but these responses nonetheless play a role in determining the extensions of natural kind terms. Despite the fact that researchers distinguish jadeite from nephrite, the Chinese word "yü" has both in its extension. The language community applies the term to both kinds, and they don't treat the application of the term to either kind as erroneous or nonliteral. On pain of claiming that uses of the term treated as appropriate are in fact treated as inappropriate, we must accept that the term's extension wasn't fully determined by the most unified, objective kind into which its earlier (i.e., pre-jadeite) paradigms fell.

The case of "water" illustrates both points. Despite the fact that D_2O and H_2O have significant molecular and behavioral differences, researchers include both in the extension of "water." As we saw, researchers could have proceeded in at least two different linguistic ways with regard to the term's extension. But there's at least room for doubt about whether researchers' decision has in fact made it so that D_2O is included in the term's extension. The language community doesn't seem to have given this decision much uptake. The ordinary English speaker would tell you that water = H_2O, as would many philosophers of language. If usage in the language community consistently excludes D_2O from the term's extension, then perhaps this case is more like the Chinese "yü": although researchers say that D_2O is a form of water, the language community includes only H_2O in the term's extension. We don't need to decide this here, though. What's important for us is this: It's implausible that natural kind terms have their extensions fully determined by the most unified, objective kinds into which their (pre-empirical research) paradigmatic applications fall. Instead, researchers and language communities can respond to relevant empirical results in various ways, and these responses can also play a role in determining terms' extensions.

It is important to note that there are discussions in Haslanger's work in which she seems to accept points like these. In a 2005 paper, for instance, she raises doubts about the revisionary/non-revisionary contrast with regard to her social constructionist accounts of race and gender. As she notes there, she had previously said that those accounts were not analyses of our ordinary

50 NONIDEAL THEORY AND CONTENT EXTERNALISM

race and gender terms; rather, they were revisionary proposals, whereby the revised concepts would offer political and theoretical advantages (Haslanger 2005, 11; see Haslanger 2000, 34). But in the 2005 paper, she raises doubts about just how revisionary those proposals were, and she appeals to content externalism to suggest that although ordinary speakers might not *think of* race and gender terms as expressing the meanings described in her account, they may be mistaken about this, just as ordinary speakers could be mistaken about the meanings of terms like "beech," "elm," "sirloin," "quark," and so on. In describing the process by which the extensions of kind terms are determined, she allows that it may involve some refining or revising.[12] This suggests that we should understand objective type externalism as allowing the same.

Haslanger's discussion of the term "incomplete" illustrates the point.[13] There, Haslanger describes how faculty at the Massachusetts Institute of Technology (MIT) might respond to empirical evidence relevant to the extension of the term "incomplete," and she takes this response as playing a role in determining the term's meaning and extension. At MIT, she says, there's a rule stipulating that students may not receive an incomplete for a course unless they've completed at least 80% of the coursework, and most faculty believe that most other faculty follow the rule. If the rule is followed, then all the paradigmatic applications of "incomplete" will be cases in which students have completed at least 80% of their coursework, and the most objective, unified type into which these paradigms fall would, as the rule says, be an institutional kind that includes only cases in which students have completed at least 80% of their work. But in fact it is common for faculty to grant incompletes to students who have completed less than 80% of their work (Haslanger 2005, 21). In this situation, it seems that the paradigmatic applications of the term "incomplete" aren't limited to instances in which the student has completed at least 80% of their coursework. Thus, if the term's extension is determined by the most objective, unified type into which the paradigms fall, the term won't refer to an institutional type whose eligibility conditions require 80% of coursework to be completed. It'll refer to some other objective type. If the extension of the term "incomplete" is fully determined by the most objective, unified type into which its paradigms fall, then there shouldn't be much

---

[12] As noted above, in the 2008 article that appeals to the Floam example, Haslanger's appeal to content externalism is meant to reveal the extensions of our ordinary type-terms.

[13] See also Haslanger 2020a and 2020b, in which she articulates how it's possible for social forces to alter the content of an externalist concept.

more to say about it: The term's extension has already been fixed. The faculty can discover what that extension is by identifying the objective kind into which the term's paradigmatic applications fall, or they could introduce a new term that seeks to pick out a different type, but the extension of the term "incomplete" isn't up to them—they play no role in determining its meaning or extension.

But Haslanger doesn't think that's the whole story about the determination of "incomplete." "Once the gap between rule and practice is pointed out," she says, "there may be controversy about what an incomplete 'really is'" (ibid. 22). Some might say that the rule determines what an incomplete really is, and the practice of giving incompletes ought to follow the rule. Others might say that the practice determines what an incomplete really is, and the rule ought to be changed (so that, say, an incomplete can be given to any student who has completed at least 50% of their coursework).

Note the parallels between Haslanger's account of this situation and LaPorte's take on his examples. Researchers discovering D_2O faced a decision about what water *really is*, and they could have proceeded as though D_2O is in the extension of "water" or not; the Chinese language community faced a decision about what yü *really is*, and they could have refused to accept that jadeite is in the term's extension or not. So too the MIT language community faces a decision about what an incomplete really is, and they can accept certain applications of "incomplete" as appropriate or decide that such uses are mistaken. In each case, the language community may respond in various ways to the results of empirical inquiry about the objective type(s) into which paradigmatic applications of the term fall, and its response will partly determine the term's meaning and extension. Researchers and language communities respond to empirical discoveries relevant to a given type-term's extension, and these responses also play a role in determining the term's extension.

With these points in mind, we are now in a position to refine the three phases in the determination and discovery of extensions on an objective type externalist account. Above, we said that in the first phase, there's a term that roughly or for the most part picks out an objective kind in the world. The objective kind attracts the term's reference and thereby fixes its extension. In the second phase, we undertake efforts to discover the extension that was determined in the first phase. In the third phase, ordinary speakers accept that the empirical results of the second phase tell them what the term has always referred to. But we've now seen reasons to doubt that the extensions of

52   NONIDEAL THEORY AND CONTENT EXTERNALISM

type-terms are determined once and for all in the first phase. In the second phase, researchers don't *discover* the term's predetermined extension; they 'choose' among several reasonable ways of proceeding, linguistically, in light of relevant research. In the third phase, ordinary speakers might revise their usage in light of relevant empirical research, but they need not and don't always.

It's unclear what these points about the second and third phases tell us about the first. Do they show that terms' extensions are indeterminate in the first phase, and the later phases determine them? Or perhaps in the first phase, a term's extension is determined by some unified, objective kind into which its paradigms fall, but that extension can change in the second and third phases. These are interesting questions, but we don't have to answer them here. What's important for us is that there's 'room' in the second and third phases for human and social forces to play a role in the determination of type-terms' extensions. Researchers' collective decisions play a role in the second phase. A language community's response to relevant research plays a role in the third phase.

Here, then, is one way to revise the three phases in the determination of type-terms according to objective type externalism.

> [Phase 1] A language community develops a term T that roughly or for the most part picks out an objective kind in the world.
> [Phase 2] Researchers investigate the part(s) of the world that T picks out. They have various options regarding what to say about T's extension, and they choose among these options. Different groups of researchers might proceed differently.
> [Phase 3] Language communities respond to researchers' results: accepting some of those results or not, changing usage in some way or not.

A sketch of the history of the term "water," for instance, might go like this. Before the 18th century, language communities had developed a term that picked out the substance that fills our lakes and streams, that falls from the sky, and that humans and other living organisms drink to survive. Maybe the term was also applied to other substances like tears[14] and urine.[15] This was

---

[14] As when one's "eyes water."
[15] As in the expression "make water." See, for example, Buck Mulligan in the Telemachus episode of James Joyce's *Ulysses*: "When I makes tea I makes tea. . . . And when I makes water I makes water" (Joyce 1986, 11).

the first phase in the determination of the term's extension. Again, we can leave it open as to whether at this point, the term's extension is indeterminate or not and, if it's determinate, just how it's determined. It may be determined by the most unified, objective kind into which its paradigms fall.

In the second phase, researchers investigate the kind(s) that the term picks out. In the 18th century, researchers like Henry Cavendish and Antoine Lavoisier delivered empirical results suggesting that (most of) the stuff we refer to with the term "water" is the same kind because it's composed of H_2O. In 1781, Cavendish "produced water when he exploded a mixture of 'inflammable air' (hydrogen) and 'de-phlogisticated air' (oxygen)" (Jacobsen 2006, 459). As an advocate of phlogiston theory, Cavendish took this result as reason to believe that 'inflammable air' is composed of phlogiston and water. Notably, Cavendish's interpretation "preserved [water's] status as a distinct chemical 'element'" (ibid., 459). He didn't take his empirical work to have revealed the essence of water. James Watt, also a phlogiston theorist, learned of Cavendish's work in early 1783 from Joseph Priestley, but Watt gave it a different interpretation. Instead of saying that water partly composes inflammable air, Priestley told Jean Andre de Luc and Joseph Black that "water is composed of de-phlogisticated air and inflammable air, or phlogiston, deprived of part of their latent heat" (ibid.). Watt, then, took water to be a compound of gases, not an element. In June 1783, Antoine Lavoisier and Pierre Simon LaPlace repeated Cavendish's experiments and interpreted the results according to Lavoisier's 'new chemistry': water, they said, is a synthesis of hydrogen and oxygen. Lavoisier's interpretation and his 'new chemistry' have of course influenced both ordinary usage and the development of chemistry as we understand it today. Although it's common to credit Cavendish with the discovery that water = H_2O, the term's extension was more plausibly determined by Lavoisier's or Watt's interpretation of Cavendish's results, not by Cavendish's own.

In the second phase, there were several competing interpretations and research paradigms relevant to the determination of the extension of the term "water." Among researchers, Lavosier's approach eventually gained the greatest influence. It went the same way among ordinary speakers in the third phase, so that they, following textbooks and intellectual elites, came to regard "water" as appropriately applied to all and only H_2O.

But things went differently with "water" and the discovery of D_2O. Before the discovery of D_2O, the language community had developed a term that picked out H_2O. Here, we can again be agnostic about just how determinate the term's extension was before the empirical results. Did the extension include only samples in which the hydrogen has no neutron, did it include all samples with isotopes of hydrogen, or was the extension indeterminate with regard to isotopes? If it had been discovered previously that water = H_2O, then the discovery precluded the possibility that D_2O would be included in the extension of the term "water." But with the discovery of D_2O, there began another phase in the determination of the term's extension. As is typical in the second phase, and as we saw above, there were several ways in which researchers might have proceeded, linguistically speaking. They could continue including only H_2O in the extension of "water," or they could 'expand' the term's extension to include D_2O. They opted for the latter.

But this doesn't seem to have gotten much uptake. In the third phase, ordinary speakers don't seem to have been much influenced by researchers' decision to count D_2O as water. Ordinary speakers, middle school and high school textbooks, and philosophers of language continue to take it that applications of "water" to substances that aren't H_2O are, strictly speaking, erroneous or nonliteral. Standard dictionary definitions say water is the stuff that forms our seas, lakes, rivers, and rain, and it's the basis of the fluids of living organisms. That description doesn't pick out D_2O. While there are trace amounts of D_2O in our oceans (about 0.0156%), D_2O isn't the basis of living organisms' fluids. Prima facie, then, although researchers discovered that D_2O is a form of water, heavy water, this didn't change the term's extension. In this case, the third phase in the determination of the term's extension was unaffected by the results of the second phase. Consequently, this ignored second phase seems to have played no role in determining the term's extension.

1.4 Three explanatory goals

As applied to social kind terms, objective type externalism has three principal explanatory goals. (1) It aims to tell us how social kind terms and concepts have their meanings, contents, and extensions determined. (2) For a specific term or concept, it aims to tell us what its meaning, content, or extension is. (3) It aims to provide us with concepts that will help undermine the influence of interconnected systems of privilege and subordination (Haslanger 2005,[16] 11; 2008, 56, 66).

[16] As noted above, in this 2005 paper, Haslanger is appealing to externalism to suggest that her accounts of race and gender terms might not be revisionary. It may be that speakers are referring to the

An appeal to the three phases described above is supposed to satisfy all three goals. That's pretty straightforward for the first two goals. The three phases themselves tell us how type-terms have their meanings and extensions determined. For a given term, then, we can identify its meaning and extension by figuring out what those three phases determined them to be. Reflecting on how those phases turned out with regard to "water," for instance, helped us determine the extension of the type term "water."

Things are more complicated for the third explanatory goal. Why should appealing to objective type externalism provide us with concepts that will help undermine systems of oppression? Haslanger's idea is that appealing to an externalist framework for social terms enables us to identify the parts of the world we're actually picking out with those terms, as compared to the parts we *think* we're picking out. And if we suppose that what we're actually picking out with race and gender terms are the groups that have suffered injustice thanks to various forms of oppression, then identifying what our terms actually pick out—instead of what we think they pick out—should help us undermine systems of oppression. As Haslanger says, "These are the groups that matter if we are going to achieve social justice" (Haslanger 2008, 66).

Why think an appeal to externalism enables us to identify the parts of the world we're actually picking out with social kind terms, as compared to the parts we *think* we're picking out? The thought is that what we think our terms refer to can be influenced by dominant mystifying ideology, but this isn't so when it comes to what our terms actually refer to.

To illustrate how an appeal to externalism might 'cut through' what speakers *think* a term refers to, consider Haslanger's discussion of the term "parent" in the context of a school district (Haslanger 2005, 99–101). If you were to ask speakers in a language community what the word "parent" refers to in communications from the school district, many would say something equivalent to *immediate biological progenitor*. That's the part of the world that most people *think* the term is used to pick out. Haslanger calls this the "manifest concept" associated with the term "parent." It's what ordinary speakers tend to think the term means and/or refers to. But if we were to

---

kinds Haslanger describes, but they're not aware that their terms have these referents. Thus, it's not plausible that Haslanger intends only for her revisionary/ameliorative proposals for race and gender terms to satisfy this third explanatory goal. In this paper and in the 2008 paper cited, externalism is supposed to cut through the mystifications of ideology and reveal the social kinds that construct interconnected systems of privilege and subordination.

appeal to externalism to identify the term's extension, we'd find that paradigmatic uses apply the term "parent" to whoever is there to pick a child up from after school activities, whoever signs permission slips for field trips, whoever is the child's legal guardian, and so on, and this can include grandparents, foster parents, adoptive parents, aunts, uncles, and others. Haslanger calls this the "operative concept" associated with the term: it's the most objective type into which the term's paradigmatic applications fall. An appeal to content externalism, then, might not reveal what we think we're talking about when we use a term, and it might not capture our intuitions about what the term refers to—that is, it might not reveal the manifest concept. But it should tell us what part of the world we're actually using our term to pick out—it will tell us the operative concept associated with the term.

This feature of externalism is especially helpful when our thoughts about what a term refers to are likely to be affected by dominant mystifying ideologies. Many have made the case that according to dominant ideology, race and gender are biological natural kinds. To be a Black woman is to have biological traits that make one both Black and a woman. To be a Latin man is to have biological traits that make one both Latin and a man. Whatever these traits are, they're biological rather than social. This view helps obscure the injustices of a White-supremacist patriarchal order: It suggests that biology determines distinct characteristics for distinct races and genders, and the social order that privileges some races and/or genders and subordinates others is only a 'natural' consequence of these biological facts. If this ideology influences what we think race and gender terms refer to, then it will make us more inclined to think that race and gender terms refer to biological kinds. And, indeed, such views are common among ordinary speakers. There's at least prima facie reason to believe that what we think race and gender terms refer to is influenced by dominant mystifying ideologies.

Accordingly, if we were to identify what ordinary speakers *think* race and gender terms refer to, we wouldn't be likely to find out what they *do* refer to; instead, we'd be likely to find what the dominant mystifying ideology 'says' they refer to: biological kinds. So if we want to identify "the groups that matter if we are going to achieve social justice" and thereby undermine systems of oppression, we should take a different approach. Haslanger suggests we identify the parts of the world that our uses of race and gender terms are actually picking out. Externalism is supposed to serve just this purpose. For a given social kind term, then, we can identify its meaning and extension by figuring out what the three phases of objective type externalism determined them to be. When we do this for race and gender terms, we'll reveal what they actually refer to—we'll identify the operative concepts. Thus, it will provide us with concepts that will help undermine systems of oppression.

To recap: Objective type externalism proposes three phases by which kind terms have their extensions determined. Appeal to these three phases is meant to satisfy the theory's three goals. As described in Haslanger's account and traditional accounts, oppression plays little to no role in these phases. Haslanger's account plausibly accepts that oppression influences the first phase, in which a type term is developed to pick out some part of the world: Prima facie, oppression influenced the development of oppressive race and gender terms. But she takes the last two phases to be undistorted by the influences of oppression, so that research into a kind term's reference will reliably discover or determine the objective kind to which it refers, and so that ordinary speakers will accept the results of that research. Insofar as the last two phases are taken as being unaffected by systemic oppression, it may be that the theory is problematically idealized, at least in part. The next section makes the case that, in fact, oppression systematically influences all three phases. Thus, because objective type externalism idealizes away from these influences, it is systematically inaccurate. We'll see in Section 3 that de-idealizing the three phases will better serve the theory's explanatory goals.

2. Oppression and the determination of type-terms

This section argues that for social kind terms, in fact each phase of objective type externalism is systematically influenced by oppression. In making the case that the influences are systematic, I won't argue that contemporary race, gender, or class oppressions are systemic. I'll follow many others in taking it that they are and in taking it that these systems include ideological, institutional, legal, and interpersonal manifestations.[17] What I'm showing is that these systems influence the processes that the externalist claims to determine the extensions of social kind terms.

Overall, the argument that each phase of objective type externalism is systematically influenced by oppression is simple. (1) At each phase, social kind terms have their paradigmatic applications—and thus their meanings

---

[17] See, for instance, Kwame Ture [Stokely Carmichael] (1966); Marilyn Frye (2000); Patricia Hill Collins (2015, 2); Vivian May (2015, 3); Ange-Marie Hancock (2007, 74).

58 NONIDEAL THEORY AND CONTENT EXTERNALISM

and extensions—fixed through processes that turn heavily on conversations about social kinds. Take "conversation" broadly, so that it includes linguistic exchanges of nearly any kind: talking about empirical results, lecturing and listening, publishing and reading papers, rumormongering, extended deliberations that lead to legal decisions, ad campaigns, propaganda, and so on. (2) Conversations (at least about social kinds) are systematically influenced by oppression. Legal, educational, institutional, and social exclusions have systematically prevented members of oppressed groups from participating in the conversations that matter most to determining terms' paradigmatic applications: conversations among academics, lawyers, medical experts, politicians, scientific researchers, architects, art and literary scholars, leaders of business, industry, and government, and so on. Moreover, these conversations have been systematically influenced by dominant oppressive ideologies that obscure the experiences of oppressed groups and justify their oppression. (3) Since meanings and extensions are determined at each phase through conversation, and since conversation about social kinds is systematically influenced by oppression, it should be that the determination of meanings and extensions at each phase is systematically influenced by oppression.

I take it that (1) is plausible on its face: linguistic exchanges among competent speakers in a language community develop new terms and fix paradigms for those terms; linguistic exchanges among researchers determine which experiments to carry out, how to set them up, how to interpret their results, and how to proceed linguistically in light of results; and linguistic exchanges among researchers, reporters, community leaders, and ordinary speakers, among others, determine how a language community will respond to relevant empirical results.

For reasons I'll make clear shortly, this chapter makes heavy use of examples to motivate (2). Before I explain why, let me note that there are several more general arguments in Chapter 3 to the effect that oppression systematically affects conversations, including conversations in which meanings and extensions are determined.[18]

I take it that the most obvious way to challenge the argument above is to concede that oppression systematically influences the relevant linguistic

---

[18] Since that chapter de-idealizes social externalism, the arguments make the case that oppression systematically influences conversations in which Burgean normative characterizations are established. The arguments can easily be recast as reaching the conclusion that oppression systematically influences conversations in which terms have their paradigmatic applications determined.

exchanges but to raise doubts about whether these influences suffice to affect what a term's meaning or extension turns out to be. The idea that an objective type term's meaning and extension are determined by an objective type in the world can make it difficult to believe that oppression's influences on conversation would matter much to the term's meaning and extension.

In order to forestall this challenge, it helps to focus on particular examples so that we can see in more detail what a term's meaning and extension were determined to be and how oppression influenced this determination. Accordingly, the following sections focus on examples. In each example, some term has had or terms have had their meanings/extensions determined by processes that were influenced by oppression, and the resulting meanings/extensions are distorted such that they help obscure oppression. Each example plays several roles in the argument.

First, each example will illustrate ways in which oppression influences one or another phase of objective type externalism. For each example, I'll point to various oppressive factors that influenced the relevant phase of determination. In some cases, I'll note that it's plausible that some of these factors systematically influence conversations about social kind terms. For instance, many of the terms we'll consider have been influenced by the exclusion or marginalization of oppressed groups from the most influential conversations relevant to determining the terms' paradigms. These exclusions are plausibly systematic. Each of these examples on its own helps justify (2) from the argument above.

But the examples also help justify (2) when taken together. The oppressive influences in the examples will affect a wide variety of terms—legal terms, economic terms, race terms, and gender terms—and these influences will issue from every 'level' of oppression: ideological, institutional, legal, and interpersonal. I take it that the best explanation for why each level of systemic oppression influences the processes that determine such diverse social kind terms is to say that oppression's influence on these processes is systematic.

Second, each example illustrates how oppression's influences are sufficient to affect social kind terms' meanings and extensions. For each example, we'll see that appealing to the ways in which oppression influenced the meaning-determining processes *explains why* the term's meaning and extension turned out as they did. For instance, why did the terms "labor" and "leisure" turn out so that women's domestic work falls into the extension of the latter term and not the former? Because of how oppression influenced the processes that determined the terms' paradigmatic applications. Women were systematically

60 NONIDEAL THEORY AND CONTENT EXTERNALISM

excluded from the relevant conversations, and patriarchal ideology centered men's experiences while marginalizing women's. Taken together, the examples give us reason to expect that in the typical case when oppression affects the phases of objective type externalism for a social kind term, it will affect the term's meaning and extension. If oppression affects the phases systematically, then the meanings and extensions of social kind terms are systematically affected.

Third, each example illustrates how meanings and extensions influenced by oppression help to obscure oppression rather than to reveal it. For instance, if women's domestic work falls into the extension of "leisure" rather than "labor," then those terms plausibly help obscure and reinforce the oppression of a system that pressures women to perform domestic work without pay or recognition. If oppression systematically affects the meanings and extensions of social kind terms, then it may well be that those terms systematically help obscure oppression.

Since Haslanger's view focuses most of all on race and gender terms, I will give them special attention, but I'll consider a variety of social terms.

2.1 Oppression systematically influences the development of social kind terms

In the first phase, a language community develops a term that picks out, at least roughly, an objective kind in the world. The idealized objective type externalist account takes it that at this point, a type term's extension is fixed by applications of the term to paradigmatic cases and an implicit extension to things of the same kind. Haslanger takes it that for race and gender terms, the objective kinds into which their paradigmatic applications fall correspond to the groups who suffer from race- and gender-based oppression. If research into race and gender terms' extensions were reliable, then, it would reveal those groups as the terms' extensions. It would reveal the operative concepts associated with race and gender terms, and these would help us undermine systems of oppression.

There are at least two ways in which Haslanger's account recognizes the influences of oppression on the determination of social kind terms. First, Haslanger takes it that race and gender terms refer to hierarchical social positions. These positions are presumably constructed, maintained, and assigned thanks to and as part of systemic oppression. Thus, systemic oppression influences the first phase in the determination of race and gender terms by constructing and maintaining the kinds to which they refer.

Second, Haslanger recognizes the influences of oppression on manifest concepts. Remember that the manifest concept associated with a term is what we *think* the term refers to, or it captures what our intuitions say about the term's meaning and extension. Haslanger notes that our manifest concepts are often susceptible to the influences of oppressive ideology.

> It is an important part of the social constructionist picture that, to put it simply, our meanings are not transparent to us: often ideology interferes with an understanding of the true workings of our conceptual framework and our language. More specifically, ideology (among other things) interferes with our understanding of our classificatory practices, suggesting to us that we are finding in nature divisions that we have played an important role in creating. (ibid. 92; see also ibid. 89, 111)

In drawing the distinction between manifest and operative concepts and aiming to identify the latter, Haslanger is concerned with circumventing the ideological interference that can affect manifest concepts. If our operative concepts can't or don't obscure oppression, then identifying them should indeed help us reveal oppression, and thus they should help us dismantle oppressive systems.

Haslanger deserves immense credit for articulating the manifest/operative distinction, for characterizing the influences of ideology on manifest concepts, and for showing how we can use content externalism to debunk the apparent authority of our manifest concepts. But what I want to point out here is that there are also ways that oppressive ideology systemically influences our *operative* concepts. This is a third way that systemic oppression can influence the first phase in the determination of a term's extension. If our operative concepts—just like our manifest concepts—can and often do help obscure oppression rather than reveal it, but we don't recognize this, then we are likely to be misled about the oppressive systems we're trying to reveal and dismantle. In this case, if we take it that operative concepts can't or don't obscure oppression, then we shall do worse at realizing our goals of revealing and dismantling oppression.

That is, failing to recognize this third way in which systemic oppression influences the first phase in the determination of a term's extension compromises the theory's ability to satisfy its third goal—its goal of revealing and dismantling oppression. If it's true that operative concepts also obscure rather than reveal oppression, then a de-idealized theory that recognizes this kind of influence will do better at serving the theory's third goal than will the idealized theory that doesn't. Below, I'll make the case that the first phase of objective type externalism is systematically influenced by oppression, and this makes it so that operative concepts associated with social kind terms at this phase systematically obscure rather than reveal oppression.

As with each phase, the overall idea is that (i) a social kind term's paradigmatic applications are determined through conversation, (ii) conversation of social kinds is systematically influenced by oppression, and so (iii) oppression systematically influences the determination of social kind terms' paradigms. Since the determination of a term's paradigms determines its meaning and extension according to objective type externalism, it follows that oppression systematically influences the determination of social kind terms' meanings and extensions.

But, again, in order to make the case that oppression affects operative concepts, and in order to illustrate how the resulting operative concepts obscure oppression, I'll focus on specific examples in which operative concepts have been influenced by oppression.

2.1.1 Political and economic terms

Elizabeth Anderson has provided reasons to think that operative concepts related to class, socioeconomic status, labor, and leisure terms have often been developed in ways that obscure gender- and class-based oppression by taking men's work and roles as paradigms.

> Economists and political scientists have traditionally defined class and socioeconomic status from the point of view of men's lives: a man's class or socioeconomic status is defined in terms of his own occupation or earnings, whereas a woman's status is defined in terms of her father's or husband's occupation or earnings. Such definitions obscure the differences in power, prestige, and opportunities between male managers and their homemaker wives, and between homemaker wives and female managers. (Anderson 1995, 71)

In developing the terms "class" and "socioeconomic status," economists and political scientists selected paradigms that center men and men's lives. The most objective type into which these paradigms fall is a social type that, as Anderson suggests, obscures differences in opportunity, prestige, and power that help maintain both class- and gender-based oppression. That is, the operative concepts associated with "class" and "socioeconomic status" obscure oppression. Since the objective types to which these operative concepts refer are social types, they presumably don't contribute to the ideology-driven appearance that gendered oppression is *natural*. But it doesn't follow that they reveal oppression. Rather, they obscure it.

Similarly, the operative concepts associated with "labor" and "leisure" obscure and help maintain gender-based oppression. Together, they normalize the oppressive idea that women's unpaid domestic work is *leisure*, thereby obscuring the injustice of a system that often expects women to perform domestic labor without compensation or recognition. Again, economists have taken paradigms for the term "labor" to be the work done by male heads of household. It's unclear just what is the most objective, unified type into which these paradigms fall, but it is clear that whatever type it is, it doesn't include women's domestic labor—that falls into the extension of "leisure" (ibid.). The operative concepts associated with "labor" and "leisure" obscure the oppression of a system that tends to make women financially dependent on husbands and fathers while also expecting them to perform unpaid domestic labor (often in addition to paid labor outside the home).

Presumably, then, the operative concepts determined for these terms help obscure oppression. Is it plausible that this is a consequence of oppression's influences on the conversations in which these terms were developed? It is. The influences are various, and they suffice to explain why the relevant operative concepts obscure the experiences and oppressions they do.

First, oppression contributed to the systematic exclusion of women from the conversations in which such terms were developed. Women, people of color, and other oppressed groups were (and often still are) excluded when terms were (and are) developed in historically White, male-dominated professions: academia, scientific research, medical fields, business, architecture, literature, industry, government, law, and so on. At another 'level' of oppression, social practices discounted women's reports of domestic work, minimizing women's claims that might challenge how the terms' paradigms were selected. If women were left out of the relevant discussions and given no credibility in them, then it would not be surprising that women's experiences and oppression would end up being obscured (see, e.g., Collins 1990; Fricker 1999, 2007; Dotson 2011; Medina 2012).

Second, oppressive legal, institutional, and social exclusions plausibly influence not only who develops social kind terms but also who they are developed *for*: Anderson suggests that theoretical and scientific knowledge is "often tailored to the needs of mostly male managers, bureaucrats, and officials exercising power in their role-given capacities" (Anderson 1995, 50). If the operative concepts were developed for people who had little or no direct experience of women's work or oppression and who had little incentive to learn about them, then again it would not be surprising if the resulting concepts were to obscure women's oppression and experiences.

Third, Anderson claims that men's work was taken as paradigmatic of *labor* thanks to the influence of a worldview that centers men and their lives while discounting and marginalizing women and women's lives (ibid. 71). I propose that this sort of influence issues from the ideology 'level' of oppression. Distorting the selection of a term's paradigms in ways that reflect dominant ideology is often sufficient to produce operative concepts that also reflect the dominant ideology. When that ideology marginalizes or ignores the lives and experiences of groups who are targeted for oppression, such operative concepts will also tend to obscure those same lives and their experiences of oppression. They will obscure oppression.

Note that although we've focused on economic and political terms here, the points raised are general. Oppressed groups aren't just excluded from the conversations in which political and economic terms are developed but from conversations in which a wide array of terms is developed. Similarly, it's not just political and economic terms that tend to be tailored to the needs of White men, and it's not just political and economic terms that tend to reflect dominant ideologies. These patterns are systematic—oppressed groups are and have been systematically excluded from various professional fields by complex networks of legal and institutional policies, social norms, and economic factors. The examples above suggest that these systematic exclusions affect the operative concepts determined when terms are developed, and they suggest that the resulting operative concepts obscure oppression. If the effects of these exclusions are systematic, then we have all we need to say that oppression systematically influences the first phase of objective type externalism. Moreover, if the concepts described above are representative of the concepts developed when oppression influences the first phase, then we should expect that oppression makes it so that operative concepts associated with social kind terms systematically obscure rather than reveal oppression.

DE-IDEALIZING OBJECTIVE TYPE EXTERNALISM 65

The examples to follow will suggest these same points and show that they hold for a diversity of social kind terms.

2.1.2 Gender terms

Similar points hold for at least some gender terms. Many trans studies scholars have described how terms related to trans persons and gender dysphoria have been developed *through* processes that exclude gender-nonbinary people and *in ways* that obscure the lives, experiences, and oppression of nonbinary persons. That is, nonbinary people have been systematically excluded from the conversations in which terms related to trans persons and gender dysphoria have been developed; these conversations have been influenced by a binary gender ideology that marginalizes gender-nonbinary persons, and the operative concepts determined in these conversations obscure the lives, experiences, and oppression of nonbinary persons.

As Dean Spade describes it, for instance, medical institutions that provide—and control access to—gender-affirming surgeries and hormones have traditionally limited the paradigms for the (outdated) terms "transsexual" and "gender identity disorder" in ways that are plausibly distorted by and in service of oppressive gender norms. Spade makes the case that medical institutions have created the social category to which "transsexual" refers[19] partly by providing gender-affirming medical treatments and partly by selecting who is eligible for such surgeries (Spade 2006, 318). Together, these two facts make it so that medical institutions have determined the paradigms for the term "transsexual." According to objective type externalism, the term's extension is then determined (in the first phase of determination) by the most unified, objective type into which these paradigms fall.

According to Spade, taking this objective type to be the term's extension serves to obscure and marginalize the lives of and oppressions faced by gender-nonbinary persons, and it reflects dominant binary gender ideology. Spade reports that in order to gain access to gender-affirming medical services, one must successfully recite "the transsexual narrative" time and again: "in meeting after meeting with medical professionals, and in session after session with counselors and psychiatrists" (ibid. 319). For instance, the "transsexual childhood" is an important, plausibly necessary, part of this narrative: one must say that one has identified with 'the opposite' sex or gender since childhood (ibid. 319–320). As trans studies scholars have long pointed

---

[19] Or *did* refer, if one thinks this social category has become extinct since Spade first wrote in 2000.

out, those seeking gender-affirming medical interventions often know what the official medical narrative is, and they know to produce it in order to satisfy medical gatekeepers (see, e.g., Stone 1987; Hausman 1995). Thus, although the trans childhood wasn't part of the definition of "gender identity disorder" in the fourth edition of the *Diagnostic and Statistical Manual of Mental Disorders* (DSM), and it isn't part of the definition of "gender dysphoria" in the DSM-5, it is claimed (sometimes falsely) by paradigms of "transsexual." And insofar as reciting the trans childhood narrative is prerequisite for the treatments that serve as necessary for joining the social category to which "transsexual" refers, it is plausibly a necessary condition for membership in the extension of the operative concept expressed by "transsexual."

Thus, the operative concept determined for "transsexual" helps to obscure oppression. And, as above, it's plausible that this is a consequence of oppression's influences on the conversations in which these terms were developed.

First, given the widespread marginalization and exclusion of gender-nonbinary persons, it's little surprise that nonbinary persons played little role in the conversations through which gender terms relevant to gender dysphoria and gender transitioning were developed. And it should be no surprise that such conversations would lead to operative concepts that obscure the experiences and oppression of those who were excluded.

Second, the necessity of reciting the official trans narrative suggests that the selection of paradigms in the relevant conversations was distorted by binary gender ideology. Binary gender ideology falsely gives us the impression that all persons are either men only or women only—no one is both, and no one is neither. These norms thus obscure the possibility of identifying with both dominant binary genders, with neither of them, or with some nonbinary gender. And thus they make it seem necessary that if one doesn't identify with one binary gender, then they must identify with 'the other.' The official trans narrative requirement is a way for practitioners to make it so that only persons who conform to binary gender roles will be included in the extension of "transsexual" (see, e.g., Stone 1987, 227–228). In this way, the requirement and its attendant selection of paradigms are clearly influenced by binary gender ideology, and they bolster binary norms by supporting the appearance that every person is either a man only or a woman only. I say the influence of gender norms is "distorting" here because it obscures rather than reveals what the paradigms have in common. It inaccurately takes the commonality to be a certain kind of childhood and disposition to conform to binary gender norms. Since binary gender ideology is oppressive, its influence is one manifestation of the influences of oppression on gender terms. Binary gender ideology makes it so that nonbinary persons are socially and institutionally marginal, ineligible for various accommodations, and vulnerable to violence (see, e.g., Engelhardt 2021, 2022; Watson 2020).

In addition, the selection of paradigms for "transsexual" plausibly helps determine paradigms for terms like "gender dysphoria" so that the operative concept for *this term* reinforces binary gender norms. Insofar as reciting the trans childhood narrative is necessary for a diagnosis of gender dysphoria (previously "gender identity disorder"), the narrative also determines the selection of paradigms for "gender dysphoria."[20] The objective, unified kind into which the paradigms fall, then, will presumably exclude those of us who experience considerable and persistent discomfort with dominant gender norms and roles, but who do not consistently identify with the norms and roles of either binary gender. In fact, identification with "the other gender" remains one of the diagnostic criteria for gender dysphoria in the DSM-5. This, again, helps reinforce binary gender norms and obscure nonbinary experience by making it seem as though persistent discomfort with one of the two dominant binary genders only ever occurs alongside identification with 'the other' binary gender role (see Engelhardt 2021).

Nonbinary people have been systematically excluded from the conversations in which terms related to trans persons and gender dysphoria have been developed; these conversations have been influenced by a binary gender ideology that marginalizes gender-nonbinary persons, and the operative concepts determined in these conversations obscure the lives, experiences, and oppression of nonbinary persons. Prima facie, these oppression-obscuring operative concepts are thanks to the influences of oppressive exclusion and ideology on the term-developing conversations.

2.1.3 Race terms

There are also numerous cases in which race terms have been developed such that their operative concepts obscure oppression rather than reveal

---

[20] Note that this is the case even if the trans childhood isn't or wasn't included as a requirement in the DSM diagnosis criteria for the term or its antecedent, "gender identity disorder." If it's true that *in practice* reciting the official narrative is or was necessary for diagnosis, then the paradigms for the operative concept will have all recited the narrative. This may not be true, but I'm following Spade and many others in taking it that we have good reason to believe that it—or at least something close to it—was.

68   NONIDEAL THEORY AND CONTENT EXTERNALISM

it. In each case, the (by now familiar) points about oppression's influences hold: the conversations in which the obscuring operative concepts were developed were influenced by oppressive ideology and systematic exclusions. And, again, these influences help explain why the operative concepts came to obscure oppression rather than reveal it.

Linda Martín Alcoff describes a number of cases in which legal decisions interpreted race terms in ways that advanced racial oppression. Some of these effectively selected paradigms for race terms—if not for the ordinary terms, then at least for their uses in the law. According to objective type externalism, this (along with implicit extension to things of the same kind) would have determined the operative concepts for those terms prior to the second and third phases.

Here's one example: In an 1854 decision, *People v. Hall,* the California State Supreme Court ruled that "we understand [the term 'Black'] to mean the opposite of 'White,' and that it should be taken as contradistinguished from all White persons" (Carbado 2009, 660). The court was considering an appeal to a murder conviction. George W. Hall, a White man, had been convicted of murdering Ling Sing, a Chinese man, partly thanks to the testimonies of Chinese witnesses. Hall appealed his conviction on grounds that a Chinese witness shouldn't have been permitted to testify against him. It was state law at the time that "no Black, or Mulatto person, or Indian, shall be allowed to give evidence in favor of, or against a white man" (ibid. 659). Writing for the court, Justice Hugh Murray[21] agreed with Hall on grounds that Chinese people are Black, because "Black" just refers to everyone who is not White. As Alcoff points out, this ruling prescribes a "Black/White binary" for conceptualizing all racial identities in the United States (Alcoff 2003, 10). If Murray accurately described or successfully prescribed paradigmatic applications of "Black" and "White," then the most unified, objective kinds into which those paradigms fell presumably made it so that "White" referred to persons of European descent, and "Black" referred to everyone else. As Alcoff points out, this made the extension of "Black" even more extensive than the "one drop rule," since one could be Black without *any* recent African ancestry.

---

[21] Alcoff names the justice as Charles J. Murray, but every other source I can find calls him Hugh Murray, and I can't find any record of a California Supreme Court justice at the time with the name Charles J. Murray. So I'm going with "Hugh."

The Black/White racial binary in the United States obscures and contributes to racial oppression. It marginalizes Latinx persons, Asians, and Indigenous Americans, and it obscures their distinctive racial experiences—including the ways in which they are alternately classified as White or Black in accordance with what best serves racial oppression. In *People v. Hall*, Chinese Americans were classified as Black so that witness testimony from Chinese Americans couldn't be used against Whites. In this case, it was disadvantageous to be classified as Black. But there are also cases in which groups were brought into the extension of "White" to their detriment. In the 1954 case *Hernandez v. Texas*, the Supreme Court of Texas ruled that Mexicans were White people of Spanish descent, to the effect that Mexican Americans could be tried by all-White juries. Peter Hernandez was convicted of a murder by an all-White jury; his lawyer, James DeAnda, appealed the conviction on grounds that Hernandez was denied a jury of his peers and thus denied a fair trial. Alcoff reports that in Texas at the time,

> Mexicans were subject to Jim Crow in public facilities from restaurants to bathrooms, they were excluded from business and community groups, and children of Mexican descent were required to attend a segregated school for the first four grades, whether they spoke fluent English or not. (Alcoff 2003, 11–12)

Nonetheless, the Texas Supreme Court ruled that since Mexicans are White, Peter Hernandez had been tried by a jury of his peers, and his trial had been fair.[22] As Alcoff sums up, "When they were classified as nonwhite, Latino/as were overtly denied certain civil rights; when they were classified as white, the *de facto* denial of their civil rights could not be appealed" (ibid. 12). Similar stories of alternating racial classification to the detriment of the groups so classified are not uncommon. Chinese Americans in Louisiana were classified as White in 1860 and as Chinese by 1870; in 1900, children of Chinese and non-Chinese parents were reclassified as White or *Black*. In 1927, the U.S. Supreme Court defined the Chinese as non-White, "thus more firmly subjecting them to all the segregationist and Jim Crow legislation then in effect" (ibid. 11). "The variable classifications," Alcoff concludes, "tell a story of strategic reasoning in which arguments for legal discriminations

---

[22] The U.S. Supreme Court later overturned the Texas Supreme Court's decision.

are deployed against people of color by whatever opportune classification presents itself in context" (ibid.).

These variable classifications are made possible by the Black/White binary at the same time that they are obscured by the operative concepts associated with "Black" and "White." So long as these operative concepts are mutually exclusive and jointly exhaustive of racial groups in the United States, then— no matter the specific extensions of the two concepts at any given time—they will obscure the distinctive racial oppressions that target Asian, Indigenous American, and Latinx persons. The Black/White binary assumes that "all racial discrimination operates exclusively through anti-black racism" (ibid. 8). This is of course false, and taking it to be true obscures the distinctive oppressions suffered by non-Black people of color. When the operative concepts associated with "Black" and "White" are jointly exhaustive, they partly constitute the Black/White binary and its associated obfuscations of racial oppression. The operative concepts associated with race terms can and often do obscure oppression.

We can explain why these operative concepts obscure oppression by appealing to the ways in which the processes involved in their determination were influenced by racial oppression: systematic exclusion of people of color from the ranks of judges and others who could influence legal decision-making, exclusion from political positions that could be used to advocate against racially oppressive policies, and historical and legal exclusion from opportunities that could build wealth and help win support for opposition to racial oppression. In addition, as Alcoff points out, the oppressive ideology of the Black/White binary plausibly influenced the relevant legal decisions, even while the decisions themselves helped reinforce the ideology.

The foregoing examples illustrate how oppression influences the first phase of objective type externalism, how these influences are sufficient to affect social kind terms' meanings and extensions, and how meanings and extensions influenced by oppression help obscure oppression rather than reveal it. Each case was influenced by oppressive ideology and systematic exclusions; this gives us enough reason to accept that oppression systematically affects the first phase. Since these influences are systematic, and since we saw diverse examples in which those influences affect meanings and extensions, it's plausible that oppression systematically affects meanings and extensions developed in the first phase. I'll now turn to the second phase.

2.2 Oppression systematically influences research into social kinds

In the second phase, empirical research is undertaken to identify the objective kind (or its essence) into which a term's paradigmatic applications fall. On the usual descriptions, this research is bound to discover what the term's extension already is and has been. In effect, the results of the research are predetermined by reference magnetism and the term's paradigmatic applications. We saw that historical examples make this account untenable. Instead, we should take it that researchers make decisions (consciously or not) about terms' extensions, and these decisions determine extensions at the second phase.

In this section, we'll see that when it comes to social kind terms, such decisions have often been influenced by oppression, and this has often resulted in terms that help obscure oppression. We can make the case that these decisions are systematically influenced by oppression by an appeal to the general argument given above (and to the arguments in the next chapter): these decisions result at least partly from conversations among researchers, and these conversations are influenced by dominant ideology and by systematic oppressive exclusions. Prima facie, then, the determination of meanings and extensions at this phase is systematically influenced by oppression.

But, as in the last section, it is helpful to illustrate how oppression influences this phase, how these influences are sufficient to affect social kind terms' meanings and extensions, and how meanings and extensions influenced by oppression help obscure oppression rather than to reveal it. We'll see that the influences in some examples are plausibly systematic, giving us further reason to accept that oppression systematically affects the second phase and the extensions determined therein.

2.2.1 "Intelligent"

Elizabeth Anderson has surveyed scholarship that reveals influences of gender-based oppression on inquiry, including empirical inquiry into the extensions of social kind terms. In many cases, it's plausible that these influences led to the determination of oppression-obscuring meanings and extensions for the relevant terms. That is, much of the scholarship Anderson describes illustrates how oppression influences the second phase of objective type externalism, how this suffices to alter terms' extensions, and how the altered extensions tend to obscure oppression. I'll take one example.

Anderson describes research involved in developing IQ tests. IQ tests are taken by many to determine the intelligence of those who take them (see, e.g., Rietveld et al. 2014). Educational systems use IQ tests to identify children for special education and gifted education programs. Researchers in the hard and social sciences study the relationships between IQ tests and class, race, genetics, and academic achievement (Martschenko 2017). Insofar as IQ tests are taken to determine the intelligence of those who take them, and insofar as they're used to divide persons into educational and professional tracks, they play an important role in our inquiry into the extension of the term "intelligent." Those who score higher on IQ tests are sorted into the loose social group to which "intelligent" refers by placement in gifted education programs and by admittance into 'high-IQ societies' like Mensa. IQ tests have been used in the United States to screen applicants for the police and military, and various institutions have had IQ requirements for admission. Researchers who use IQ tests typically take those who score higher as being more intelligent—as being better candidates for inclusion in the extension of the term "intelligent." IQ tests are a tool developed in service of research into the extension of the term "intelligent"; they are taken as tracking, at least loosely, the kind to which the term refers.

As many have pointed out, this research has been influenced by and has helped reinforce various oppressions. Anderson describes how research involved in developing IQ tests (i) drew on oppressive gender ideology and (ii) helped obscure and reinforce gender-based disparities in educational opportunities (Anderson 1995, 77–78). As usual, it's plausible that the first helps explain the second. Of course, the systematic exclusion of women from the professions, educational opportunities, economic freedoms, and so on, that would have enabled them to contribute to the relevant research helps explain (ii) as well.

On the first IQ tests developed by Lewis Terman, girls scored significantly higher than boys did. Since school grades didn't differ by gender, and since grades were taken as being an independent measure of intelligence, Terman took the results of the first test as undermining the test's claim to validity. So Terman modified it. He "eliminated portions of the test where girls scored higher than boys and inserted questions on which boys scored higher than girls" (ibid. 77). But Terman wasn't consistent in eliminating or adjusting portions of the test that showed gender differences. In particular, he didn't address subsets of the test on quantitative reasoning, which "conformed to prevailing ideological assumptions about appropriate gender roles" (ibid.). When the results of Terman's IQ test challenged dominant gender ideology, he had it adjusted. The research was influenced by oppressive gender ideology.

Moreover, in developing the test this way, Terman's research helped obscure and reinforce gender disparities in educational opportunities. As Anderson points out, it is plausible to take school grades as evidence of the validity of IQ test results and to take IQ test results as evidence of "children's innate intelligence" only if "schools provide fair educational opportunities to all children with respect to all fields of study" (ibid. 78). If there are gender disparities in how students' grades are assessed, in how children are encouraged or discouraged to pursue certain fields, in support given to students pursuing various fields, and so on, then these disparities would explain gendered differences in grades in the relevant fields. Indeed, Anderson points to "those schools that discourage girls from pursuing math and science" on the assumption that "girls have inferior quantitative reasoning ability." These schools fail to recognize that "lack of encouragement can cause relatively lower performance on math tests" (ibid.). In this case, girls' lower grades in math and science are explained by manifestations of gender-based oppression in their school environment. But thanks to IQ tests, girls' grades are instead taken as being explained by a gendered difference in innate abilities for quantitative reasoning. In this way, research on IQ tests serves to obscure the injustices of discouraging girls from pursuing math and science and more general gendered inequality in educational opportunities.

Research into the extension of "intelligent" has also been influenced by and helped obscure racial exclusion and marginalization. Donna Y. Ford points out that African Americans, Hispanic Americans, and Native Americans are "consistently under-represented in gifted programs," and this underrepresentation is thanks primarily to students' performance on traditional intelligence tests (Ford 2005). These results are the sort that ought to challenge the test's validity, just as Terman took the gender-differential results on his original test to do. But researchers using IQ tests have accepted these results; prima facie, this is because, like Terman's quantitative reasoning results, they conform to prevailing racial ideology. But by continuing to take IQ tests to identify 'innate intelligence,' research into the extension of "intelligent" skews that extension toward Europeans, people of European descent, and people who speak European languages. More plainly, IQ tests and their use in determining the extension of "intelligent" reinforce notions of European and White supremacy. In turn, they present the exclusion of people of color from gifted programs as a consequence of differences in 'innate intelligence;' thus, they present that exclusion as warranted, not a consequence of oppression. But there's evidence that these exclusions are thanks to oppression. Frasier et al. (1995) and Harmon (2002) have argued, for instance, that racial stereotypes play a role in keeping teachers from referring students of color to gifted programs. In this case—as with schools that discourage girls from pursuing math and science—using IQ tests to determine the extension of "intelligent" obscures injustices in how educational opportunities are distributed while reinforcing oppressive ideology.

In sum, research on the extension of "intelligent" was influenced by oppressive race and gender ideologies and by widespread marginalization of women and people of color from the professions, educational opportunities, and economic freedoms crucial for participating in research relevant to the term's extension. These influences are evident in the ways IQ tests have and have not been altered to conform to dominant ideologies. Using IQ tests to determine the extension of the term has reinforced oppressive race and gender ideologies that assume White men to be more intelligent than women and people of color are, and they have obscured the social and institutional factors that contribute to the marginalization of women and people of color from specific educational opportunities.

2.2.2 Race and gender terms 1: Sexual ambiguity

Similarly, research into the extensions of race and gender kind terms has historically been influenced by oppression, and it has led to extensions that conceal oppression. Siobhan B. Somerville's influential work on 19th-century scientific research on evolution, sexuality, gender, and race describes various cases in which that research was influenced by intersecting oppressive ideologies—not to mention, of course, that European researchers at the time were nearly all middle- to upper-class cis White men. In many of these cases, these ideologies influenced how researchers elected to proceed linguistically, determining paradigmatic applications such that terms came to obscure oppression rather than reveal it.

For instance, Somerville gives reason to think that dominant binary gender norms and associated "anxieties about gender boundaries" influenced how researchers understood race terms, gender terms, and terms for sexual orientations (Somerville 2000, 26). This influence was mediated through the methodologies of comparative anatomy of the time, and together they prompted researchers to "racialize sexual ambiguity" (ibid. 27). Here's an account of the relevant background assumptions of comparative anatomy:

> The surface and interior of the individual body rather than its social characteristics, such as language, behavior, or clothing, became the primary sites of its meaning. "Every peculiarity of the body has probably some corresponding significance in the mind, and the causes of the former are the remoter causes of the latter," wrote Edward Drinker Cope, a well-known American paleontologist, summarizing the assumptions that fueled the science of comparative anatomy. (ibid. 23)

In this context, to say that a body exhibits "sexual ambiguity" is to say that it doesn't conform to expectations for one or the other binary European genders. Somerville provides an 1867 study of African women by W. H. Flower and James Murie as one example.

> The characteristics singled out as "peculiar" to this race [the "protuberance of the buttocks" and the "remarkable development of the labia minora"] fluttered between genders, at one moment masculine, at the next moment exaggeratedly feminine. (ibid. 27)

In a binary gender system that presents itself as natural, inevitable, and grounded in bodies that signify minds, there should be no such bodies. Rather, bodies should conform to European expectations for gendered bodies and thereby signify conformity to the gender binary more generally. Bodies that didn't conform thus signified minds that didn't conform to gender roles, and they thus challenged the alleged inevitability and naturalness of the binary gender system. This was the cause of anxieties about gender boundaries.

In order to manage these anxieties, Flower and Murie posited that the 'ambiguous' bodies were "sufficiently well marked to distinguish these parts [buttocks and labia minora] from those of any ordinary varieties of the human species" (ibid. 26). That is, in order to help maintain the European binary gender system, Flower and Murie proposed that the threatening bodies are not "ordinary varieties" of the human species; instead, they took the sexually ambiguous bodies to be paradigms of a different 'variety'—a racial kind.

> Flower and Murie constructed the site of *racial* difference by marking the sexual and reproductive anatomy of the African woman as "peculiar"; in their characterization, sexual ambiguity delineated boundaries of race. (ibid. 27)

The binary gender system then could be taken as applying only to 'ordinary'—that is, White European—bodies, and the bodies of African women could be paradigms of a non-ordinary racial kind. Other researchers took a similar approach to paradigms of racial kinds.

> Starting with [George] Cuvier, this tradition of comparative anatomy located the boundaries of race through the sexual and reproductive anatomy of the African female body, ignoring altogether the problematic absence of male bodies from these studies. (ibid. 26)

With this approach, the naturalness of the binary gender system can be preserved because it can still hold for the White European bodies that matter. Any bodies that challenge the gender system, meanwhile, can be dismissed by positing racial differences.

Take these points in the context of research into the extensions of kind terms. Upon discovering 'sexually ambiguous' persons who challenged the White European gender binary, biologists, comparative anatomists, and sexologists could have responded differently. Rather than racialize bodies exhibiting 'sexual ambiguity,' they could have expanded the extensions of "man" and "woman" to include 'sexually ambiguous' bodies. Flower and Murie thought that paradigms of gender terms were sexually unambiguous White bodies, and they thought that the African bodies they studied were in many ways similar to their gender paradigms but had some physical differences. But there are also differences between H_2O and D_2O, and yet researchers decided to include both in the extension of "water." Obviously, Flower and Murie and their colleagues could have responded in an analogous way: they could have expanded the extensions of their gender terms.

But to proceed this way would have threatened the European gender binary. If Somerville's analysis is correct, then the paradigms of the relevant race terms were selected *so that* they wouldn't fall into the extensions of "woman" and "man" (and related terms in other European languages). The point of taking allegedly sexually ambiguous African bodies to be paradigms of a racial kind was to maintain the European gender kinds and to help obscure the nonnaturalness of the binary and hierarchical European gender system. Researchers' decisions about how to proceed linguistically in the second phase of objective type externalism were made to conform to dominant gender ideology. These decisions were thus influenced by oppressive ideology (and presumably also by systemic exclusion). Consequently, these decisions established paradigmatic applications for race and gender terms such that the terms' extensions served to obscure and reinforce the European gender binary.

In addition, researchers' decisions about how to proceed linguistically for race and gender terms helped establish and reinforce White supremacist ideology. Far from providing us with concepts to resist interconnected systems of oppression, researchers' decisions helped establish them. On the one hand, by determining the racial kind in such a way that its members could not fall into the extensions of either "man" or "woman," researchers' decisions situated African bodies as outside a gender binary that is plausibly prerequisite for being perceived as intelligibly human. Lori Watson makes a related point about gender-nonconforming persons.

> Gender non-conforming persons . . . are perceived as occupying a space of contradiction: human and not intelligibly human. Their bodies and self-presentation do not fit within the schema of intelligible humanity. Normative notions of humanity carry with them the gender binary. (Watson 2020, 240)

If this is right, and if research into 19th-century racial kind terms for Africans excluded them from the extensions of "man" and "woman," then the second phase in the terms' determination precluded normative notions of humanity from applying to Africans. In this case, the second phase of objective type externalism was not only influenced by oppression; it also contributed to it. Points similar to the foregoing also apply to linguistic labor for "lesbian" (see Somerville 2000, 27–29).

On the other hand, as binary sexual differentiation came to be racialized as White, it came to be taken as evidence of evolutionary progress and, thus, as justification of White supremacy (see Schuller 2018, 37–38). Somerville reports that Darwinists at the time adopted the idea that bodies that weren't 'sexually ambiguous' were evidence of advanced evolution toward civilization.

> One of the basic assumptions within the Darwinian model was the belief that, as organisms evolved through a process of natural selection, they also showed greater signs of sexual differentiation. Following this logic, various writers used sexual characteristics as indicators of evolutionary progress toward civilization. (Somerville 2000, 29)

In an 1894 work titled *Man and Woman*, for instance, the influential British sexologist Havelock Ellis appealed to these ideas to hypothesize that industrialization in Europe had brought about "more marked sexual differences" than "are usually to be found in savage societies" (Ellis 1911, 13, cited in Somerville 2000, 29). Similarly, in their 1889 *The Evolution of Sex*, biologists Patrick Geddes and J. Arthur Thomson contrasted 'primitive' gender ambiguity and 'civilized' differentiation: "Hermaphroditism is primitive; the unisexual state is a subsequent differentiation" (Geddes & Thomson 1889, 80, cited in Somerville 2000, 29).

For these biologists, sexologists, and comparative anatomists, then, research into the extensions of race and gender terms didn't reveal oppression or concepts that could be used to dismantle systems of oppression. Instead, their research prompted linguistic decisions such that (i) the presence or absence of 'sexual ambiguity' became a mark of racial difference, and (ii) racial differences were taken as being evidence of evolutionary progress toward civilization. These decisions helped justify both the European gender binary and White supremacy. Presumably, these decisions seemed plausible thanks to dominant race and gender ideologies, and the non-accidental absence of racial and gender minorities from the relevant research meant that these decisions were less likely to be challenged. That is, this research that established paradigmatic applications for race and gender terms was influenced by oppression; since the research established paradigmatic applications for the terms, the objective type externalist should say that the research affected the terms' meanings and extensions. Prima facie, the most unified, objective types into which the relevant paradigms fall are types that obscure and reinforce oppressive race and gender ideologies. The objective type externalist should say, then, that oppressive influences affected the theory's second phase and led to the determination of meanings and extensions for race and gender terms such that they obscured oppression.

2.2.3 Race and gender terms 2: Sentimentalism

Kyla Schuller focuses on a different paradigm in early race and gender science but reaches the same conclusions: research into race and gender kinds was influenced by and helped reinforce race- and gender-based oppressions. Schuller focuses on what she calls "Sentimentalism" or the "the sentimental politics of life." While 19th-century Sentimentalist accounts of race took it to be biological, they didn't take individual biology as predetermining aptitudes and behaviors (Schuller 2018, 11). Instead, Schuller proposes, these 19th-century life scientists took the entire nervous system to be *shaped by its sensations*, "[acquiring] its structure from the sensations [it] habitually pursues" and passing its adaptations to offspring (ibid. 8). In addition, they thought that bodies receiving the same sensations were thereby "a fractional element of a larger and more comprehensive being, called society" (Horace Bushnell 1852, 15, cited in Schuller 2018, 9). Consequently, she says, life scientists of the time took race as demarcating

> the accumulated physical effect of a group's relative achievement of the seven cultural traits defined as determinant of civilization: sexual differentiation, monogamous marriage, Christian faith, arts and literacy, domestic architecture, capitalistic accumulation, and democratic government. (Schuller 2018, 12)

Thus, races were taken as being collective cultural achievements and ongoing collective cultural projects. Achieving and maintaining the traits "determinant of civilization" shaped a race's habitual experiences and thus, according to Sentimentalists, physically determined both the nervous systems of individual members and the "more comprehensive being" they composed. As these effects accumulate over individual lifetimes and (via transmission to offspring) generations, they determine biological races. According to Schuller, then, the view of race and evolution at the time allowed that a society could regulate how it would evolve and thus maintain or direct the biological race(s) of its members (ibid. 37).

Thus, although Sentimentalist research into the extension of "race" identified physiological traits, these traits weren't the deterministic traits we tend to associate with biological accounts of race. Nonetheless, this conception of race was still influenced by White-supremacist ideology, and it still gave ersatz justification to abuses targeting people of color, to racial exclusion, and to gender-based oppression.

It was influenced by White-supremacist ideology in that, unsurprisingly, the seven alleged determinants of civilization privilege White European cultures and mark all others as relatively inferior. As with the more familiar biological accounts of race, the Sentimentalist account was mutually reinforcing with racial oppression and helped obscure the injustice of it.

The Sentimentalist account offered justification for various abuses of people of color and poor people by endowing "white bodies, and the wealthier classes of African Americans, Latinx, and Native Americans" with distinctive abilities to internally process and respond to stimuli (ibid. 12). Sentimentalists didn't take bodies privileged by race and/or wealth as merely biologically determined to be superior; rather, they were conceived as capable of improving on their biological inheritance and, thereby, capable of taking control of themselves and their lives, eligible to be praised for their achievements.

The racially oppressed, by contrast, were thought to have nervous systems "incapable of internal response," and they were thus often taken as being "benumbed to both progress and pain" (ibid. 4). Conceiving of racialized groups this way satisfied demands to justify various abuses.

> The racialized could be recruited from across the Americas, Africa, and Asia for multiple forms of unfree and free labor, forced reproduction, and/ or coerced experimentation on the grounds that they lacked the nervous capacity to feel any harm. (Ibid. 14)

The Sentimentalist account offers justification for racial exclusion and gender-based oppression by positing human evolutionary stages as fragile 'achievements' and by taking White women to be distinctively vulnerable to influences that might threaten these achievements. Sentimentalists took it that if a civilized society were, as a body, to be exposed to sensations that undermine the determinants of civilization, then it might degenerate. So civilization had to be protected from such sensations. On the one hand, this involved identifying—often by race—both (i) those persons or groups who were a threat to a civilization and must die and (ii) those whose lives must be protected (ibid. 15). On the other hand, it prompted an account of sex differentiation that would 'stabilize' the vulnerable White race.

Recall that on the 'self-regulating' account of evolution, human nervous systems are shaped by their sensations, and the resulting nervous structures are passed to offspring. The emergent view of sexual differentiation proposed that among Whites—who were taken as being alone among the races in exhibiting sexual differentiation—this is true of females and not males (ibid. 37). This 'impressibility' was meant to be a physiological fact about women, and it thus posited a physical difference between women and men.

Thus, although Sentimentalists' view on racial classifications of the 19th century contrasts with the biological determinist view, this doesn't challenge the view that sex/gender as a biological binary emerged and solidified at this time (ibid. 16–17), and Schuller echoes the claim above that sex differentiation was taken as grounds for racial classification.

> The discourse of thorough divergence in the character, physiology, mentality, and emotion of men and women emerged in both conservative and feminist discourse of the nineteenth century and served to diagnose a specialized trait that allegedly only the civilized had developed. (Ibid. 16)

As we saw above, research into the extensions of gender terms led to biological accounts of sex/gender. These newly emerging biological accounts of differential sex gave rise to "new binaristic accounts of body morphology, identity, and relationality" (ibid. 17) and to corresponding practices:

> A flurry of new and long-lasting tactics of sex difference emerged in this period, including policed dress; sex- and race-segregated bathrooms; restrictions on abortion and contraception; sex- and race-based admissions policies to newly established educational and professional institutions; the gradual consolidation of modern sexuality; and feminist claims for political rights. (Ibid. 16)

This account of binary sex/gender difference, along with the Sentimentalist account of racial difference, served as justification for race- and gender-based oppression. The distinctive 'impressibility' of White women meant that they were especially vulnerable to the sorts of sensations that could result in degeneration, and this was used to justify restrictions on both women's activities and the freedoms of racialized groups. "To these leading evolutionists, restricting the suffrage and deporting African Americans were necessary measures to . . . remove contaminating influences" from White civilization (ibid. 37).

Sentimentalist research into the extensions of race and gender terms was influenced by White-supremacist ideology, binary gender ideology, and the systematic exclusion of women and people of color from opportunities

82 NONIDEAL THEORY AND CONTENT EXTERNALISM

to contribute to the research. These influences pushed the research toward views of race and gender that offered justification for White-supremacist ideology, abuses targeting people of color, racial exclusion, and gender-based oppression. It didn't reveal oppression or concepts that could be used to dismantle systems of oppression. Instead, like the comparative anatomists' research, it led to paradigmatic applications for race and gender terms that fell into objective types that helped obscure oppression.

2.2.4 Manifest and operative concepts, dubious research

Let me be clear that my claim in this subsection is not only that dubious research has influenced the *manifest concepts* associated with race and gender, and it's not only that this research *misidentified* the bases of race and gender classifications. Researchers plausibly did influence our manifest concepts, and what they reported about races and genders was inaccurate. But they also influenced race and gender terms by partly determining their paradigmatic applications. Researchers took it that paradigmatic applications of "man" and "woman" were White Europeans occupying traditional binary gender roles. They took it that paradigms of non-White race terms exhibited 'sexual ambiguity' and lacked "cultural traits defined as determinant of civilization." Objective type externalism takes the results of empirical research as authoritative: researchers are best positioned to tell us what a term's paradigms and extension are, and if I don't know what the paradigms are, or if I use the term idiosyncratically, then it's the researchers' paradigms—not mine—that determine the term's extension (see Haslanger 2008, 63). According to the objective type externalist account, then, race and gender terms' extensions should have been determined by the most unified, objective types into which researchers' paradigms fell. By determining the paradigms for the terms, researchers played a role in determining the operative concepts associated with race and gender terms. For race and gender terms, this process and its result were influenced by oppression. A theory that ignores this influence will conceal oppression's influence on our terms, and it is likely to misidentify the extensions of terms so influenced. A de-idealized theory would fare better.

None of this should be surprising. It's long been recognized that research into social kinds is influenced by various oppressive forces and effects: dominant ideology, differential access to education, corporate and government funding that privileges work that reinforces oppressive hierarchies, prestige rankings, and so on. Predominantly White male researchers have for over a century delivered empirical findings that support hierarchical race and gender systems, telling us that our race and gender terms refer to kinds that make those hierarchies biologically determined, evolutionarily advantageous, optimal for humankind, and so on. These results weren't accidental; rather, assumptions about race and gender hierarchies were plausibly definitive of various scientific methodologies of the time (see, e.g., Somerville 2000, 17–29; Schuller 2018, 8–37).

I should also emphasize some of these same points to explain why outdated research is relevant to objective type externalism. It may be tempting to say that race and gender terms didn't refer to what early researchers said they did because *that's not what races and gender are*. Race terms refer to races; gender terms refer to genders; whatever they are, they aren't the things those early researchers said they were, so the terms' extensions shouldn't have been influenced by any of that research.

But if researchers select a term's paradigms, then since objective type externalism says a term's paradigms partly determine which most unified, objective type it refers to, researchers play a role in determining a term's extension. It's not easy to tell what the relevant objective types are, given the paradigms described above. But the people who selected the paradigms chose them in a way that suggests that they, the types, would help obscure oppression. That's at least prima facie reason to think that that's how those types are, absent a social-metaphysical account of what objective types could have been available for the paradigms to fall into.

It may be that subsequent researchers selected (or will select) different paradigms for the relevant terms and they thereby determined (or will determine) different extensions for them. This is of course possible on the objective type view, just as Haslanger allows that the MIT faculty could change what "incomplete" refers to (Haslanger 2005, 21–22). But this possibility shouldn't make us think that the earlier researchers discussed above didn't determine extensions for race and gender terms at one time. Similarly, the fact that the MIT faculty could have changed the extension of "incomplete" in 2005 shouldn't make us think that the term never had its pre-2005 extension. As LaPorte says and as Haslanger's examples suggest, it's possible for researchers and language communities to change the extensions of their terms (or, if you prefer, to replace old terms with new homophones). For the objective type externalist, one way to do it is to change the term's paradigmatic applications. In the cases discussed above, researchers were influenced by oppression to determine the paradigmatic applications of race and gender

84 NONIDEAL THEORY AND CONTENT EXTERNALISM

terms in ways that seem to result in extensions that obscure oppression. This shows that systemic oppression influences the second phase of objective type externalism in ways that can distort extensions. Whether our present terms still have those extensions or not is immaterial.

2.3 Oppression systematically influences responses to empirical research

In the third and final phase, ordinary speakers respond to empirical findings and researchers' linguistic decisions. The traditional account of natural kind externalism typically overlooks this step. Instead, it's taken for granted that whatever researchers discover or decide with regard to a term's extension, ordinary speakers shall accept it and follow researchers in their use of the term. Or, in some cases, the thought is that after the first phase, ordinary speakers play no role in either determining or discovering the extensions of kind or type-terms. The term's extension is determined by a reference magnet as early as the first phase, and this extension is discovered by researchers in the second phase. After that, ordinary speakers can use the term as researchers decide to do (i.e., correctly) or not (i.e., incorrectly), but the term's extension has already been determined and discovered.

But this ignores the sort of possibility that played out with the Chinese term "yü." Recall that the term was applied exclusively to nephrite for thousands of years; upon the introduction of jadeite (which is superficially similar to nephrite but has a different chemical composition), there was initially some hesitation to apply "yü" to both chemical kinds. People who were experienced with working nephrite by hand suspected early on that nephrite and jadeite were different substances, and this was eventually confirmed by determining their chemical compositions: jadeite is $NaAl(SiO_3)_2$, and nephrite is $Ca_2(Mg,Fe)_5Si_8O_{22}(OH)_2$. If ordinary speakers had no choice but to follow researchers' determinations, then the language should have started treating nephrite and jadeite as different kinds by now. Presumably, this would mean that "yü" applies to nephrite while applications of the term to jadeite are treated as nonliteral or erroneous. But in fact "yü" has both nephrite and jadeite in its extension. Ordinary speakers' uses of "yü" didn't just follow chemists' jadeite/nephrite distinction.

Prima facie, then, ordinary speakers play a role in the determination of type-terms' extensions at the third phase. They can follow researchers' usage or not. Or, if there are competing research programs, the language community may follow some researchers' usage and not others or none at all. There's nothing requiring a language community to follow empirical researchers' usage for a kind or type term; if a language community does follow some researchers' usage, there's no guarantee that the influential research will be the best research, and of the groups that might influence a language community's use of a term, there's nothing limiting those groups to researchers: the community could follow usage developed by pseudoscientific research, by propagandists, by a popular uprising, and so on. Prima facie, whichever usage a community does follow will determine the paradigms for the term in its ordinary or popular uses. In this way, ordinary speakers play a role in the third phase of determining type-terms' extensions.

The mere fact that ordinary speakers play this role doesn't entail that the third phase is systematically influenced by systemic oppression. But there are various reasons to think it is. As suggested in the previous paragraph, the potential influences on a language community's usage are legion; where a language community is beset by systemic oppression, many of those possible influences will be oppressive and systematic; if some of these are actual then the third phase shall be systematically influenced by oppression. Here's a list of the relevant sorts of possible influences; it is incomplete but I hope suggestive. Some of these are discussed in the next chapter.

(1) Prima facie, ordinary linguistic usage is influenced by patterns of semantic deference, whereby some speakers accept other speakers' usage or use-rules for a term as standard or normative (Putnam 1975; Burge 1979, 1982, 1986a, 1986b). In a society with hierarchical social positions, people with higher social standing are more likely to receive semantic deference for a term than those with lower social positions are, all else being equal. Consequently, hierarchical social positioning will affect patterns of semantic deference and thereby affect linguistic usage. Since hierarchical social positions are systematic and oppressive, the influence on linguistic usage shall be systematic and oppressive (see, e.g., Pohlhaus 2012; Engelhardt 2019a, 2019b).

(2) In language communities with dominant ideologies, linguistic uses that advance, reinforce, or cohere with those dominant ideologies will be more likely to be influential than uses that conflict with them will be, all else being equal. In a language community in which dominant ideologies are oppressive, then, oppressive dominant ideologies

will likely influence linguistic usage. Since the influences of dominant ideologies tend to be systematic, this influence would presumably be systematic too (see, e.g., Mills 1997, 1998, 2007; Dotson 2011; Mason 2011; Engelhardt 2019a, 2019b).

(3) In a language community that isn't small and localized, the ability to influence ordinary linguistic usage will depend greatly on one's ability to access public platforms like TV, radio, internet, and so on, and to influence ordinary speakers via these platforms. At present, one's ability to do the latter will be greatly enhanced if they can afford to hire or otherwise make use of famous spokespeople, marketing teams, lobbyists, and others, or if they can speak uninterrupted on mass media, if they can garner positive coverage from news media, if they can start or buy a news outlet, and so on. Where the ability to afford or otherwise make use of these is systematically influenced by oppression, oppression will systematically influence ordinary linguistic usage (see, e.g., Collins 1990; Fricker 1999, 2007; Dotson 2011; Medina 2012).

(4) In language communities with dominant ideologies, the ability to influence dominant ideology will often depend on how ideologies are distributed, maintained, and passed between generations. In our culture, for instance, the ability to influence dominant ideology might depend on the ability to influence how history is taught in schools, how public debates are framed, how news narratives are framed, which events are covered on the most influential news outlets, which legal and institutional policies are adopted, and so on. Where hierarchies of oppression systematically influence which people can influence dominant ideology in these ways, oppression will systematically influence how dominant ideologies evolve, and this will, via point (2) above, influence which linguistic uses get more widespread uptake (see, e.g., Collins 1990; Stanley 2015).

These give us reason to accept that systemic oppression systematically influences which applications of social kind terms are treated as paradigmatic by ordinary speakers. Since a term's paradigmatic applications partly determine which unified, objective type the term refers to, they give us reason to accept that oppression systematically influences the extensions of social kind terms at the third phase.

Along similar lines, we can again appeal to the general argument developed at the beginning of the section. Meanings and extensions at this phase are determined partly in conversations, broadly construed, and these conversations are influenced by dominant ideology and by systematic oppressive exclusions. Prima facie, then, the determination of meanings and extensions at this phase is systematically influenced by oppression. Here, the salient form of 'conversation' involves perhaps everyone in the language community and perhaps all of their public discussion, as well as news reports, movies, political slogans—any linguistic exchanges that influence which applications of a term are paradigmatic.

But, again, it is helpful to illustrate oppression's influences and its effects on meanings and extensions. As usual, we'll see that the influences in some examples are plausibly systematic, giving us further reason to accept that oppression systematically affects this phase and the extensions determined herein.

First, notice the variety and extent of factors that reinforce dominant race and gender ideology, according to which race and gender are biological kinds. These factors encourage us to use race and gender terms so that their paradigmatic applications conform to the dominant ideology. For gender, the dominant ideology is reinforced in medical institutions by assigning binary genders to newborns according to external sex organs—gender is simply 'read' as a biological fact. It's reinforced by legal institutions when the gender assignment is documented on a birth certificate. It's reinforced linguistically and socially by the gendered pronouns that correlate to the birth assignment and by the gendered styles and colors of dress customarily adopted for infants. It's reinforced again when educational institutions segregate children according to birth assignments. And so on, with institutions, laws, social norms, and linguistic practices all reinforcing gender ideology throughout one's life.

As many have pointed out, all these factors work together—as a system—to reinforce a biological understanding of gender. They thereby also work as a system to reinforce dominant uses of gender terms according to which the paradigmatic applications are biologically determined. By making it seem obvious that fetuses, newborns, and toddlers are to be taken as paradigmatic applications of gender terms, for instance, these factors make it seem obvious that membership in the extensions of gender terms is biologically determined. They constitute a system that influences which applications of gender

88 NONIDEAL THEORY AND CONTENT EXTERNALISM

terms are taken as paradigmatic, and they do so in such a way as to reinforce dominant, oppressive, binary gender ideology. This system thus illustrates how gender oppression systematically influences the third phase of objective type externalism. Analogous points are plausible for race terms, for which the paradigms will again include fetuses, newborns, and toddlers, as well as persons from any and all cultures—even cultures with different racial classification systems—suggesting that biological and not social features determine membership in a term's extension.

Second, there are systematic efforts to suppress resistance to the systemic, oppressive influences just described. Let me first describe the resistance: social construction projects. Many social construction projects seek to 'debunk' biological accounts of race and gender and replace them with social construction accounts. If successful, such projects would presumably influence paradigmatic applications of race and gender terms. They seek to influence not only how ordinary speakers think about race and gender terms but how they use them. If a social construction project were to affect ordinary usage enough to change a term's paradigmatic applications, it would likely affect which operative concept the term expresses. Affecting ordinary usage this much probably takes more than publishing papers on race or gender, of course, but many social construction projects plausibly do involve more. Various kinds of work help 'spread the word' that race and gender are socially constructed. Social construction accounts are promoted, defended, or assumed in classrooms at various educational levels, in literature and film, on social media, in activist organizing, in the pages of *Teen Vogue*. These are social-political projects that influence (or try to influence) how ordinary speakers use race and gender terms. Rather than being oppressive, however, they aim to be liberating.

Such social construction projects have become the targets of governmental, legal, institutional, and social efforts to enforce dominant race and gender ideologies. One way to reinforce such usage is to challenge, undermine, or delegitimize the academic disciplines that often develop and teach social construction accounts of race or gender. For our purposes, what's important about these efforts is that by targeting social construction accounts, they plausibly aim to reinforce uses of race and gender terms such that their paradigmatic applications conform to dominant ideology. Since many of these efforts result in state, legal, and/or institutional policies, they end up exerting systematic influences on usage in those states, legal systems, and/or institutions.

In fall 2018, Hungary's government decided to withdraw accreditation from gender studies programs. Zsolt Semjen, a deputy for Hungary's prime minister, told Agence France-Presse that gender studies is "an ideology not a science," adding, "No one wants to employ a gender-ologist" (Redden 2018). In winter 2022, the Wyoming Senate voted to defund and remove all classes in gender and women's studies from the University of Wyoming system (Greenberg 2022). David Paternotte says that media articles attacking gender studies are widespread, and they create a climate that's hostile to gender studies—and, presumably, a climate that's hostile to social construction accounts of race and gender. Premilla Nadasen describes further manifestations of this climate, calling it:

> . . . a broader problem of intimidation and harassment, almost a kind of bullying. I think in some places the conversation often centers around abortion, and that has been the kind of launching pad for thinking about the crisis of quote, unquote gender ideology. In other places it's about reproductive rights. In other places it's about same-sex marriage. In other places it's about the breakdown of the two-parent heterosexual family, or even childcare. . . . In all of these cases the culprit becomes women and gender studies scholars. They become the reason for the supposed breakdown in family values. (Redden 2018)

In Brazil, two state bills—one passed in 2015 and one in 2018—made similar attacks on gender studies. The 2015 bill banned learning materials with information on "gender ideology"; the 2018 bill banned school policies or activities "likely to apply 'gender ideology' or the terms 'gender' or 'sexual orientation.'" While both of these bills were struck down in Brazil's Supreme Court in May 2020, the Florida state legislature passed a similar "Don't Say Gay or Trans" bill in 2022 (Cabrera 2020).

Women's and gender studies haven't been the only targets of these efforts, of course. There have also been widespread efforts to delegitimize other scholarly traditions that adopt social construction accounts of race and to prevent such traditions—or anything remotely similar to them—from being taught in public schools. Most recently in the United States, these efforts have targeted what has been called "critical race theory." While that term, "critical race theory," does pick out a scholarly tradition that adopts a social constructionist account of race, the term has been applied much more widely in popular and political discourse. In the context of the efforts to reinforce traditional, White-supremacist accounts of race and racism and to prevent resistant accounts from getting wider uptake, "critical race theory" refers not only to the view that race is socially constructed but also to any educational frameworks that concern institutional racism, the 1619 Project, White privilege, antiracism, or other facets of systemic racial oppression. In 2021, at least 36 U.S. states adopted or introduced laws or policies that restrict the teaching of "critical race theory," institutional racism, White privilege, or other topics related to systemic racial oppression.

These are just the examples that attempt to delegitimize social construction accounts in schools. They aren't the only efforts to diminish the influence of social constructionist accounts of race and gender, and they aren't the only attempts to have a systematic influence on which applications of race or gender terms are taken as paradigmatic. So-called bathroom bills prohibit trans women from using women's restrooms and other gender-segregated public facilities, and they prohibit trans men from using men's restrooms and other gender-segregated public facilities. Among other objectionable consequences, these bills enforce the dominant view that excludes trans women from among the Haslangerian paradigms for the term "woman." They make it so that, by law, either trans women aren't women at all, or they are non-paradigmatic women who are prohibited from using women's public facilities. These bills thus make it less likely that the paradigmatic applications of the term "woman" include trans women. The same goes for bills prohibiting trans women and men from participating in gender-segregated sports along with other women and men, bills that prohibit or all but prohibit changes to gender markers on official documents like licenses and passports, and bills that make it prohibitively difficult to access gender-affirming medical interventions. They make it so that trans women are either non-paradigmatic women who are legally forbidden from participating in women's sports or not women at all, so that trans men are either non-paradigmatic men who have "F" on their official documents or not men at all, and so that only wealthy and/or politically connected trans women will satisfy the criteria to fall within the extension of the dominant term "woman."

Florida's aforementioned "Don't Say Gay or Trans" bill prohibits educators from talking about sexual orientation or gender identity at many grade levels, according to the text of the bill. According to the American Civil Liberties Union (ACLU), it bans "classroom discussions related to sexual orientation and gender identity," including discussions in which students talk about "their LGBTQ+ family members, friends, neighbors, and icons" or "their [i.e., students'] own lives, experiences, and families"; regarding LGBTQ+ persons, it denies "their very existence" (ACLU of Florida, n.d.). With regard to the extensions of gender terms, the bill shrinks the possibility that school-age children in Florida will know that there exist trans men and women, thereby making it ever more unlikely that children in Florida will grow up and accept that trans women are paradigmatic women and trans men are paradigmatic men.

These are just some of the more obvious ways that laws, policies, and institutional rules are used to enforce and reinforce uses of race and gender terms such that their paradigmatic applications conform to dominant, oppressive ideology.

The foregoing points suggest that all levels of systemic oppression—ideological, legal, institutional, and social—contribute to influencing which applications of race and gender terms are taken as paradigmatic, such that ordinary speakers' uses of the terms will conform to dominant, oppressive ideologies. We thus have reason to suppose that oppression systematically influences the extensions of social kind terms at the third phase of their determination. Since dominant gender and race ideology make various aspects of race- and gender-based oppression seem 'natural' or 'inevitable,' they help to obscure oppression. Thus, we should think that oppression systematically influences the third phase of objective type externalism with the consequence that race and gender terms obscure oppression. Taking this in conjunction with the results of Sections 2.1 and 2.2, we should conclude that oppression systematically influences each phase of objective type externalism, that these influences suffice to affect the meanings and extensions of terms, and that the distorted terms tend to obscure oppression.

3. The de-idealized theory improves upon its predecessor

Section 2 made the case that oppression systematically influences all three phases of objective type externalism's account of the determination of kind terms. In its idealized version, however, the theory doesn't recognize this influence, while the de-idealized version does. In this section, I'll make the case that because of this difference, the de-idealized version better serves each of the theory's main goals. In Section 3.1, I'll outline the idealized theory's idealizations and sketch the de-idealized theory; I'll make the case that the latter better serves the idealized theory's goals in Section 3.2.

3.1 Ideal and nonideal phases

In developing her account of objective type externalism, Haslanger brought together scholarship on race and gender and work on content externalism, and her view led to advances in both areas. It showed how natural kind externalism can be extended to objective type-terms, and it suggested that externalism can be used to debunk mystifying ideology. Objective type externalism's account of how social kind terms have their extensions determined, however, overlooks the systematic influences of oppression. It idealizes.

In the first phase, members of a language community develop an objective type term by fixing its paradigmatic applications and implicitly extending the term's reference to the most unified, objective type into which those paradigms fall. It's important to Haslanger's project to suppose that in a community structured by oppression, this process makes it so that social kind terms typically refer to social kinds that contribute to oppressive structures. If our social world is structured to produce social kinds that contribute to oppression, then when we name parts of the social world, we're likely to pick out and name those oppression-contributing kinds.

But this overlooks that in communities structured by oppression, the process of developing terms, of 'picking out and naming' parts of the world, is also likely to be influenced by oppression. We saw in Section 2.1 that oppressive laws, institutions, and social hierarchies make it so that oppressed groups are systematically excluded from the most influential conversations in which terms are developed; meanwhile, oppressive ideologies make it so that when we pick out and name parts of the social world, we're most likely to pick out parts that reinforce our ignorance, not disabuse us of it. For instance, we pick out gender kinds that obscure nonbinary lives and oppression, we pick out race kinds that obscure Indigenous American experiences and oppression, and we pick out political and economic kinds that obscure unpaid domestic labor. In overlooking these influences, objective type externalism tacitly accepts an idealized social ontology, idealized institutions, and an idealized cognitive sphere. Here's what we said about these idealizations in Chapter 1:

> [*Idealized social ontology*] Ideal theory tends to represent humans as "the abstract and undifferentiated equal atomic individuals of classical liberalism," thus abstracting away from "relations of structural domination, exploitation, coercion, and oppression" (Mills 2005, 168).

[*Ideal social institutions*] Ideal theory represents "fundamental social institutions such as the family, the economic structure, the legal system" as they would be in an ideal-as-idealized model, thus abstracting away from "how their actual workings may systematically disadvantage women, the poor, and racial minorities" (ibid., 169).

[Idealized cognitive sphere] Ideal theory won't "recognize, let alone theorize" the ways in which oppression influences agents' social cognition, thus abstracting away from "the distinctive role of hegemonic ideologies and group-specific experience in distorting our perceptions and conceptions of the social order" (ibid., 169).

Objective type externalism's last two phases accept the same idealizations. Phase 2 takes it that empirical research will identify the most unified, objective type into which all or most of a social kind term's paradigmatic applications fall. It's assumed that this phase and its results won't be significantly influenced by unequal social positioning among researchers, systematic exclusion of oppressed groups from research opportunities, or dominant ideology. But we saw that empirical research is systematically influenced by all of these. Phase 3 assumes that the language community will accept the best empirical results relevant to some social kind term and adapt usage accordingly. But as we saw, various oppressive factors influence how our language community uses its social kind terms, from long-standing institutions that reinforce uses that conform to dominant ideology to legal, institutional, and social backlash against efforts to debunk such ideology-confirming uses.

In order to de-idealize the theory, we can de-idealize each phase. Broadly, that means that for each phase, instead of assuming the above idealizations, we reject them and recognize the influences of systemic oppression. On the one hand, this could mean simply that at each phase, we don't assume that oppression won't influence the determination of meanings and extensions. For any given term, it's an empirical question whether oppression influenced the determination of its meaning and extension at each phase, and we answer the question by empirical means: social analysis, historical scholarship, and so on. Call this the "weak de-idealization." On the other hand, we can propose that for every term—or at least every social kind term—oppression systematically influences each phase in the determination of its meaning and extension so as to obscure oppression. Call this the "strong de-idealization." The weak de-idealization differs from both the strong de-idealization and the idealized theory in that it's agnostic about whether oppression systematically influences objective type externalism's three phases. The strong de-idealization assumes that it does. The ideal theory assumes that it doesn't.

But in practice, I don't think there should be much of a difference between these two 'strengths' of de-idealization. That's because there are many and various ways that oppression can influence any given phase in a term's determination, and the effects of oppression's influences can be just as diverse. Given this, when it comes to identifying how oppression has affected a given term's meaning or extension, it doesn't help us much to say simply that each phase was affected by oppression. As in the examples that I discussed in the previous section, we should try to identify specific influences and their effects. Similarly, while it's important to acknowledge that oppression systematically affects the determination of meanings and extensions (at least for social kind terms), it's not enough to say so and then leave it there. For each term, we should try to say which features of systemic oppression affected each phase and how these influenced the term's meaning and extension. Since these may differ for different terms developed at different times, in different places, in different contexts, and so on, the best we can do for any given term is to deploy empirical methods to identify the relevant influences and effects. Thus, even if we adopt the strongly de-idealized phases and assume that every phase in the determination of social kind terms is influenced by oppression, we'll still have to deploy the same empirical methods appealed to in the weakly de-idealized phases to identify just what these influences were and what effects they had.

Thus, when speaking generally, we should leave it open exactly how each phase of de-idealized objective type externalism is influenced by oppression. The specifics will have to be filled in for each term and in light of relevant empirical inquiry. As a rule, we should be looking for how oppression has influenced each phase for any given social kind term. Who is excluded from the institutions at which the research was undertaken? How was public response influenced by dominant ideology? Who had their contributions minimized? How was the research distorted by ideology? And so on. Section 2 can be taken as illustrating what this might look like for the terms discussed.

There may be exceptions in which the extension-determining processes aren't influenced by oppression, and there will surely be attempts to carry out the processes without the influence of oppression. But the former will be rare, and the latter will most often have only mixed success. Systemic oppression is pervasive and crafty, and it finds its way into places one might not expect. The de-idealized phases tell us it finds its way into the objective type externalist's phases, but they don't and can't give us a recipe for exactly how that happens for each term. We have to look at the actual world to find out how oppression influences it.

This is not to say that de-idealized objective type externalism doesn't idealize at all, and it's not to say that the de-idealized theory is the same as the ideal theory but with the idealizations 'deleted,' as it were. The de-idealized theory is still a theory, and so it will still adopt those idealizations that are advantageous. For instance, it shall still model speakers without representing their middle names, heights, or birthdays. Presuming that these don't systematically affect the processes that determine our terms, it is helpfully simplifying for the theory to abstract away from these features of our world. Of course, however, the de-idealized theory won't adopt all the same idealizations as the ideal theory.

Moreover, the de-idealized theory's social model isn't the same as the ideal model but with the problematic idealizations about oppression 'deleted.' Rather, the de-idealized theory's model of society is informed by the extensive scholarly literatures on White supremacy, patriarchy, colonialism, hetero-patriarchy, imperialism, misandrogyny, and so on. For any given term, these are the literatures that will tell us how systemic oppression influences the phases of its determination. (Thus, theorists who adopt or deploy objective type externalism should be well versed in this literature, especially in light of the systems that produce ignorance of systemic oppression discussed in Chapter 1.)

It can be helpful to compare the de-idealization here to a de-idealization reviewed in Chapter 1. Recall Lynne Tirrell's de-idealization of Wilfrid Sellars's account of language games. Sellars proposes that all entrances into language games are *neutral*, in that all speakers are granted the same powers and permissions upon entrance. For any given speaker entering any given language game, Sellars assumes that his language entrance won't be influenced by oppression. But Tirrell points out that in language games structured by oppression, speakers will seldom enter language games with the same powers and positions. In order to account for this, Tirrell introduces *non-neutral* language entrances, in which speakers are granted differential powers and permissions, often in accordance with their hierarchical social positioning. The introduction of non-neutral entrances is a modification to central features of Sellars's account. It rejects the assumption that language games and entrances aren't affected by oppression, and it enables the theorist to appeal to relevant scholarship and empirical information to acknowledge when and how they are. With regard to objective type externalism, the situation is similar. The de-idealization rejects the assumption that oppression doesn't significantly influence the determination of social kind terms' meanings and extensions, and the de-idealized phases enable the theorist to appeal to relevant scholarship and empirical information to acknowledge when and how oppression does influence social kind terms' meanings and extensions.

3.2 The de-idealized theory is superior

Above, I outlined three goals of objective type externalism: (1) It aims to tell us how social kind terms and concepts have their meanings, contents, and extensions determined. (2) For a specific term or concept, it aims to tell us what its meaning, content, or extension is. (3) It aims to provide us with concepts that will help undermine the influence of interconnected systems of privilege and subordination.

If the idealized theory fails to acknowledge systematic influences on how social kind terms and concepts have their meanings, contents, and extensions determined, then it is inadequate with regard to its first goal. I've made the case that because the theory is idealized, it does fail to acknowledge systematic influences of oppression on all three phases in the determination of the extensions, meanings, and contents of social kind terms and concepts. Consequently, the account given by the theory in order to satisfy its first goal is systematically inaccurate. The de-idealized theory, by contrast, corrects this systematic inaccuracy; it doesn't foreclose the possibility of oppression's systemic influence, and it calls us to identify its influences in each case. If all else is equal, then, the de-idealized theory should serve the first goal better than its idealized counterpart does. Since the only difference between the two theories is that one recognizes the influences of oppression and the other doesn't, all else *is* equal, and we should accept that the de-idealized theory serves the first theoretical goal better than the ideal theory does.

Things are much the same with regard to the second explanatory goal. The idealized theory fails to account for a systematic influence on the meanings, contents, and extensions of social kind terms and concepts. When we apply the idealized theory to determine the meanings, extensions, or contents of specific social kind terms or concepts, the results it delivers are likely to be inaccurate. The idealized theory accepts that a kind term's extension is identified or determined by relevant research, but it fails to acknowledge that such research and its popular uptake can be influenced by oppression. There are at least two reasons why this failure makes the idealized theory worse at satisfying its second goal.

First, oppression can influence how ordinary speakers respond to empirical research. For instance, although the best research into gender kinds might reveal that trans women and men are paradigmatic women and men, respectively, oppressive influences—including ideological, institutional, legal, and interpersonal influences—might prevent (many of) the social kind terms in popular usage from counting trans women and men as paradigms. In such a case, because the idealized theory fails to recognize the influences of oppression on popular uptake, it will say that the extensions of "woman" and other gender terms are identified by the best gender research; consequently, it will say that the paradigmatic applications of "woman," for instance, include trans women. The idealized theory's account of the term's paradigmatic applications will thus be inaccurate, and since the externalist says a term's extension is determined by its paradigms, the idealized theory's account of the term's extension will be inaccurate.

Second, even if the idealized theory is sometimes accurate about the extensions of social kind terms that are influenced by oppression, it makes inaccurate predictions about how such extensions may change. It predicts that a social kind term's extension will change only if there's a change to either the best relevant research or to the reference magnet that attracts the term's reference. But, as we saw, in a society structured by oppression, a social kind term's extension can also change thanks to the influences of oppression, as when legal decisions fix the extensions of race terms in ways that reinforce oppression or stifle resistance to it. Since this can occur thanks to a legal decision, it can occur without a change in reference magnets or in the best available research, contrary to what the idealized theory posits.

Since all else is equal between the two versions of the theory except that the de-idealized theory recognizes the influences of oppression, and since the idealized theory's failure to recognize these influences makes it inaccurate, we can see that the de-idealized theory serves the second goal better than the idealized version does.

With regard to the third goal, I reviewed many ways in which the idealized theory makes it more difficult for us to recognize the influences of systems of privilege and subordination. I take it that, all else being equal, a theory that obscures such influences is less help to us in undermining those influences than is a theory that reveals them. Again, since all else is equal between the idealized and de-idealized theories, but the de-idealized theory helps reveal influences of systems of oppression that the idealized theory obscures, we should conclude that the de-idealized theory better serves this third goal than its idealized predecessor does.

We saw that oppression systematically influences each of the three phases in the determination of social kind terms in ways that conceal oppression and its effects. In the first phase, we saw that oppressive ideologies and systematic exclusions make it so that terms are often developed in ways that 'center' the privileged, obscure the lives and experiences of the oppressed, and make it more difficult to reveal oppression or its effects. We saw that the operative concepts associated with the terms "class," "socioeconomic status," "labor," and "leisure" were developed in ways that help obscure class- and gender-based oppression while the operative concepts associated with "gender dysphoria" and terms related to gender transitioning help obscure the lives of and oppressions faced by gender-nonbinary persons. We saw that the race terms "Black" and "White" were developed such that their associated operative concepts served to obscure and justify racial oppression partly by marginalizing and obscuring the distinctive racial experiences of Latinx persons, Asians, and Indigenous Americans.

At the second phase, empirical research into social kinds is shaped by oppressive ideology, by the legal, institutional, and social forces that exclude women and people of color from participating in empirical research and by the oppressive structures that shape social kinds themselves. We saw that research that's been thus influenced by oppression can in turn affect social kind terms' paradigmatic applications and operative concepts. For instance, research on IQ tests plausibly helps determine paradigmatic applications of the term "intelligence" so that its extension reinforces oppressive race and gender stereotypes and obscures race- and gender-based exclusion and discrimination in professional and educational opportunities. Similarly, empirical research relevant to race and gender terms influenced paradigmatic applications of those terms in such ways that their extensions served to obscure and/or justify the European gender binary, the gender hierarchy, racial hierarchies, labor exploitation, and more.

At the third phase, there are manifold ways in which a language community's response to empirical research is influenced by oppression. After outlining four general ways in which oppressive social structures make it likely that linguistic usage is influenced by oppression, we focused on race and gender terms. We saw that the health system, the legal system, and the educational system all enforce uses of gender terms that conform to dominant ideology. And we saw that state, legal, and institutional systems are deployed in ways that inhibit uses of race and gender terms that would challenge dominant ideology. Insofar as uses of race and gender terms that conform to dominant ideology help obscure oppression, these points give us reason to believe that oppression and its effects are more likely to be obscured when oppression influences the third phase.

By abstracting away from the influences of oppression, the idealized account of objective type externalism ignores all of these ways that oppression influences the processes that determine social kind terms' meanings and extensions. By failing to account for these influences, it makes it seem as though the relevant processes are not so influenced by oppression. Accordingly, it obscures how oppression and its effects influence social kind terms and the processes that give them meanings and referents. The de-idealized theory, by contrast, calls us to reveal these influences and their effects on our terms. The de-idealized theory thus serves the third goal of objective type externalism better than its idealized predecessor does.

4. Conclusion

De-idealizing objective type externalism produces a theory that better serves its goals than the idealized theory. We saw that systems of oppression systematically influence the processes that, according to objective type externalism, determine the extensions and meanings of social kind terms and the extensions and contents of social kind concepts. These influences come from various 'levels' of systems of oppression—ideological, legal, institutional, interpersonal—and it's plausible for many of them that they occur systematically. Granted that there are systems of race, gender, and class discrimination in our language community, and given the widespread and multilevel influence that the foregoing has shown them to have on our social kind terms and concepts, it's plausible to infer that oppression systematically influences our social kind terms/concepts and the determination of their extensions, meanings, and contents. By idealizing or simplifying away from oppression and its effects, the idealized version of objective type externalism fails to recognize systematic influences on the meanings, extensions, and contents it aims to explain, and it obscures some aspects of the systems of oppression that it has been used to try to reveal.

In the next chapter, I raise similar considerations regarding social externalism: the traditional account of social externalism abstracts away from the influences of oppression on our terms and the processes that determine their extensions and meanings. That is, it idealizes. I'll make the case that oppression systematically influences the processes that, according to social externalism, determine terms' meanings and extensions. Since the idealized theory fails to account for these systematic influences, its accounts of meanings, extensions, and the processes that determine them are systematically inaccurate, and it obscures oppression. A de-idealized version of the theory would correct these shortcomings. If we consider social externalism in light of the goals we attributed to objective type externalism, we should again conclude that the de-idealized theory is an improvement over the idealized traditional theory.

3

De-idealizing social externalism

0. Introduction

This chapter motivates and develops a de-idealization of social externalism. Much of its overall organization mirrors the previous chapter. In Section 1, I'll motivate social externalism, review its explanatory goals, and sketch how it satisfies them. I'll say that on the idealized account of social externalism, there's no consideration of whether the processes that determine the meanings and extensions of social kind terms are influenced by oppression. It's assumed that the theory can idealize away from oppression and its effects without compromising its explanatory success much. Section 2 argues that oppression systematically affects the processes that, according to social externalism, determine the meanings and extensions of social kind terms. I'll make the case in two ways: I'll point to several influences that are systematic, and I'll show that the influences of oppression are widespread and come from various 'levels'—ideological, legal, institutional, interpersonal. The latter points suggest that the best explanation for why oppression influences our terms in so many ways and at so many levels is to suppose that its influence is systematic. Section 3 then introduces modifications to develop the de-idealized theory, and it makes the case that the de-idealized theory better serves social externalism's goals. By idealizing or simplifying away from oppression and its effects, the idealized version fails to recognize systematic influences on the meanings, extensions, and contents it aims to explain. By modifying the theory to account for these influences, the de-idealized theory gives us an account of social kind terms' extensions and how they're determined that is systematically more accurate than the idealized theory. In addition, the de-idealized theory reveals effects of oppression that are obscured by the idealized theory.

Nonideal Theory and Content Externalism. Jeff Engelhardt, Oxford University Press. © Oxford University Press 2024.
DOI: 10.1093/oso/9780197754191.003.0003

1. Social externalism

This section motivates[1] social externalism and reviews how it satisfies its explanatory goals. I'll take it that when we apply social externalism to social kind terms, its explanatory goals are similar to those we attributed to objective type externalism in the previous chapter.

1.1 Motivating social externalism

Social externalism is most often motivated by appealing to Tyler Burge's tharthritis thought experiment. The tharthritis thought experiment is most often interpreted as making the case that many meanings and contents are determined by features of one's social environment (outside one's body). If some meanings and contents are determined by one's social environment, then such meanings/contents are not fully determined by what's going on in one's body. If so, then the thought experiment establishes content externalism—the view, you'll recall, that some meanings/contents aren't fully determined by what's happening in one's body and brain.

Whereas Putnam appealed to the reasonable idea that thinkers tend to think and refer to the kinds of things in their environment (rather than about superficially similar kinds not in their environment), Burge appeals to a related intuition: that we tend to use the meanings that our peers and others in our community are using, to refer to the things that others in our community are referring to, and to think about the things that others in our community are thinking about. Accordingly, the thought is that the meanings and contents that members of a community are deploying can play a role in determining the meanings and contents of some individual community member's words and concepts. For a thinker could have little understanding of the words or concepts they're deploying while taking it that they use those words/concepts with the meanings and contents deployed in their community. In such a case, facts about the meanings and contents used in the community would partly determine the individual's meanings and contents. This sort of possibility extends well beyond natural kind terms and their associated contents. For just about any term, one could have little understanding of

---

[1] As in the previous chapter, the point of motivating the theory isn't to convince anyone to adopt it. It's to help clarify it and to show readers unfamiliar with the theory why anyone would believe it.

DE-IDEALIZING SOCIAL EXTERNALISM 103

its meaning while taking oneself to use it with the meaning used in the community. So too for just about any concept.

The tharthritis thought experiment illustrates this point with the term "arthritis." Suppose that Sam has various beliefs about arthritis. She believes her father has it in his knees. She believes her partner's sister takes medication for it. She thinks daytime TV often has commercials advertising treatments for it. And so on. She thinks about arthritis, and sometimes she utters the word "arthritis" as a way to refer to the same thing that those around her refer to when they say it. In addition, Sam suspects she has arthritis in her thigh, and she would express the content of her suspicion by saying, "I have arthritis in my thigh." As we deploy the word and concept, however, arthritis doesn't occur in thighs. It is a rheumatoid condition that afflicts joints only. So when Sam tells her doctor of her suspicion, she is promptly corrected, and she accepts the correction. She had a false belief about arthritis.

Now take a counterfactual situation in which what goes on inside Sam's body and brain is exactly as it is in the actual situation, in which Sam's utterances of and history of exposure to words that sound like "arthritis" are exactly the same, and in which Sam is again inclined to say, "I have arthritis in my thigh," just as she is inclined to say, "There are advertisements for arthritis medication on daytime TV." When she says such things and has associated beliefs, she takes herself to be talking and thinking about the same thing that others in her community are talking and thinking about when they use the word "arthritis." The one difference is that Sam's counterfactual community deploys the term and concept slightly differently. Instead of limiting their application of the word form "arthritis" and the concept it expresses to rheumatoid conditions of the joints, they also apply it to rheumatoid conditions more generally. In this community, the extension of the word and concept *does* include rheumatoid conditions that afflict the thigh. Accordingly, when Sam tells her physician, "I have arthritis in my thigh," she isn't promptly corrected; instead, the physician takes this to be a live possibility.

Whereas Sam's utterance is taken as false by definition in the actual situation, her utterance in the counterfactual situation is possibly true. But if what Sam says in both situations is the same, then it should be that if one is false by definition, then the other one is too. Instead, Sam seems to be saying two different things in the two situations.

Granted that Sam is, as she takes herself to be, deploying the same concept and term that others in her community deploy, then this would explain the difference in what she says. In the actual situation, members of Sam's community talk about a condition that afflicts only joints, as evidenced by the physician's correction. Say that this condition is *arthritis*, and say that the concept ARTHRITIS has all and only instances of this condition in its extension. In the counterfactual situation, community members think and talk about a different condition. The condition they concern themselves with includes arthritis *and* other rheumatoid conditions, including those that afflict the thigh. Say that this condition is *tharthritis*, and the concept THARTHRITIS has all and only instances of tharthritis in its extension. Since the concepts ARTHRITIS and THARTHRITIS have different extensions, they presumably have different contents. If Sam is deploying the concept that people in her community are deploying in each situation, she is deploying different concepts in the two situations. She deploys ARTHRITIS in actuality and THARTHRITIS in counterfactuality.

Similarly for the terms she utters in each situation. In the actual situation, the word "arthritis" refers to arthritis. In the counterfactual situation, the same word form, "arthritis," isn't used to refer to all and only instances of arthritis (as we know it). Rather, the term used in the counterfactual condition has a different extension: it includes arthritis *and* other rheumatoid conditions. The terms in the two situations have different meanings and extensions.

What's going on in Sam's body in each situation is the same, though. Since her concepts nonetheless have different contents in the two situations, it must be that something other than what's going on in Sam's body partly determines the contents of her concepts. Similarly, mutatis mutandis, for the meanings and extensions of the words she uses.

If Sam's concepts in these cases are partly determined by what's happening in her social situations, then her concepts aren't fully determined by what's going on inside her body. And the same goes for the meanings of her words. Content externalism is established. And, as noted above, this point seems to generalize to nearly any term or concept. For just about any term or concept, one could have little understanding of its meaning or content while taking oneself to use it with the meaning/content used in the community. As Burge says of the tharthritis thought experiment,

> Such arguments go through for observational and theoretical notions, for percepts as well as concepts, for natural kind and non-natural kind notions, for notions that are the special preserve of experts . . . [and for] any notion that applies to public types of objects, properties, or events that

are typically known by empirical means. (Burge 1986a, 6; see also Burge 2007, 287–289)

This version of content externalism, then, has at least two noteworthy differences from the view motivated by the Twin Earth thought experiment. On the Twin Earth thought experiment, it's the meanings/contents of natural kind terms/concepts that aren't fully determined by what's going on in the individual's body. As we saw in the previous chapter, natural kind externalism is often taken to be restricted to natural kind terms/concepts. And this is so, presumably, because of how the relevant meanings/concepts are 'externally determined'—they're determined by the kinds in a language community's natural environment. So natural kind externalism, as traditionally understood, is (i) limited to natural kind terms/concepts and (ii) requires differences in natural environment to ground differences in meaning/content. The view motivated by the tharthritis thought experiment, by contrast, doesn't accept either (i) or (ii). It applies much more generally. And instead of changes in the natural environment, it turns on changes in social environment.

1.2 The division of linguistic labor

The tharthritis thought experiment gives us reason to believe social externalism, and it suggests that the meanings, contents, and extensions of an individual's terms and concepts can be determined by the individual's social environment. But it doesn't tell us much about how a social environment determines meanings, contents, or extensions. We'll need to know that if we're to appeal to social externalism to tell us the meanings and extensions of social kind terms.

The traditional answer is that at least in many social environments, there is a division of linguistic labor. As we saw in Chapter 2, the idea of the division of linguistic labor probably originated with Putnam. He says,

> Whenever a term is subject to the division of linguistic labor, the "average" speaker who acquires it does not acquire anything that fixes its extension. In particular, his individual psychological state certainly does not fix its extension; it is only the sociolinguistic state of the collective linguistic body to which the speaker belongs that fixes the extension. (Putnam 1975, 146)

Where there is a *nonlinguistic* division of labor, a community is divided so that some community members do work that produces, say, fruits and vegetables that other members of the community can consume as food. Although it may be that everyone or almost everyone in the community can eat the produce grown by community members, relatively few grow that food themselves. Indeed, it may be that many who enjoy fruits and vegetables in the community don't know how to grow them themselves, don't have the space for growing food, don't have access to seeds or sunlight, and so on. The community together depends for its fruits and vegetables on both (a) those who produce them and (b) those who make the fruits and vegetables available to the community (through shipping, distribution, etc.).

The same goes for the division of linguistic labor. For many terms in a language, there are some speakers in the language community who cannot say with much precision what the term means or what it refers to; for any such term, these speakers have not "acquire[d] anything that fixes its extension," as Putnam says. Instead, the term's extension is fixed by "the sociolinguistic state of the collective linguistic body to which the speaker belongs." Just as there are people in the division of labor who can and do grow vegetables and others who can't or don't, some people in the division of linguistic labor can say with precision what a term means and refers to while the rest of us can't. We who can't define a term with much precision depend on those who can to provide us with terms with precise meanings and identifiable extensions, just as non-farmers depend on farmers for fruits and vegetables.

Return to the example of the terms "topside" and "sirloin" (Yli-Vakkuri & Hawthorne 2018, 7–8). Many competent speakers of English don't know the difference between topside and sirloin, but their uses of the terms "topside" and "sirloin" have different meanings and extensions and express different concepts. If I ask, "May I please have sirloin?" in a restaurant, for instance, I and everyone around me will take it that I have ordered sirloin and not topside. If the dish comes out and I say it's not what I was picturing when I said "sirloin," those who can define "sirloin" with more precision (perhaps a waitress or chef, or a butcher seated near me) can explain to me what sirloin is—they can tell me what I was referring to when I ordered using the word "sirloin." Prima facie, in this situation, I should accept that they're right: I should accept that those who can define the term with more precision and who can tell sirloin from other cuts of meat are in a better position than I am to say what my own utterance of "sirloin" meant and referred to. If I took myself to be communicating with other English speakers using

English words in the ways they're typically used, and if I recognize that the waitress knows better than I do what the English word "sirloin" means and refers to when used in the typical way, then I should accept that the word's meaning wasn't determined by whatever I was picturing or thought I was saying. Alternatively, if I accept correction from others, then that's evidence that I did take myself to be using the word as those around me use it, whether or not I was aware of taking myself thus and no matter whether I had explicitly intended to do.[2] Either way, in the usual case, a person who can't tell sirloin from topside or other cuts of meat will (and ought to) defer to those who can make such distinctions when it comes to the meaning and extension of the term "sirloin." Prima facie, it's part of linguistic practice in our language community that we give *semantic deference*: with regard to the meaning and extension of some term, those who are less competent in the term's use and less knowledgeable about the part(s) of the world to which it refers defer to and accept correction from those who are more competent with regard to the term's use and more knowledgeable about the part(s) of the world to which it refers.

We can imagine 'chains' of semantic deference that ultimately lead to the most competent and knowledgeable members of the language community. I know next to nothing about sirloin, topside, and the rest, so I defer to the waitress. The waitress may in turn defer to a chef or butcher; butchers and chefs might defer to those who have the most expertise among them, or perhaps they defer to experts in cattle biology, scholars of butchery, or some such. We might imagine that, ultimately, there are some who earn semantic deference from all others by appealing to relevant empirical facts, drawing distinctions, producing counterexamples, and deploying other linguistic resources in order to elicit others' assent regarding the meaning and extension of "sirloin" and related terms.

In the tharthritis thought experiment, something similar holds for the actual and counterfactual terms associated with the word form "arthritis." Sam's physician elicits assent from Sam regarding the use of "arthritis"; Sam's physician might give semantic deference to other physicians and to rheumatologists; among rheumatologists, there are presumably some who can appeal to empirical research, draw distinctions, and so on, and thereby

---

[2] "The subject's willingness to submit his statement and belief to the arbitration of an authority suggests willingness to have his word taken in the normal way—regardless of mistaken associations with the word" (Burge 2007, 131).

earn semantic deference from the rest regarding "arthritis." Of course, the patterns of semantic deference differ in the counterfactual scenario as compared to actuality. In actuality, speakers defer to those who say that "arthritis" has in its extension only those rheumatoid conditions that afflict joints. In the counterfactual scenario, those who receive semantic deference say that "arthritis" also has in its extension rheumatoid conditions that afflict thighs.

Prima facie, what makes the difference in the two scenarios is that the speakers who elicit semantic deference from others in each situation give different accounts of the meaning and extension of the word form "arthritis." If so, then we have an account of how terms have their meanings and extensions determined by a speaker's social environment—by "the sociolinguistic state of the collective linguistic body to which the speaker belongs," as Putnam says. (1) Patterns of deference among competent speakers lead ultimately to speakers—call them "experts"—who can elicit assent from all others about what the term picks out in the world and how best to articulate the term's meaning. (2) The experts' assent-eliciting account of what a term picks out gives the term's extension; (3) their assent-eliciting account of how best to articulate a term's meaning—which account is "usually arrived at through reflection on *archetypical applications*"—gives the term its meaning (Burge 2007, 259; see Yli-Vakkuri & Hawthorne 2018, 7–8[3]). Here's how Burge puts it while making a point about synonymous expressions:

> What does *having the same meaning* involve in the cases of empirically applicable terms? Synonymies are grounded in practice: *the most competent speakers would use the two relevant expressions interchangeably....*
>
> 'Greatest competence' consists in abilities to draw distinctions, to produce precisifications, to use numerous linguistic resources, to offer counterexamples to proposed equivalences—that elicit the reflective agreement of other competent speakers. We may imagine a vast, ragged network of interdependence, established by patterns of deference which lead back to people who would elicit the assent of others. (Of course, we idealize from this network; a person's degree of competence may vary over time and with

[3] Here's how John Hawthorne and Juhani Yli-Vakkuri put it: "To paraphrase Putnam, the division of labour here can be pictured as one in which there are some people whose job it is to eat sirloin, others whose job it is to cook sirloin, and yet others whose job it is to know the difference between sirloin and other cuts of beef. All three groups of people use the term 'sirloin,' but the extension of 'sirloin' is fixed (holding other facts about the world fixed) by the way the third group uses the term" (Yli-Vakkuri & Hawthorne 2018, 7–8).

the case at hand, and may develop or regress.) To put it crudely, a person counts as among the *most competent* if he or she would be *persuasive* to other competent speakers in the use and explication of the language. The point about persuasion is fundamental. I shall develop it by considering the dialectic that typically leads to statements that explicate meaning. . . .

The dialectic attempts to arrive at what might be called *normative characterizations*. These are statements about *what Xs are* that purport to give basic, 'essential', and necessarily true statements about *Xs*. They are used as guides to certifying the identity of entities: something that is cited as an *X* but does not fulfill the condition laid down by the normative characterization will not normally be counted an *X*. A subclass of normative characterizations not only purport to state facts that set norms for identification; they also provide linguistic meaning—set a norm for conventional linguistic understanding. ('A knife is an instrument consisting of a thin blade with an edge for cutting, fastened to a handle'; 'To walk is to move on foot at a natural unhurried gait'; 'A baby is a very young child or very young higher animal.') (Burge 2007, 259, original emphases)[4]

As is suggested by Burge's examples—"knife," "walking," "baby"—he takes *empirically applicable terms* to include more than those terms for which there is relevant scientific research. The term "knife" presumably does not refer to a natural kind, and there isn't (so far as I know) scientific research that aims to identify the most unified, objective type to which the term "knife" might refer. Elsewhere, Burge takes it that points like the foregoing apply to "sofa," "brisket," "clavichord," "contract," and "red" (ibid. 107–110). And, as we saw above, Burge takes it that social externalism applies to "any notion that applies to public types of objects, properties, or events that are typically known by empirical means" (Burge 1986a, 6; see also Burge 2007, 287–289).

Accordingly, the process that determines the meanings and extensions of the relevant terms on this account doesn't necessarily involve scientific research. It could, of course, but whether it does or not is determined by how the patterns of deference turn out and who they lead to. If it's true for the term "arthritis" that semantic deference leads back to scientific researchers into rheumatoid conditions, that's because those researchers elicit the assent of other competent speakers: In discussions regarding the meaning and

---

[4] As I'll discuss more in the next subsection, he's here arguing that we can doubt synonymies between empirically applicable terms.

110   NONIDEAL THEORY AND CONTENT EXTERNALISM

extension of the term, speakers familiar with the relevant research elicit the assent of those who aren't familiar with it, and among those familiar with the relevant research on arthritis, those with the greatest competence elicit the assent of the others. At the end of the network of semantic deference, there are the researchers into rheumatoid conditions who can draw distinctions, produce precisifications, offer counterexamples to proposed equivalences, and thereby elicit the reflective agreement of other competent speakers. Having success in relevant scientific research is presumably helpful in (and sometimes part of) eliciting the reflective agreement of other competent speakers, but it's not necessary for it.

For terms like "sofa," "contract," and "knife," there isn't any scientific research that aims to identify the most unified, objective kinds into which paradigmatic sofas, contracts, or knives fall. But still, according to Burge, there are discussions regarding the meanings and extensions of the terms, and in these discussions some speakers elicit the assent of others. Collectively, these discussions establish patterns of deference—"vast, ragged network[s] of interdependence"—that lead to speakers who would elicit assent from others regarding the appropriate application and explication of whichever term or terms are at issue. Whoever is at the end of a chain of semantic deference for a given term plays the role that experts on rheumatism play for "arthritis." That is, whichever speakers are at the end of the chain of deference for a term give the normative characterizations that determine that term's extension and conventional linguistic meaning.

Thus, a term's meaning and extension are determined by whichever speakers stand at the end of the patterns of semantic deference for that term. Patterns of deference for a term T are themselves determined by discussions regarding T's meaning and extension. By eliciting the assent of other speakers in these discussions, some speakers emerge as those to whom the rest of us give semantic deference for the term.

Burge says that these speakers—those at the end of chains of deference—exhibit *greatest competence*. "A person counts as among the *most competent*," he says, "if he or she would be *persuasive* to other competent speakers in the use and explication of the language" (ibid. 259). He then expands on his point about persuasion.

> I have pointed up the central role of persuasion in the dialectic [that leads to expert normative characterizations]. To understand the dialectic one

must understand the nature of persuasion. Sometimes we see the most competent speakers as creating new uses through impressive employment of verbal resources. In such cases, persuasion in the strict sense need not be involved. Imitation may be based primarily on the attractiveness of the style of speech, the power or status of the speaker, or the impressionability of the hearer. But often when someone is seen as more competent it is because he or she is persuasive on matters about which there are objective rights and wrongs and on which substantive reasons have a bearing. The agreement reached is not to a decree, nor is it merely the result of practical reasoning about how to adjust our usage for smoothest communication. The agreement concerns the proper ordering of applications of a term which we have already made or are disposed to make and, ultimately, the correct characterization of the examples that those applications pick out. In the course of the dialectic, we *stand corrected*: we recognize ourselves as convicted of *mistakes*, not merely infelicitous strategies for communication. We come to know something that characterizes empirical entities and sets standards for characterizations to which we regard *ourselves* as antecedently committed. Thus the most competent speakers are pre-eminent not merely because they impress the impressionable. Their influence is based on persuasion that is subject to dispute and cognitive checks. (Ibid. 260, original emphases)

On Burge's view, it may happen that speakers elicit the assent of others by virtue of their power, status, or speaking style, but he sets these possibilities aside—they don't involve persuasion in the strict sense, he says. When the dialectic does involve persuasion in the strict sense, a speaker elicits assent from others because she has been "persuasive on matters about which there are objective rights and wrongs and on which substantive reasons have a bearing." Authority in the dialectic, Burge says later, "derives in part from an ability to answer doubts—to persuade oneself and others" about the relevant term's core applications and about the use-rules to which we hold ourselves responsible (ibid. 262). In Burge's paradigmatic case, then, the persuasion is epistemic: we give and receive assent on epistemic and empirical grounds. If I have disagreed with a speaker who later wins my assent and the assent of others regarding a term, I should—on epistemic grounds—recognize myself as having previously made a *mistake*. I stand corrected.

1.3 Cognitive value, conventional linguistic meaning, terms, and concepts

In the previous chapter, I took it that whatever determines a term's extension thereby also determines both the term's meaning and the content of the associated concept. Burge develops a distinction that prevents me from adopting that sort of compression in this chapter. The distinction is between what Burge calls "cognitive value" and "conventional linguistic meaning" (ibid. 269). Roughly, the latter is a term's meaning, and the former is the content of a concept or a concept itself (ibid. 272). While many philosophers of language and mind take it that word meanings are determined by the contents of concepts they express, Burge rejects this orthodoxy. (Yli-Vakkuri and Hawthorne take it to be orthodoxy. See Yli-Vakkuri & Hawthorne [2018, 18].) Burge makes his case in several ways, but it suffices for our purposes to review just one. As we saw, Burge takes it that a term's conventional linguistic meaning is determined via a dialectic that leads—by semantic deference—to speakers who give a characterization that sets a norm for conventional understanding of the term's meaning. For instance, that process might lead to a norm for understanding the meaning of the term "sofa" as "piece of furniture [meeting conditions X, Y, and Z] meant for sitting." Burge points out, however, that a person who raises doubts about the claim "sofas are pieces of furniture . . . meant for sitting" will rightly be attributed different doubts and beliefs from the person who raises doubts about the claim "sofas are sofas" (Burge 2007, 269). Thus, we shouldn't take it that the phrases "sofa" and "piece of furniture . . . meant for sitting" express concepts with the same content; if they did, then we wouldn't attribute different beliefs to the two doubters. Instead, we can say, with Burge, "One must assign different cognitive values or units of potential information—to the conventionally synonymous phrases ('sofa' and 'piece of furniture . . . meant for sitting')" (ibid.).

It doesn't follow from this point that the cognitive value associated with a term has some *different* normative characterization. Rather, in the typical case, "the best understanding one can achieve of a cognitive value is that offered by accepted normative characterizations and whatever background information accompanies them" (ibid. 272). Moreover, Burge warns us against supposing that "cognitive value" and "conventional linguistic meaning" refer to different *entities*. Rather, he says, "one might take the expressions as labels for different methods of interpretation" (ibid. 270n15). He doesn't commit to this position either, however.

Still, in order to mind the distinction between cognitive value and conventional linguistic meaning, I'll take it that the process described in the previous subsection does not tell us the concept that a term expresses. It tells us only the meaning of the relevant term(s).

But even with this position, we should keep in mind a caveat about meanings. Burge doesn't just think that the aforementioned doubts about meaning-giving characterizations are intelligible and distinct from the necessarily false doubts—for example, that sofas are sofas. He takes it that our linguistic practice of entertaining doubts about meaning-giving characterizations is (further) evidence that such characterizations are revisable. In speaking of the truth of meaning-giving characterizations that elicit speakers' agreement, he says, "There is no transcendental guarantee that people cannot agree in making mistakes" (ibid. 262). For any given term, a meaning-giving characterization that was agreed upon at one time could later come to be regarded as false. "Dialectic ending in reflective equilibrium among competent speakers," Burge says, "is a defeasible but reliable tool for individuating conventional meanings" (ibid. 271). We should take meaning-giving characterizations as being open to revision and doubt; they're as close as we'll come at any given moment to identifying a term's meaning and the content of the concept that the term expresses, but they may nonetheless be mistaken.

1.4 Social externalism's explanatory goals

I'll take it that social externalism's explanatory goals are similar to objective type externalism's. In the discussion of objective type externalism, I outlined goals specific to Haslanger's application of the view to social kind terms and concepts. Since social externalism has been taken as applying to social kind terms—to all empirically applicable terms—since its introduction, there's no need to develop a distinctive account of the view as it applies to race terms, gender terms, and so on. So we can take the first two explanatory goals to be quite general. (1) Social externalism aims to tell us how empirically applicable terms have their meanings and extensions determined. And, (2) for a given term, it aims to tell us what its meaning and extension are. But since my focus in this book is on our social terms and concepts, and especially on those terms/concepts that may be influenced by and/or contribute to oppression, I'll be especially concerned with those same terms here.

114   NONIDEAL THEORY AND CONTENT EXTERNALISM

For similar reasons, I'll again be concerned with whether or not the traditional account of social externalism can help us reveal oppression. Although Burge doesn't seem to intend for social externalism to achieve this end, there have been cases in which social externalism has been deployed to identify the concepts associated with race terms.[5] And Haslanger herself appeals to social externalism in some places to support or supplement her project of providing us with concepts that will help undermine the influence of interconnected systems of privilege and subordination (see Haslanger 2005,[6] 11, 17; 2006, 107; 2008, 63, 66). It is appropriate then to say that some have appealed to social externalism to reveal oppression.

Whether social externalists have deployed the theory to reveal oppression or not, however, it's important for our purposes to keep track of how the theory does in this regard. Whether it's true or not that the theory *aims to* reveal oppression, we should, all else being equal, prefer a theory that reveals oppression to one that obscures it. Accordingly, I will consider the extents to which the idealized and de-idealized versions of social externalism reveal or obscure oppression. But we shouldn't take it that if the de-idealized theory satisfies this goal better than the idealized theory does, then the de-idealized theory better satisfies the goals of social externalism. On that score, we should focus only on the first two explanatory goals above.

How does social externalism satisfy goals (1) and (2)? The process described above is supposed to tell us how empirically applicable terms have their meanings and extensions determined, satisfying the first goal. Competent speakers engage in discussions about the meanings and extensions of empirically applicable terms in the language; some speakers earn deference from others with regard to questions about the meanings and extensions at issue in these discussions. Among the speakers who earn deference from others, there will be a subset whose claims about meaning and extension also elicit assent from the speakers to whom others have deferred.

---

[5] See, for example, Appiah (1996). Plausibly, though, Appiah doesn't adopt an *idealized* social externalism. Appiah proposes that our current race concepts are best clarified by appeal to long-dead intellectual elites who held pseudoscientific ideas about race—one may doubt whether these are meant to be the speakers who exhibit the greatest competence and who would elicit assent from other competent speakers today.

[6] As noted in Chapter 2, in this 2005 paper, Haslanger is appealing to externalism to suggest that her accounts of race and gender terms might not be revisionary. It may be that speakers are referring to the kinds Haslanger describes, but they're not aware that their terms have these referents. Thus, it's not plausible that Haslanger intends for her revisionary/ameliorative proposals for race and gender terms to satisfy only this third explanatory goal. In this paper and in the 2008 paper cited, externalism is supposed to cut through the mystifications of ideology and reveal the social kinds that construct interconnected systems of privilege and subordination.

In this subset, there may be another subset who earn deference, and so on. The patterns of deference established in these conversations lead ultimately to speakers who can elicit assent from all others about (i) what the term at issue picks out in the world and (ii) how best to articulate its meaning. In providing their account of (i), these speakers give the term's extension; in providing their account of (ii), they give the term's conventional linguistic meaning. As noted above, these accounts are open to revision, and we as a community might later regard the speakers' accounts as mistaken. But they are, at a given time, the best accounts of a term's meaning and extension that we can achieve.

The theory then satisfies the second goal by appeal to this process. For any given term, we can identify its meaning and extension by figuring out what the process determines them to be. In order to determine the meaning and extension of "arthritis" in the actual world, for instance, we would figure out which speakers stand at the end of the patterns of deference regarding the term's meaning and extension. Suppose that it's experts in rheumatoid conditions. Then, we identify what these experts say about (i) what the term picks out and (ii) how best to articulate its meaning. The first tells us the term's extension; the second tells us its meaning.

2. Oppression and the division of linguistic labor

On Burge's account, a term's meaning and extension are determined by the accounts of meaning and extension that elicit assent from competent speakers in the relevant dialectic. Those who give the assent-eliciting accounts—the most competent speakers or 'the experts'—receive semantic deference from others in the dialectic because they are persuasive in the strict sense. It's ultimately persuasion in the relevant dialectic, then, that determines which accounts and which people determine a term's meaning and extension. Burge takes it that in the usual case, accounts and speakers receive semantic deference from others because they are persuasive on matters of objective fact. He acknowledges but idealizes away from the possibility that speakers and accounts may receive semantic deference thanks to their power or authority. Presumably, this includes power and authority granted by and/or embedded in systems of oppression. This section makes the case that in fact oppressive systems and power relations systematically influence semantic deference and the dialectics over meaning. As in the previous chapter, I won't argue that contemporary race, gender, or class oppressions are systemic. I'll follow many others in taking it that they are and in taking it that these systems include ideological, institutional, legal, and interpersonal manifestations.[7] My aim here is to show that these systems influence the social externalist's meaning-determining processes—in particular, they influence semantic deference in the division of linguistic labor. I'll make the case that these influences are systematic in several ways. Overall, I'll give examples in which semantic deference is influenced by ideological, institutional, legal, and interpersonal manifestations of oppression. I propose that these examples are representative of oppression's systematic influences on the division of linguistic labor. I take it that the best explanation for why systemic oppression influences semantic deference in so many ways and at so many levels is to say that oppression's influence on it is systematic. In addition, I'll sometimes make the case that a specific vector of influence is systemic. For instance, when I'm describing the influence that hierarchical social positioning has on semantic deference, I'll make the case that since hierarchical positioning is systematic, so are its influences on semantic deference. Since idealized social externalism overlooks a systematic influence on its meaning-determining processes and the de-idealized version doesn't, we have reason to think, all else being equal, that the de-idealized version is superior. The final section of the chapter will outline the de-idealized view and make the case that de-idealized social externalism better serves the three goals reviewed above.

In the subsections that follow, I'll survey some of the ways that oppression influences our practices of semantic deference. I aim to illustrate the extent and variety of oppression's influences; for the sake of clearer exposition, I try to discuss one influence at a time, but in fact they are mutually reinforcing. My remarks on how interpersonal interactions influence semantic deference, for instance, help elaborate on the ways that ideology influences the same—and vice versa. While this may make it more difficult to appreciate each influence on oppression individually, it should also make it clearer that the best way to understand how oppression influences semantic deference is by thinking of that influence as systematic. The influences surveyed here are interdependent because they result from and reinforce common systems of oppression.

---

[7] See, for instance, Kwame Ture [Stokely Carmichael] (1966); Marilyn Frye (2000); Patricia Hill Collins (2015, 2); Vivian May (2015, 3); Ange-Marie Hancock (2007, 74).

I'll make the case that various levels of oppression influence semantic deference in the division of linguistic labor by appeal to three broad ways in which oppression influences patterns of semantic deference: by licensing systematic patterns in corrections, by maintaining conversational ranks, and by enforcing norms of semantic deference. In order to understand these influences, it will be helpful to have tools for articulating what happens in the dialectics themselves and how those happenings influence patterns of semantic deference overall: when and how semantic deference is given, how deference to *more* competent speakers constitutes deference to the *most* competent, and so on. In the next subsection, I'll introduce some tools for that purpose.

2.1 Tools

This subsection appeals to Mary Kate McGowan's account of *covert exercitives* to motivate the idea that we can identify patterns of semantic deference by identifying 'conversational moves' that (a) enact 's-rules' of semantic deference and (b) occur systematically. I'll say that if we have reason to think an s-rule of semantic deference is enacted systematically, that's reason to believe that there's a pattern of deference that corresponds to that rule. I'll use these ideas in making the case that oppression has systematic influences on semantic deference.

2.1.1 S-rules, g-rules, and exercitives

Covert exercitives are 'conversational moves' that enact s-rules. *Conversational moves* are just contributions that participants in a conversation make to that conversation: asking a question, answering a question, changing the subject, complimenting someone, following up on a point, and so on. Following McGowan, I'll use "s-rules" to refer to rules that govern just one specific conversation (McGowan 2009, 396). For instance, if you and I agree in our conversation to use "Yard Narc" as a code name to refer to my neighbor (just in case he hears us), and we agree not to use his name, then we've plausibly set an s-rule. Henceforth in our conversation, it's permissible to use "Yard Narc" to refer to my neighbor, impermissible to use "Yard Narc" to refer to someone else, and impermissible to use my neighbor's real name. While we might deploy this rule again in other conversations within my neighbor's earshot, the rule doesn't govern conversations more generally. If

118 NONIDEAL THEORY AND CONTENT EXTERNALISM

I were talking to someone else, I couldn't simply use "Yard Narc" and success-fully refer to my neighbor without having first introduced the rule. *G-rules*, by contrast, do govern conversations more generally. Prima facie, there's a g-rule in many languages that makes it permissible to use a person's name to refer to them, and it is impermissible to use a code name for that person unless the code name has been introduced and accepted in the conversation.

McGowan points out that (i) every move in a rule-governed activity enacts s-rules that govern that activity and (ii) conversation is a rule-governed ac-tivity. Since covert exercitives are conversational moves that enact s-rules, every conversational move is a covert exercitive. Our interest shall be in how covert exercitives can enact specific kinds of s-rules, namely s-rules of semantic deference. After clarifying what exercitives are in general and motivating McGowan's case for covert exercitives, I'll develop the idea that there are s- and g-rules of semantic deference that can be enacted by covert exercitives or by traditional Austinian exercitives.

An exercitive is a speech act that "confers or takes away rights or privileges" (Austin 1962, 120; see also McGowan 2004, 95). In standard examples of exercitives, a speaker with the authority to confer or take away rights or privileges does so by performing a speech act. By virtue of my authority as a parent, I may say "bedtime is 8:00 p.m." and thereby set a rule giving my child some privileges (e.g., to stay awake past 7:00 p.m.) and taking away others (e.g., to play outside past 9:00 p.m.). Following McGowan, I'll use "Austinian exercitives" to refer to these exercitives that seem to require salient authority.

McGowan makes the point that exercitives are also performed by speakers who have much more mundane, perhaps seldom noticed, authority—namely, the authority of any participant in a rule-governed activity. She points out that in a rule-governed activity, every 'move' in the activity changes what is subsequently permissible in that activity (McGowan 2009, 396; see Lewis 1979, 342–346). If we're playing chess and you capture one of my rooks, then since you moved, that makes it newly permissible for me to take my turn; since your move captured my rook, it makes it newly impermissible for me to involve my rook in play on the board; since your move leaves a previously occupied space unoccupied, it makes it permissible for me to move to or through that space; and so on. To put it another way, every move in a rule-governed activity confers or takes away rights or privileges—every move is an exercitive. McGowan calls these sorts of exercitives "covert exercitives."

That's not to say that everything one does while participating in a rule-governed activity is an exercitive. If you sneeze or scratch your nose, that doesn't change what's permissible in our chess game. Sneezing isn't a *move* in chess, and it's only moves—contributions to the activity in question—that confer or take away rights or privileges in the activity.

Conversations are rule-governed. On McGowan's use, "rules" includes norms, and an activity is rule-governed in her sense if some contributions to the activity count as out of bounds.

> By rule-governed, I mean any activity governed by norms. The 'rules' in question need not be explicit, formal, exceptionless or even consciously recognized. If at least some behaviours (as contributions to the activity in question) would count as out of bounds or otherwise inappropriate (as contributions to the activity in question) then that activity is rule-governed in the relevant sense. Conversations, dancing, playing music, walking, chess, checkers, and baseball are all rule-governed in the appropriate sense. (Ibid. 395)

Are there contributions to conversations that count as out of bounds? Yes. At any given point in a conversation, for instance, a certain amount is presupposed by the discussants, and it is inappropriate to make conversational moves that seem to ignore what's presupposed. If we run into one another at the grocery store, and you tell me you're there buying food for your beloved cats, it's out of bounds for me to ask, "Do you have any pets?" (see ibid. 396; Lewis 1979, 339). I've violated the rule that forbids ignoring what's been presupposed. Similarly, there are rules determining the referents of definite descriptions used in a conversation at a time. If Kate and Jim are talking about Kate's house, saying things like "The house is beautiful, but the property needs work" and "We rent the house," it's out of bounds for either discussant to use the phrase "the house" to refer to some other house. For instance, it's out of bounds for Jim to say of his own home, "The house will have to be sold when I move" (see McGowan 2009, 394). Since some contributions to conversation are out of bounds, conversation is a rule-governed activity.

To show that every contribution to conversation is an exercitive, McGowan appeals to *rules of accommodation*, as developed by David Lewis. Broadly, the idea is that the rules governing a conversation tend to evolve to make permissible what the participants treat as permissible. "Presupposition," Lewis says, "evolves according to a rule of accommodation specifying that any presuppositions that are required by what is said straightaway come into existence, provided that nobody objects" (Lewis 1979, 347). In the example above in which you were buying cat food, an utterance of yours presupposed that you have pets—namely, cats. What you said required the presupposition that you have pets; since I didn't object, the presupposition straightaway came into existence, so that it was a permissible contribution to the conversation. More generally, the 'state of play' (what Lewis calls "conversational score") in a conversation "does tend to evolve in such a way as is required in order to make whatever occurs count as correct play" (ibid.). In the example with Kate and Jim, if Kate doesn't object to Jim's use of "the house," then subsequently in the conversation, "the house" refers to Jim's house and not Kate's. Why? Because it's required to make Jim's conversational contribution count as correct play.

In these cases, the moves made by the conversational participants conferred or took away rights or privileges. The conversational move that introduced the presupposition that you have cats made it thereafter inappropriate for me to ask whether you have pets, and it made it appropriate for me to make conversational moves that presuppose that you have cats. Bringing into existence the presupposition that you have pets took away the 'privilege' of appropriately asking whether you have pets and conferred the privileges associated with helping myself to the presupposition thereafter. Jim's use of "the house" to refer to his own house made it thereafter appropriate to use the term with the same referent and inappropriate to use it for a different house. These moves were covert exercitives, and as such, they enacted s-rules that changed what was subsequently permissible in the activities to which they contributed.

2.1.2 Exercitives and patterns of semantic deference

Consider paradigmatic instances of semantic deference: Sam defers to her physician about the extension of the term "arthritis"; I defer to the waitress about the extension of "sirloin." Although there's little explicit discussion of a term's meaning or extension, these cases instantiate the dialectic Burge describes. In each case, one competent speaker elicits assent from another with regard to the appropriate applications or explications of an empirically applicable term. The speaker who elicits assent from the other(s) earns their semantic deference. And in each case, the more competent speaker enacts an s-rule. When the physician corrects Sam's use of "arthritis," Sam assents to a rule such that the term doesn't apply appropriately to rheumatoid conditions that occur in thighs. From then on, it's appropriate in the conversation to apply the term to conditions that occur in joints, and it's inappropriate to apply the term to conditions of the thigh and other non-joints. When the waitress explains to me what sirloin is and I accept her account, I assent to a rule such that "sirloin" applies to cuts of meat like the one on my plate (and perhaps not to the sort of thing I was imagining when I ordered). If no one who is present to the exchange objects, then the waitress's explanation has enacted an s-rule making it appropriate to apply "sirloin" to some things and inappropriate to apply it to others. She, like Sam's physician, has enacted an s-rule.

I described the enacted s-rules as determining appropriate and inappropriate uses of the term(s) at issue. As Burge describes the dialectics that arrive at meaning-giving characterizations, though, something more happens: the person who elicits assent from her peers also thereby receives semantic deference from them. Or, from the perspective of those giving assent: by accepting the waitress's proposed rule for appropriate use of "sirloin," I also give her semantic deference regarding the term. I don't just adopt the waitress's characterization of the term; I defer to her. Sam doesn't just accept her physician's account of arthritis; she also gives him deference regarding the term. Understood this way, we might say that an additional s-rule is enacted in these cases. The physician enacts an s-rule making it appropriate for Sam to defer to him regarding "arthritis," inappropriate for the physician to defer to Sam regarding the term, and inappropriate for Sam to refuse to give semantic deference to her physician regarding the term.[8] If everyone at the table assents to the waitress's account of what sirloin is, then she enacts an s-rule making it appropriate for us to defer to her, inappropriate for her to defer to us, and inappropriate for one of us to later refuse to defer to her.

We might say that these s-rules are enacted thanks to a rule of accommodation for semantic deference. Recall that rules of accommodation make it so that 'conversational score' evolves so as to make whatever happens count as

---

[8] Three notes: (1) I take it that with regard to a given term, the semantic deference relation is asymmetric. A butcher may defer to a doctor regarding "arthritis," and the same doctor might defer to the same butcher about "sirloin," but it can't be that each defers to the other about the same term. (2) We might think that the s-rule makes it appropriate for Sam to defer to her physician about other medical terms as well. It may well do. I take it that whether it does or not is indeterminate unless or until it becomes determinate by virtue of how the conversation evolves. (3) One might also think that the physician isn't enacting an s-rule but abiding by (or perhaps enforcing) a *g-rule*. The g-rule would say that Sam and other nonexperts ought to defer to medical experts regarding "arthritis" and other medical terms. I have no problem with the proposal that this could happen in a physician's office. I don't adopt this interpretation here just because it wouldn't illustrate what I'm trying to illustrate: that s-rules of semantic deference can be enacted in conversation. You needn't think this is what happens in every case like the one described in order to accept my point; you need only accept that it could go this way.

122 NONIDEAL THEORY AND CONTENT EXTERNALISM

correct play, provided no one objects. Presumably, there are standing norms or g-rules of semantic deference for at least some terms. It is appropriate for me to give semantic deference to physicists regarding the applications and explication of "muon," "gluon," and "quark," and it is inappropriate for a physicist with expertise relevant to those terms to give me deference regarding those terms. It is inappropriate for a botanist to defer to me regarding "beech" and "elm," and it is appropriate for me to give semantic deference for those terms to a botanist. And so on. It might be that for any given term that's subject to the division of linguistic labor, there are, at a time, norms of deference specifying who should semantically defer to whom regarding that term. But as long as there are *some* such norms, then no matter what they are, we can think of them as components of the state of play or conversational score. As with rules of accommodation generally, the rule of accommodation for semantic deference would make it so that these norms—these components of conversational score—evolve so as to make whatever happens in the conversation count as appropriate.

> Norms for semantic deference evolve according to a rule of accommodation specifying that any norms of deference that are required to make a conversational contribution appropriate straightaway come into existence, provided that nobody objects.

Suppose it wasn't already appropriate for me to defer to the waitress about the application and/or explication of the term "sirloin." (Perhaps the culture at this restaurant has a the-customer-is-always-right type of policy, so there are norms making it inappropriate for the waitstaff to correct customers.) In order for her to appropriately correct me regarding the term, the norms of semantic deference governing our conversation have to change; they have to make it so that it is appropriate for me to defer to her. When she does correct me, then if no one objects, the s-rule of semantic deference is enacted—unless or until something else happens to change the conversation's s-rules of semantic deference again.

You don't have to accept that there's a rule of accommodation for semantic deference to accept the point that's important for us here. I think appealing to the rule of accommodation is helpfully clarifying, but if you don't, you can reject the proposal. For my purposes, you need to accept only that appealing to s-rules is an acceptable way to understand what happens when semantic deference is given. If you think there's a better way to understand it, that's

DE-IDEALIZING SOCIAL EXTERNALISM   123

fine, as long as you think the appeal to s-rules is one acceptable way to do it. I'll take it that when semantic deference is elicited in the dialectics as Burge describes, we can think of it as enacting an s-rule of semantic deference. I'll take it that whenever semantic deference is earned, an s-rule of semantic deference is enacted, and vice versa: whenever an s-rule of semantic deference has been enacted, henceforth someone is receiving semantic deference.

As we saw above, the semantic deference established in conversations like these is supposed to lead ultimately to speakers who can marshal examples, empirical data, and linguistic resources to elicit assent from all other speakers. There are a few ways we might think of this. First, we could take it that semantic deference is transitive. When Sam's physician corrects her and she defers to him, he has presumably learned how to articulate and apply the term "arthritis" from someone else—a professor at his medical school, perhaps, or a researcher on rheumatoid conditions. Since this person has elicited the physician's assent, he has given them semantic deference. If the semantic deference relation is transitive, then since Sam defers to her physician and her physician defers to, say, his medical school professor, then Sam also defers to the professor. Ultimately, then, the chain of semantic deference leads to whoever can elicit assent from everyone else.

Second, it presumably happens in some cases that speakers enact s-rules that call for 'direct' semantic deference to the speakers who can elicit assent from everyone else—that is, deference goes to the relevant speakers without 'going through' intermediaries. In his account of the U.S. race concept, for instance, K. Anthony Appiah proposes that in the 19th century, "ordinary speakers, when queried about whether their term 'race' really referred to anything, would have urged you to go to the experts" (Appiah 1996, 41–42). If such a conversational move were to be made and accepted, it would enact an s-rule making it appropriate to defer to the experts regarding the appropriate applications and explication of the term "race." ("The experts," Appiah says, were "the medical doctors and anatomists, and later, the anthropologists and philologists and physiologists" [ibid. 42].) It would enact an s-rule of semantic deference in the conversation.

Prima facie, s-rules like this could also be enacted in ways that are less overt. In a conversation about the appropriate applications and/or explication of the term "race," for instance, one might interject, with practiced assuredness, "As a medical doctor, I can tell you that the term 'race' is best understood as . . . " If no one objects, then in the usual case, a move like this enacts an s-rule making it appropriate to give semantic deference to the speaker. In addition, if the speaker's prefatory remark is taken as indicating that he's speaking "as a medical doctor," then the s-rule may make it appropriate to give semantic deference not only to the speaker himself but to medical doctors generally. Or, if it is otherwise salient in the conversation that the speaker is a medical doctor and participants carry on as though his being a doctor is what licenses him to define the term, this might suffice to establish an s-rule that calls for more general deference to medical doctors.

In cases like these, the participants abiding by the s-rule would give semantic deference 'directly' to the experts (e.g., the medical doctors) who can elicit assent from everyone else. There's no need to say that semantic deference is transitive. Moreover, if an s-rule like this were to be enacted systematically, then there's reason to think that there would be a corresponding g-rule. There'd be reason to think that there's a general rule governing conversations in the community calling for semantic deference to the experts. There'd be a pattern of semantic deference that leads back to the speakers who elicit assent from all others.

Elsewhere, I've proposed that "if some s-rule is enacted systematically, then there is a corresponding g-rule" (Engelhardt 2019a, 4). The idea behind the proposal is this: s-rules that are enacted systematically thereby hold systematically, and rules that hold systematically are g-rules. Note that if a rule holds *systematically*, it doesn't follow that it holds *unconditionally*. For instance, the sanctioned rule in *The Merriam-Webster Dictionary* for slang use of "sick" to mean *impressive* makes it appropriate in contexts in which slang is appropriate and inappropriate otherwise. The g-rule making such uses of "sick" appropriate holds systematically but not unconditionally. If such a rule for "sick" is enacted systematically, it is presumably followed systematically, and there would seem to be nothing more to a rule's *holding* systematically than its being enacted and followed systematically. In developing the slang use of "sick," speakers presumably enacted an s-rule making it appropriate to use "sick" this way, even though this rule contravenes the more formal g-rule for the term. When this s-rule was enacted systematically, it was presumably followed systematically, so that the rule held systematically. Again, that's not to say that the rule held *without exception*. There may well be well-circumscribed contexts in which another s-rule is in force—in more formal conversations, for instance. But if the s-rule generally holds in informal contexts, then it plausibly holds systematically.

And, if g-rules are rules of a system, then it would be appropriate to say of any rule that holds systematically in a language community that it is a g-rule.

DE-IDEALIZING SOCIAL EXTERNALISM   125

Thus, s-rules that hold systematically are (or at least correspond to) g-rules. So I take it that if an s-rule calling for deference to experts regarding some term were enacted systematically, there'd be a pattern of semantic deference leading ultimately to those deferred-to experts.

Third, we might take it that when an s-rule regarding a term's use is enacted in a conversation, deference goes not only to the speaker who enacted it *in that conversation* but also to the speaker or speakers to whom the rule can ultimately be traced. Suppose that the waitress who corrected my use of "sirloin" said that sirloin is "a cut of meat—especially beef—from the part of the hindquarter just in front of the round." When no one objected, she—call her Sylvia—enacted an s-rule governing our conversation that made it appropriate to explicate the term this way and to apply it accordingly. Suppose also that Sylvia read this definition in a dictionary, and until enacting this s-rule herself in conversation with the people at my table, she was never a participant in a conversation when this s-rule was enacted. So Sylvia never participated in a conversation in which an s-rule made it appropriate for her to give semantic deference to someone else with regard to "sirloin." Moreover, although she recalls reading the definition and the dictionary in which she read it, her source doesn't credit anyone with being the author of the entry or the rule it expresses. So there's no person known to her whom she could say she defers to for the definition. In a case like this, I take it to be intuitive and in keeping with the spirit of Burge's view to say Sylvia is giving semantic deference to *whoever* arrived at the normative characterization that Sylvia follows, even if Sylvia's never been in conversation with that speaker, even if Sylvia doesn't know who they are, and even if Sylvia hasn't ever and will never consider whether there is such a person. Here's one way to think of it: just as I give semantic deference to Sylvia in our conversation because I follow the s-rule she enacted, so too does Sylvia give semantic deference to whoever ultimately enacted (in conversation decades ago, perhaps, with the editors of the dictionary's second edition) the rule she follows.

If this is along the right lines, then there's a pattern of semantic deference that leads from Sylvia to whoever it was who elicited assent from other competent speakers involved in writing the rule in the dictionary. We can apply this idea more broadly as well. Since I—thanks to Sylvia—also follow the rule in Sylvia's dictionary, then by the same reasoning, I give semantic deference to the same person or people as Sylvia does. And, if the rule from Sylvia's dictionary is enacted systematically, then (a) by the reasoning above, there's a corresponding g-rule that governs use of the term "sirloin," and (b) those

126 NONIDEAL THEORY AND CONTENT EXTERNALISM

who follow the g-rule give semantic deference to the same person(s) as Sylvia and I do. Common adherence to the g-rule suggests that patterns of deference for the term "sirloin" lead ultimately to whoever enacted the rule that appears in the dictionary.

I don't claim that these are the only ways that eliciting assent in individual conversations might establish patterns of deference that lead ultimately to the most competent, as Burge says. It's just that it's helpful for our purposes to have some models of how it could happen. It'll help us think about how patterns of deference are established in more detail, and that will help us determine how oppression might influence those patterns.

Now I'll describe three ways that oppression can influence which s- and g-rules of semantic deference are enacted in the dialectics that lead to meaning-giving characterizations. We'll see in this discussion that the influences come from at least four different 'levels' of oppression: ideological, legal, institutional, and interpersonal. In discussing corrections in Section 2.2, I'll make the case that they're influenced by all four levels. In discussing ranks in Section 2.3, I'll argue that they're influenced by the institutional and interpersonal levels of oppression. In discussing enforcement in Section 2.4, I'll make the case that it's influenced by the legal, institutional, and interpersonal levels. In addition, I'll make the case at various points that some of these more particular influences (e.g., oppressive social ranks) themselves systematically influence semantic deference in the division of linguistic labor.

2.2 Corrections

Corrections are a standard feature of Burge's examples of semantic deference. The physician corrects the patient's use of "arthritis" (Burge 2007, 104–105). A lawyer may correct her client's use of "contract" (ibid. 110). A speaker who makes mistakes about the range of things to which "red" applies is corrected by their friends.

> They think that fire engines, including *that* one, are red. They observe that red roses are covering the trellis. But they also think that *those* things are a shade of red (whereas they are not). Second looks do not change their opinion. But they give in when other speakers confidently correct them in unison. (Ibid.)

And so on. When corrections are accepted, they establish an s-rule of deference to the person giving the correction—the corrector elicits assent from the corrected with regard to the meaning and/or extension of the relevant term. Recalling the points raised above, we add that the rules of deference enacted by such corrections lead ultimately to the speakers who give characterizations that set norms for identification and/or for conventional linguistic understanding (ibid. 258–259). If the correcter has on another occasion accepted correction from (or otherwise given semantic deference to) another speaker, A, and if deference is transitive, then the person who was corrected also defers to A; if A has accepted correction from B, then all three defer to B; if B has accepted correction from C, then all four defer to C—and so on up until everyone in the pattern of deference gives semantic deference to the speaker(s) who set(s) the norms governing the term's meaning and extension. That is, these sorts of interactions establish the patterns of deference that ultimately determine which speakers will fix the meanings and extensions of terms.

Here's what this means for us: If oppression systematically influences which corrections are given and accepted with regard to some term, then it systematically affects the pattern of deference for that term, and it affects who determines that term's meaning and extension. If so, then it would presumably affect the term's meaning and extension. Moreover, suppose oppression systematically affects the corrections given and accepted not only for some terms but generally; that is, suppose that oppression's systematic influence on corrections (and thus on patterns of deference, meanings, and extensions) is general, not limited to some terms or others. In that case, oppression would seem to have a systematic effect on our division of linguistic labor generally and on the meanings and extensions it determines.

Are there reasons to think that oppression in our language community systematically affects which corrections are given and accepted for terms generally? There are. Indeed, there are reasons to think that each of the aforementioned 'levels' of oppression—ideological, institutional, legal, and interpersonal—affects corrections and their acceptance.

First, several authors have made cases suggesting that dominant oppressive ideology influences which corrections are made and accepted in public discourse, such that corrections that reinforce dominant ideology are more likely to be made and accepted while normative characterizations that challenge dominant ideology are more likely to be rejected. For instance, Gaile

Pohlhaus Jr. has argued that it's routine for dominantly situated knowers (e.g., White, cis men under White-supremacist, cis heteropatriarchy) to dismiss conversational contributions that challenge the representations of the world developed in dominant discourses (Pohlhaus 2012). She points, in part, to public responses to cases in which a well-known figure has challenged dominant race- or gender-based ideology: then President Barack Obama's remarks on the 2009 arrest of Professor Henry Louis Gates Jr., Justice Sonia Sotomayor's claim that "she would hope a wise Latina would make better judgments than a white male without her life experiences," and quotations from Reverend Jeremiah Wright's sermons during the 2008 presidential campaign (ibid. 732–733). To propose a normative characterization for a term that challenges dominant ideology is also to make a conversational contribution that challenges dominant ideology. To dismiss a conversational contribution is to prevent it from being accepted—it prevents the relevant conversational move from affecting the conversation's score, from getting uptake in the conversation. Thus, prima facie, Pohlhaus's point entails that normative characterizations that challenge dominant ideology are more likely to be rejected. I've made the case elsewhere that similar points are made in the works of Iris Marion Young, Charles Mills, and Kristie Dotson (see Engelhardt 2019a, 12–19). And, as I argue in Section 2.4, Mills even gives reason to think that normative characterizations of terms that advance dominant ideology are *enforced*. Prima facie, whenever there is a general argument to the effect that speakers are more likely to accept conversational contributions that reinforce dominant ideology and/or reject contributions that challenge it, then we can derive from the argument the more specific point about conversational contributions that offer or presume *normative characterizations* that either reinforce or challenge dominant ideologies. Insofar as these patterns in acceptance/rejection are a consequence of the systematic reinforcement of dominant ideologies, it's so far plausible that they occur systematically.

Second, it's plausible that systemic oppression warps interpersonal interactions such that persons with more social privilege are more likely to give corrections and to have their corrections accepted than persons with less privilege are. This is suggested by discussions of 'mansplaining' and other kinds of 'splaining (e.g., Whitesplaining, thinsplaining), testimonial injustice, silencing, quieting, smothering, and more (see, e.g., Solnit 2014; Fricker 2007; Langton 1993; Hornsby 1995; Dotson 2011; Kukla 2014). In each of these, speakers in dominant positions correct (dismiss, preempt, discredit, disempower, etc.) speakers in subordinate positions. The hierarchies that position some speakers as dominant and others as subordinate are a consequence of systems of oppression. In many cases, the phenomena are distinct from other conversational phenomena because the dominant speaker leverages social power derived from oppressive hierarchies. In one of Miranda Fricker's examples of testimonial injustice, for example, the social power given to men over women under patriarchy and the social power of stereotypes of women as irrational lend force to conversational moves that discredit women by invoking 'female intuition' (Fricker 2007, 9; Langton 2010, 459–464). Thus, it's plausible that these corrections are enabled by and a consequence of oppressive systems. Thus, it's plausible that oppression systematically affects which corrections are given and accepted. Consequently, it's plausible that oppression systematically affects g-rules of semantic deference.

Let me illustrate this point with mansplaining, Whitesplaining, and so on. The paradigmatic examples of mansplaining come from Rebecca Solnit's essay "Men Explain Things to Me."[9] In one, Solnit is at a party describing a book she'd written when an "imposing man who'd made lots of money" interrupts her to describe a book on the same topic, a book he thought made a more important contribution to the same literature (Solnit 2014, 1). He hadn't read the book, though, just a summary. If that weren't epistemically arrogant enough, the book he went on to describe was the same book Solnit had already been summarizing—the book she had written. He didn't know it because he hadn't read it.

As this example suggests, not all instances of mansplaining involve correction, and, a fortiori, not all involve correction regarding the use or explication of a term. Accordingly, I don't claim that all instances of mansplaining enact s-rules of semantic deference. But some mansplainings do involve semantic correction; call these "semantic correction mansplainings." I say that these enact s-rules of semantic deference.

In one notable example, for instance, a non-gynecologist man corrected a woman gynecologist regarding the use and explication of "vulva" and "vagina" (Perlman 2019). As we saw above, corrections on the use or explication of a term plausibly enact s-rules of semantic deference, provided no one objects. Had no one objected to the mansplainer about "vulva" and "vagina,"

---

[9] Solnit doesn't use the term "mansplaining" in the essay, but as Kate Manne says, Solnit is the foremother of the concept, if not the term (Manne 2019, 295).

then the rules governing the conversation would have evolved so as to make the correction appropriate. Recall that I suggested the following rule of accommodation above:

> Norms for semantic deference evolve according to a rule of accommodation specifying that any norms of deference that are required to make a conversational contribution appropriate straightaway come into existence, provided that nobody objects.

If this rule or something similar had been in force, and had no one objected, then an s-rule of semantic deference would have straightaway come into existence to make the correction appropriate. (We might suppose that the epistemic norm that calls non-gynecologists to defer to gynecologists about gynecological terms 'previously' would have made the correction inappropriate, but the rules evolved to accommodate the correction and make it appropriate by the 'new' s-rule of semantic deference.)

More generally, if a rule of accommodation for semantic deference (or something like it) governs conversation in our linguistic community, then when a semantic correction mansplaining occurs and no one objects, an s-rule of semantic deference is enacted.

Similarly, mutatis mutandis, for Whitesplaining, thinsplaining, and so on. John Blake defines "Whitesplaining" this way:

> An affliction that's triggered when some white people hear a person of color complain about racism. They will immediately explain in a condescending tone why the person is wrong, "getting too emotional" or "seeing race in everything." (Blake 2019)

As with mansplaining, some instances of Whitesplaining are semantic corrections—maybe the paradigmatic cases involve a correction about the appropriate applications of the term "racism." As above, if a rule of accommodation for semantic deference (or something like it) governs conversation in our linguistic community, then when a semantic correction Whitesplaining occurs and no one objects, an s-rule of semantic deference is enacted.

What do the s-rules enacted by these 'splainings say? According to those who have experienced mansplaining and called attention to it, it is a gendered phenomenon: The speakers who mansplain do so *because they are men* and *because* those to whom they mansplain are not.[10] Similarly, those who experience and write about Whitesplaining say racial positions make it the kind of conversational contribution that it is—it's a conversational move in which a White person corrects a person of color, even about the proper applications of "racism." Prima facie, whatever s-rules evolve to accommodate some mansplaining, Whitesplaining, and so on, are such that they make it appropriate to make conversational contributions of the kind that mansplaining is, Whitesplaining is, thinsplaining is, and so on. That is, in some given conversation in which, say, mansplaining occurs, the rule that evolves to make that mansplaining appropriate should *make mansplaining appropriate*. If mansplaining *is* a conversational contribution that turns on discussants' gendered positions, the s-rules that accommodate mansplainings should also turn on discussants' gendered positions. If Whitesplaining *is* a conversational move that turns on discussants' positions in oppressive racial hierarchies, then the s-rules that accommodate Whitesplainings should also turn on discussants' positions in oppressive racial hierarchies. Thus, we might say that in the case of semantic correction mansplainings, the accommodating s-rules make it appropriate for men to correct non-men; when no one objects to Whitesplaining, it enacts an s-rule that makes it appropriate for people of color to give semantic deference to White people; similarly for richsplaining, thinsplaining, and so on. However, we might say that each case turns on oppressive hierarchical positioning, and so the rules enacted in each case do too: They call speakers with lower positions in oppressive hierarchies to give semantic deference to speakers with higher positions in those hierarchies.[11] It could be that both of these s-rules are enacted by a given 'splaining, and it could be that exactly which s-rules are enacted in a given case is indeterminate. Fortunately, we don't have to decide the matter here. For our purposes, it suffices to say that *whatever* s-rules are enacted by semantic correction mansplainings, Whitesplainings, richsplainings, and so on, it's plausible that they turn on oppressive hierarchical positioning. This suffices to establish

---

[10] Keep in mind, however, that how a person is gendered is partly influenced by how they're racialized, how their class markers are read, whether they're read as fat, and so on (see, for example, Davis 2003, 72; Zheng 2016, 405–406; Engelhardt 2022, 3). Thus, although discussion of mansplaining focuses on gender relations, those relations themselves are partly structured by White supremacy, class oppression, fatphobia, colonialism, and so on. The same point applies, *mutatis mutandis*, for the positions/relations crucial to Whitesplaining, thinsplaining, and so on.

[11] This is not to presume that positions in these hierarchies are fixed across conversations or that they are determinate in all conversations. Provided that there are some cases in which oppressive positions are determinate and 'splainings turn on those positions, then there will be cases in which 'splainings enact s-rules that turn on positioning in oppressive hierarchies.

that oppressive hierarchical positioning affects s-rules of semantic deference by influencing which corrections are made and accepted.

With regard to systematic patterns of semantic deference, then, the question is whether oppressive hierarchical positioning also affects *g-rules* of semantic deference.[12] I'll give two reasons to think it does. If it does, then it systematically affects patterns of semantic deference.

First, oppressive hierarchical positioning is systematic. Although speakers' social positions may vary from context to context and carry different significance in different contexts, they are not wholly arbitrary, and they have a systematic (which, again, is not to say exceptionless) influence on how we're positioned relative to one another in conversations. If oppressive positioning affects which s-rules are enacted in conversation, then since these positions are systemic, it's at least prima facie plausible that their influences are too. If s-rules that turn on hierarchical positioning are enacted systematically, then there are corresponding g-rules that turn on hierarchical positioning. Thus, if oppressive hierarchies influence conversations such that s-rules calling for disempowered speakers to defer to privileged speakers are systematically enacted, then oppressive hierarchies affect g-rules of semantic deference.

Second, it's plausible that oppressive g-rules of semantic deference are grounded in (or are specifications of) more general oppressive norms of

---

[12] Above, I considered the possibility that each kind of 'splaining enacts different s-rules, so that, for example, mansplaining enacts gendered s-rules, Whitesplaining racial s-rules, and so on. If all of these correspond to g-rules, it may seem that these will 'conflict' so that they can't all be g-rules at the same time. I don't think this is right. Rather, so long as each g-rule (or an s-rule corresponding to each) is systematically enacted, they can all be maintained. For example, suppose that a poor White trans woman without a visible disability is talking with a wealthy disabled Asian man. The relevant g-rules would call the woman to defer to the man, the Asian man to defer to the White woman, the person with a disability to defer to the person without, the trans person to defer to the cis, and the poor person to defer to the wealthy. If an s-rule of semantic deference is enacted in the conversation, and if this s-rule calls for deference from one of these speakers to the other (rather than to, say, medical doctors generally), then the s-rule they enact will conflict with one of the g-rules established by mansplaining, Whitesplaining, and so on. But that won't extinguish whichever g-rule is broken. It'll just be one case in which a conversation evolves such that that g-rule isn't maintained. Suppose the woman in the situation doesn't defer to the man, and thus the g-rule calling for women to defer to men is broken. So long as the rule calling for women to defer to men (or an s-rule corresponding to it) is systematically enacted in other conversations, it will remain in force—just not in this particular conversation. The same goes for the other g-rules of deference noted above and for g-rules generally. Compare: If there are *some* conversations in which humble chemists defer to non-chemists about chemical terms, diffident lawyers defer to non-lawyers about legal terms, or coy philosophers defer to non-philosophers about terms like "knowledge," these few and scattered conversations don't suffice on their own to extinguish the g-rules calling for non-chemists to defer to chemists about chemical terms, non-lawyers to defer to lawyers, and so on. So long as the relevant rules are systematically enacted or maintained, the g-rules remain in force. Similarly, if mansplaining, Whitesplaining, thinsplaining, and so on, occur systematically, then they will systematically enact the oppressive s-rules, and there will be corresponding oppressive g-rules—even if there are also conversations in which these rules aren't followed. Again, g-rules needn't be exceptionless.

epistemic deference. That is, it's plausible that there are norms that call, generally, for oppressed people to give epistemic deference to privileged people. Whatever reasons support belief in these norms should also support belief in g-rules that call for oppressed people to give *semantic* deference to privileged people. Compare: Prima facie, we owe general epistemic deference to botanists for botanical terms and with regard to botanical matters; that's no reason to doubt that there's also a related norm of semantic deference. Indeed, it's reason to think there *is* such a norm of semantic deference. The apparent existence of general oppressive norms calling for oppressed people to give epistemic deference to privileged people is reason to suppose that there is also the more specific oppressive norm or g-rule calling for oppressed people to give *semantic* deference to privileged people.

With regard to oppressive racial positioning, Charles Mills plausibly identifies the general epistemic norm as the "governing epistemic principle" in postcolonial European political systems:

> In general, over a period of centuries, the governing epistemic principle could be stated as the requirement that—at least on controversial issues— nonwhite cognition has to be verified by white cognition to be accepted as valid. (Mills 1997, 60)

Prima facie, when the verification isn't given, non-White cognition can instead be *corrected*. Blake's remarks on Whitesplaining provide an illustration of just how far this rule seems to extend. Blake points out that when someone Whitesplains, it reverses the epistemic norms we might expect to be in force and instead presumes that Whites deserve semantic deference when it comes to "racism."

> The implication [of Whitesplaining]: These white people know more about how racism operates than those who've struggled against it for much of their lives.
>
> To become a victim of "whitesplaining" is infuriating. Imagine a plumber trying to tell a pilot how to land a plane or a man trying to tell a mother what it feels like to give birth. (Blake 2019)

If Mills is right, then the epistemological absurdity that Blake notes for Whitesplaining isn't limited to "racism" and racism; it applies to nearly all topics and nearly all terms.

134 NONIDEAL THEORY AND CONTENT EXTERNALISM

In addition, various phenomena discussed in the social epistemology literature and elsewhere suggest the existence of norms that call speakers to give generalized epistemic deference to speakers with more privilege: testimonial injustices that discredit disprivileged speakers and give inflated credibility to people with privilege (Fricker 2007, 17–30; Medina 2012, 56–64), the stereotypes of oppressed groups as epistemically inferior (Fricker 2007, 30–60; Langton 2010, 459–464), misogynistic ideology that pressures women generally to give men deference, admiration, and support (Manne 2019, xix, 271), and so on. These all point to general norms that make it appropriate for less privileged people to defer to people with privilege on an apparently unrestricted range of topics, as if people with more privilege are generally in better epistemic positions than those with less. Whatever reasons support belief in these norms should also support belief in g-rules that call for oppressed people to give semantic deference to privileged people. And just as the epistemic norms are apparently unrestricted with regard to range of topics, the g-rules of semantic deference are apparently unrestricted with regard to the terms to which they apply. For any term, the g-rules make it so that less privileged people should give semantic deference to people with privilege.

Thus, again, it's plausible that oppression systematically affects which corrections are given and accepted, and it's plausible that oppression systematically affects g-rules of semantic deference. That is, it's plausible that oppression systematically affects patterns of semantic deference.

So far, we've seen two reasons to think that oppression affects which corrections are given and accepted. I'll give one more and then turn to other reasons to think that oppression systematically influences patterns of semantic deference.

In the foregoing, I've argued that when oppression influences epistemic deference, it also influences semantic deference. For the most part, the philosophical literature on how and when oppression influences epistemic deference has focused on interpersonal interactions—on the interpersonal level of oppression. However, some have shown that other levels of oppression also have an influence on epistemic deference. If it's plausible that whenever epistemic deference is thus influenced, so is semantic deference, then these works also give us reason to suppose that semantic deference is influenced by these other levels of oppression. I'll review one proposed phenomenon that evidences legal and institutional influences on epistemic deference, and I'll spell out how these influences extend to semantic deference.

Michael Doan characterizes *epistemic redlining* as "the practice of denying conferrals of credibility to residents of specific municipalities, generally because those municipalities are deemed to be in a state of 'financial emergency'" (Doan 2017, 184). Epistemic redlining is of course meant to draw partly on the well-known idea of *redlining*, developed by John McKnight.

> "Redlining" refers to the practice of denying financial services (e.g. mortgages, home repair loans) to residents of specific neighborhoods, generally because they are people of color and/or poor, and not because of their actual credit ratings or creditworthiness (Bartelt 2010; Ladd 1998). The practice is called 'redlining' because it literally involves drawing red lines on maps to delineate areas where banks will refuse to invest (Ibid. 183)

Whereas redlining involves the denial of financial services to entire communities because its members are people of color and/or poor, *epistemic* redlining denies credibility to entire communities on grounds that they are deemed to be in a state of financial emergency.

Why is being in a state of financial emergency grounds for denying credibility to an entire municipality? The answer also explains why epistemic redlining is a consequence of oppression at the legal and institutional levels. Doan focuses on epistemic redlining as a consequence of Michigan's emergency manager law, or Public Act (PA) 436 (2012). This law allows the governor of Michigan to appoint an "emergency manager" (EM) for municipalities deemed to be in a financial emergency. EMs aren't elected by the citizens of the municipality, and they needn't consult or seek approval from the municipality's elected officials or its electorate while making their plans or executing them. Moreover, EMs have authority over not only the municipality's financial operations but also political, administrative, and curricular operations. Speaking of PA 4, an earlier PA that functioned similar to PA 436, Doan says,

> PA 4 not only allows an EM to assume the responsibilities of all local elected officials, but as economist and local government finance specialist Eric Scorsone notes, it also gives an EM several "quasi-judicial powers related to breaking contracts" (2014, 39). Specifically, the law grants an EM the power to modify or terminate existing collective bargaining agreements and to negotiate or ban entry into new ones; to contract out public services to private companies and sell off public assets, including buildings and infrastructure;

and to dismiss public officials, set aside minimum staffing requirements, and consolidate or dissolve local departments. (Doan 2017, 180–181)

And, citing Michele Wilde Anderson, he adds:

> PA 4 enables the suspension of a city's charter and strips all elected officials of their powers, "imposing the authority of the state through an appointee of the governor" who is accountable to no one else, and effectively stripping city residents of local citizenship rights (581). (Doan 2017, 181)

Doan sums up the effect of appointing an EM in a later paper: it "suspend[s] democracy at the municipal level and strip[s] residents of local citizenship rights with the declared purpose of balancing the books" (Doan 2018, 3).

When EMs are appointed in such cases, citizens in the municipality are denied credibility. Thus, the EM law enables the governor of Michigan to deny credibility to entire municipalities. It's both Michigan's legal system and the state's institutional governing structures that enable epistemic redlining.

Two aspects of the law and its implementation can help show why Doan thinks that appointing an EM denies credibility to a municipality's citizens. First, Doan and others have made the case that state emergency intervention statutes like Michigan's PA 436 drastically oversimplify the factors that contribute to financial emergency by codifying into law the assumption that if a municipality is in a financial emergency, then it must have been mismanaged (Doan 2017, 182–183). There can of course be many causes for a financial emergency, and few of them reduce to mismanagement: shifts in federal and state revenue-sharing policies, federally subsidized suburbanization, regional unemployment and underemployment thanks to outsourcing and offshoring of labor. Doan cites law professor Peter Hammer's summary of the situation in Flint, Michigan, for instance:

> The primary, non-structural reason Flint was in financial distress was the direct result of state revenue sharing policy. This fact does not get the public attention it deserves. The State of Michigan created the very financial distress in Flint and other cities that it then used to supposedly justify the need for Emergency Managers. (Ibid. 183, emphasis removed from original)

Given the various possible contributing factors, it would be prima facie best to consider municipal financial emergencies on a case-by-case basis (as had been done in the United States before the 1970s). Instead, statutes like PA 436 presuppose that mismanagement is the problem, and so an EM is the solution. In effect, the statute communicates that if a municipality has an EM, then it has been so badly mismanaged that legal consequences suspending its charter and stripping all elected officials of their powers are appropriate. Thus, the appointment of an EM discredits the municipality's charter and its elected officials. Since an EM can be appointed even if there's little reason to believe that the financial emergency resulted from mismanagement, this discrediting can be unwarranted. When the discrediting is in fact grounded in the municipality's racial composition (about which I'll say more below) rather than its management, the municipality and its citizens plausibly suffer an unwarranted credibility deficit.

Second, there are further reasons to think that when an EM is appointed, the municipality's citizens—not only elected officials—suffer a credibility deficit. For one thing, as noted above, appointing an EM strips residents of their citizenship rights. For another, by stripping their elected officials of power, appointing an EM dismisses the representation that voters elected. Moreover, since EMs are neither elected nor re-elected, residents are denied some of their usual avenues for influencing what decisions are made by local officials. Without the usual official routes for influencing municipal plans and actions, citizens must find other ways to have their voices heard, but Doan argues that the processes that discredit city officials for mismanagement extend to discrediting all citizens of the municipality. He cites Peter Hammer again, referring to the Flint water crisis from April 2014 to June 2016, during which tens of thousands of Flint residents were exposed to dangerous levels of lead, and legionnaires' disease killed at least 12 people. "Flint residents had knowledge of the water crisis almost immediately upon the switch to the Flint River [as a water source]," but they weren't taken seriously as knowers (ibid. 179). Writing elsewhere with Sharon Howell and Ami Harbin, Doan says the governance in Flint and other municipalities with EMs situated "non-experts as lacking the credibility to speak truthfully about the quality of the water flowing from their taps, let alone about the state of their own health and well-being" (Doan et al. 2019, 68). As Doan puts it, the EM law codifies into law hierarchical valuations of ways of knowing such that "the 'fiscal responsibility' of local governments comes to be regarded as a proxy for the credibility of entire populations" (Doan 2018, 14). When an EM is appointed to a municipality, then its members are plausibly discredited. If the appointment is thanks

138 NONIDEAL THEORY AND CONTENT EXTERNALISM

to racial oppression, then the municipality's residents shall be discredited thanks to racial oppression.

Are municipalities assigned EMs thanks to oppression? Doan thinks so. Municipalities put under emergency management in Michigan have been predominantly African American, to the effect that between 2007 and 2013, 51.7% of Michigan's Black residents were subjected to emergency management, as compared to only 2.7% of the state's White residents (Doan 2017, 182). Indeed, a 2016 study found that a municipality's percentage of Black population is "an independently significant predictor" of where an EM would be appointed in Michigan; Doan takes this to suggest that "race has, in fact, played a role in the distribution of EMs" (ibid. 184). Doan claims that just as a community's racial makeup—not its members' creditworthiness—made it subject to redlining, so too a community's racial composition makes it subject to epistemic redlining.

So epistemic redlining denies credibility to entire communities, and it results from oppression codified in laws and institutions. It is an epistemic effect of oppression at the levels of laws and state institutions. When an entire community is discredited, it is of course less likely to receive epistemic deference. If being less likely to receive epistemic deference results in being less likely to receive semantic deference, then epistemic redlining also reveals a way in which oppression at the levels of laws and state institutions affects semantic deference.

Howell, Doan, and Harbin provide what may be an example.[13] They describe activist organizing to resist water shutoffs in Detroit and to address toxic tap water in Flint. These included efforts to use stories and evidence from citizens of Flint and Detroit to challenge the dominant narratives that Flint had clean drinking water and that Detroit water shutoffs were just and fair. As part of these efforts, coalitions among activist groups "attempted to shift the idea of 'criminality' away from those who could not afford to pay for water, or who were turning water back on to meet basic needs, and on to those being paid to turn water off" (Doan et al. 2019, 74). The authors are pointing to a difference in normative characterizations for the extension of one word form. EMs, backed by the governor and legal statutes, had applied the term to those who could not afford to pay for water or who were turning

---

[13] I say they *may* provide an example because I'm drawing on their report of what activists were trying to achieve, and the description they give doesn't (for good reason) make it certain that activists were intending to engage in a dialectic over the meaning and/or extension of the term.

it back on; presumably, they took it to be inappropriate to apply the term to those they were paying to turn water off. Community organizers advanced the reverse: they proposed that "criminality" applies to those shutting water off, not those who can't afford to pay or who turn it back on. Presumably, the activists could have drawn distinctions, produced precisifications, used linguistic resources, and so on, in attempt to elicit assent from others, including other activists, EMs, and state officials. Perhaps they did: in a theater project developed to make more people aware of the crises in Flint and Detroit, "the people of Detroit indicted Mayor Duggan (played by Michael Doan), Governor Snyder (Fred Vitale), and EMs Kevin Orr and Darnell Earley" (ibid. 13). And, presumably, the activists could have offered meaning-giving characterizations to explain the extension of "criminality" that they thought appropriate. So too for the EMs and others who advanced the government's account of the extension of "criminality." In an idealized Burgean dialectic over the term, the disagreement would be decided by which speakers are most persuasive in the strict sense. But epistemic redlining put community activists at a disadvantage. They were unjustly discredited, and thus they were seldom even given opportunities to speak at City Council meetings, and they were dismissed as "dumb," "unscientific," and "lazy" (ibid. 5, 2, 10). They were dismissed by those with the power to enforce laws, to raise water prices, to bring foreclosure against those who couldn't pay inflated water prices, and so on. Epistemic redlining inhibited the activists' ability to earn semantic deference for their normative characterizations.[14] Epistemic redlining results from the legal and institutional levels of oppression, it affects semantic deference, and it systematically affects poor communities of color. It gives us reason to think that oppression—as embedded in state institutions and legal systems—systematically affects which corrections are made and accepted. Thus, it systematically affects patterns of semantic deference.

2.3 Ranks

By "ranks," I mean the positioning in a conversation that endows different speakers with different powers and permissions. In a more formal

---

[14] Activists did eventually gain national media attention, of course, and Snyder and Earley were criminally charged for their roles in the water crises in January 2021.

140   NONIDEAL THEORY AND CONTENT EXTERNALISM

or traditional classroom setting, for instance, the prevailing norms might make it impermissible for students to speak unless and until called upon by the instructor. The instructor has powers and permissions that the students don't: she is permitted to speak without having to be called upon, and she has the power to decide whether the students have permission to speak or not. The classroom norms endow different speakers with different powers and permissions. I'll use the term "ranks" to refer to the different positions. Given the norms in this context, *instructor* and *student* are different ranks.

Differential ranks are a common but often unacknowledged feature of examples of semantic deference. When the physician corrects the patient's use of "arthritis" in Burge's example, the physician doesn't offer much to support the correction or to persuade the patient. He appeals briefly to the dictionary, but otherwise it seems to be granted that the physician has the authority to correct the patient.

> Generally competent in English, rational, and intelligent, the patient reports to his doctor his fear that his arthritis has now lodged in his thigh. The doctor replies by telling him that this cannot be so, since arthritis is specifically an inflammation of joints. Any dictionary could have told him the same. The patient is surprised, but relinquishes his view and goes on to ask what might be wrong with his thigh. (Burge 2007, 104–105)

Similarly, Burge begins his example with the legal term "contract" like this: "A fairly common mistake among lawyers' clients is to think that one cannot have a contract with someone unless there has been a written agreement" (ibid. 109). Presumably, we're to imagine that a lawyer in conversation with such a client would be appropriately positioned to correct her client, just as the physician is in a position to correct the patient.

The norms governing a visit to the physician or a consultation with a lawyer aren't as rigid as those governing the classroom described above. A patient could speak permissibly without waiting to be called upon by the physician, and the same goes, mutatis mutandis, for the client and lawyer. But, plausibly, the conversational participants do have different ranks, and these are pertinent to the corrections made in each example. Prima facie, it's appropriate for the physician to correct the patient's use of a medical term, but it would be inappropriate for the patient to *correct* the physician's use. The patient might make other moves that focus the conversation on the physician's use of a term—asking for clarification, expressing confusion, and so on.[15] If the physician has permission to correct the patient but not vice versa, then they have different permissions in the conversation: they have different ranks. So too, mutatis mutandis, for the lawyer and client with regard to legal terms.

We can use Lynne Tirrell's distinction between neutral and nonneutral language entrance transitions to elaborate on our understanding of ranks.[16] When a speaker enters into a conversation and is counted as a participant, an entrance transition occurs. Wilfrid Sellars had supposed that all such transitions are *neutral*: everyone who joins a conversation is granted, upon joining, the same permissions and powers. Tirrell points out, however, that in social contexts shaped by oppression, entrance to language games is *nonneutral*: conversational participants enter a conversation with differential powers and permissions. Under patriarchy, for instance, "men tend to have greater game-assigned powers, women fewer, and the powers women do have tend to support men's enhanced status" (Tirrell 2018a, 9). More generally, "oppression systematically denies persons authority on the basis of identity factors and so shapes who actually counts as a player in the language game" (ibid. 16–17; see Tirrell 2018b, 125).

Take it that nonneutral entrance transitions give speakers different ranks in a conversation. If language transitions were neutral, everyone would have the same rank (at least when a conversation begins). Since they are not, there are different ranks. Since language entrance transitions are systematically warped by oppression, so are ranks. Since ranks also systematically affect who can and can't appropriately give corrections, then oppression also systematically affects who can and can't appropriately give corrections. Oppression has a systematic effect on which corrections will be made and accepted. In the division of linguistic labor, the corrections that are systematically given and accepted determine patterns of deference, and thus they determine who determines terms' meanings and extensions. By systematically

---

[15] Here's how I characterize the difference between corrections and similar conversational moves elsewhere: "Suppose Amir is in his first year studying English and I'm a fluent speaker tutoring him. In this case, it is permissible for me to correct Amir's usage, not just object to it. When I merely object, it is Amir's prerogative to withdraw his move or defend it; when I correct his use, the presumption is that his move is thereby withdrawn, though he may query my correction, protest, and, with enough evidence, have his move reinstated. On the other hand, it is impermissible for Amir to correct my usage. He may request explanation, express confusion, and so on, and, with effort, he may get me to withdraw a move I've made, but it is my prerogative to withdraw the move or not. This difference in our permissions is due to our difference in rank (at the time) when it comes to . . . English" (Engelhardt 2019a, 5).

[16] I learned of Tirrell's work on nonneutral entrance positions after publishing my own work on ranks cited in the previous footnote.

affecting which corrections are appropriate and which aren't, oppression systematically affects patterns of semantic deference and the determination of meanings and extensions. These observations support the points developed in the previous section, on corrections.

But, in addition, Tirrell makes the case that oppression affects the efficacy of moves made in a language game. "A woman's nonneutral entrance," for instance, "limits her position-specific game-assigned powers, her positional authority, and undermines her power to exercise her expertise authority" (Tirrell 2018a, 22). There are several ways that oppression can limit a speaker's conversational powers; among them, Tirrell says, is that "oppressed people often face default *challenges*" (ibid. 24, emphasis added). Gendered oppression, for example, often makes it so that when a speaker is read as a woman, her gender is "prima facie justified grounds for challenge" (ibid.; see also Kukla 2014).

Challenges are familiar features of conversation. If I say the storm will pass this evening and Sam has reason to think it won't, she might challenge the content of my claim. Alternatively, suppose a student in the sort of formal, traditional classroom described above announces to the class that, henceforth, all students may speak without first having to be called upon by the instructor. In this case, the instructor might challenge the student's authority: he doesn't have the authority in the classroom to give others permission to speak; only the instructor has that authority. When a challenge is made, the speaker who has been challenged might have the opportunity to justify the content of her claim (e.g., that the storm will pass) and/or to establish her authority to perform the act in question (e.g., the act of giving all the students permission to speak). If she successfully meets the challenge, then others in the conversation can treat her claim as justified or her act as warranted. But if she fails to meet the challenge, then, all else being equal, others shall treat her claim as unjustified, her act as unentitled. If I don't meet Sam's challenge, then others should carry on as though it isn't established that the storm will pass this evening. The student is in no position to establish his authority to give out permissions to speak, and so his attempt to give those permissions should fail.

Some *challenges* need to be justified. Tirrell gives a case in which she, Tirrell, says that Tom Brady (a football player) is a great quarterback; her brother challenges, "What do you know about football?" Tirrell then demands that he justify his challenge by appealing to her prima facie authority as a New Englander: "I'm a New Englander! Everyone here knows all about the Pats" (Tirrell 2018a, 24). Her brother then offers justification for his challenge by making the case that football is outside the domain of Tirrell's expertise, and Tirrell finally meets her brother's challenge by citing relevant statistics.

Take this in the context of corrections and other moves made in the dialectics that arrive at meaning-giving characterizations. Suppose an oppressed person offers a normative characterization for a term's meaning or extension. If her position as oppressed makes it so that challenges to her authority are prima facie justified, then in the usual case she will have to show that the challenge isn't justified and/or to meet the challenge. Speakers who are privileged won't have these additional hurdles to having their normative characterizations accepted. So oppressed speakers will be disadvantaged. Notice that this extends to every move. Oppressed speakers' normative characterizations will be open to challenges that are prima facie justified, and so will any corrections or challenges that oppressed speakers make to *others'* uses, normative characterizations, objections, or challenges. Thus oppression influences which normative characterizations will be given, accepted, corrected, and rejected; it influences how normative characterizations will be refined and by whom. That is, it influences both semantic deference and the norms that characterize terms' meanings and extensions.

These influences result from the ranks assigned to speakers in social situations ordered by oppressive hierarchies. Although conversational participants' specific powers and permissions will of course vary widely with context, oppressive hierarchies are embedded in our systems of oppression. It is part of our oppressive systems that oppressed speakers' ranks are subordinate to those of the privileged. Since the oppressive rankings are systematic, their effects should be too. We should take it that the influences that ranks have on semantic deference, meanings, and extensions are systematic.

When considering how conversational ranks affect the division of linguistic labor, it's helpful to keep in mind that oppression assigns and enforces ranks in various ways. Perhaps most generally, the oppressive hierarchies of race-based, gender-based, and other oppressions are, at present, social rankings. They can manifest in any and all interpersonal interactions. Prima facie, these are the sorts of ranks to which Tirrell is referring above and to which Mary Kate McGowan refers here:

Since a system of oppression ranks people according to their membership in socially marked groups and since this ranking involves treating persons

144 NONIDEAL THEORY AND CONTENT EXTERNALISM

in some categories differently than persons in other categories, this system is clearly norm-governed. (McGowan 2009, 397)

These general ranks are plausibly established and reinforced at various levels of oppressive structure. In many examples of semantic deference, institutional ranks plausibly play a role in establishing a speaker's power or permission to correct others. It's not hard to imagine that when a physician corrects a patient's use of "arthritis" or any other medical term, the patient is inclined to accept partly thanks to the physician's positioning in the medical institutions and practices that structure doctor-patient interactions. The practices—licensing procedures, institutional certifications, and so on—of medical institutions situate medical doctors as experts to whom the rest of us should defer, at least when it comes to medical matters. To put it another way, it's plausible that medical-institutional practices include norms or g-rules that make it appropriate for patients to defer to physicians about medical matters, inappropriate for physicians to defer to patients about medical matters, and (perhaps) inappropriate for patients to defer to persons who are not institutionally recognized experts. If so, then since g-rules of semantic deference determine patterns of semantic deference, we can say that there are ranks that (i) are established by institutional norms, practices, and so on, and that (ii) influence patterns of semantic deference. Call these "institutional ranks." Medical systems establish institutional ranks, and there are plausibly many others. A lawyer's permission to correct a client's use of "contract" is partly endowed by the institutional ranks of the legal system. In a classroom, an instructor's permission to correct a student is partly thanks to the instructor's institutional rank. Where there is a 'chain of command' and associated ranks, as in a military or paramilitary organization, there are often strong (and sometimes explicit) norms calling for lower ranks to accept corrections from their 'superiors,' thereby establishing norms of semantic deference as well. Less formally, within a research lab, there are often norms that make it appropriate for, say, the lead researcher to correct research assistants with regard to terms relevant to the research but not vice versa. And so on. In all of these cases, institutions and their practices influence semantic deference by establishing institutional ranks and situating them in norms or g-rules of semantic deference.

It doesn't matter whether we take it that institutional ranks influence patterns of semantic deference, that institutionally established norms of semantic deference constitute institutional ranks, or some other order of explanation. What matters for our purposes is that if oppression systematically influences which persons are more likely to occupy higher ranks, then oppression systematically influences patterns of semantic deference. If oppression makes it so that privileged persons are systematically more likely to occupy higher institutional ranks, for instance, then it shall make it so that many institutions are set up such that the speakers who are normatively situated so as to receive semantic deference are more likely to be the beneficiaries of systems of oppression.

I don't suppose that readers need to be convinced of it, but it's plausible that oppression does make it so that privileged persons are systematically more likely to occupy higher institutional ranks. In the United States, the paths that most commonly afford access to higher institutional ranks require wealth, elite social networks, and success navigating various institutions—all things that are more easily accessible for privileged people, thanks to oppression. The most common paths to becoming a lawyer or medical doctor, for instance, go through college and medical school or law school. It often costs tens or hundreds of thousands of dollars in payments or debt to attend college and these graduate schools, with the more elite schools typically costing more. Aside from the costs of attending, the time spent not working full time can be prohibitive if you don't have other ways to meet the costs of living or if you have to support your parents or children. Class oppression thus puts several obstacles in the way of those who might try to acquire higher institutional ranks, as do various interdependent oppressions. The legacies of slavery, Jim Crow, mass incarceration, and racial oppression generally make it so that Black people in the United States systematically have less wealth and less access to wealth than Whites do. The legacy of colonization and the associated exclusions of Indigenous peoples of North America have had similarly devastating effects on the wealth of Indigenous people. The wage gaps that distinguish the higher pay of White men from equally qualified White women, Black women, Puerto Rican women, and others, make it so that women without financial support from family or elsewhere are less likely to be able to afford the costs associated with becoming a lawyer, medical doctor, and so on. This only scratches the surface of the wealth-related obstacles that systemic oppression puts between oppressed groups and higher institutional ranks. I've said nothing, for instance, of the costs typically necessary to gain entrance to colleges and graduate schools or the costs that accrue after medical school or law school. Moreover, the obstacles that oppressed people face in navigating

146 NONIDEAL THEORY AND CONTENT EXTERNALISM

institutions and gaining access to elite social networks are similarly abundant and interconnected.

There are manifold feedback loops among these obstacles that make it ever more difficult for oppressed people to obtain higher institutional ranks. Let me note one that draws on Tirrell's nonneutral entrance transitions. Oppressive hierarchies make it so that conversational participants make nonneutral entrance transitions in accordance with oppressive hierarchical positioning: lower positions in the hierarchy tend to have fewer conversational powers and permissions. Consequently, speakers with lower positions in oppressive hierarchies are less likely to receive semantic deference in the dialectics that determine meanings and extensions. Individual speakers, however, might pursue more and greater conversational powers—more powerful nonneutral entrance transitions—by trying to obtain higher institutional ranks like *lawyer* or *medical doctor*. Obtaining higher institutional ranks typically requires navigating various institutions such that one can graduate or earn promotion, get letters of recommendation, get credit for one's successes, earn relevant certifications, maintain a position long enough to become eligible for promotion, and so on. In many kinds of institution, this will often involve navigating conversations in such a way that one's contributions are recognized and credited, so that one's expertise can be recognized, so that potential recommenders can be impressed, so that respect can be earned from colleagues, and so on. Plausibly, then, obtaining higher institutional ranks is much more difficult if one has fewer conversational powers and permissions or if one's authority is systematically denied in conversational contexts. Of course, this is exactly what systemic oppression achieves with regard to oppressed persons. As Tirrell says, "Men tend to have greater game-assigned powers, women fewer, and the powers women do have tend to support men's enhanced status" (Tirrell 2018a, 9). And "oppression systematically denies persons authority on the basis of identity factors" (ibid. 16–17; see Tirrell 2018b, 125). And

> a woman's nonneutral entrance limits her position-specific game-assigned powers, her positional authority, and undermines her power to exercise her expertise authority. Disregarded expertise authority impedes contributing to projects about which one cares, and in so doing, thwarts one's developing further capacities. Such disregard undermines autonomy and creative effectiveness; it literally stunts one's growth. (Tirrell 2018a, 22)

So here's the feedback loop: First, institutional ranks help reinforce oppressive hierarchical ranks by tending to grant more conversational powers and permissions to people who are more privileged by oppressive hierarchies. Second, oppressive hierarchies establish nonneutral entrance transitions, so that oppressed persons have fewer conversational powers and permissions to begin with. Third, having fewer conversational powers and permissions makes it so that oppressed persons are less likely to obtain more conversational powers and permissions by obtaining higher institutional ranks. Institutional ranks reinforce both oppressive hierarchies and nonneutral entrance transitions, and nonneutral entrance transitions reinforce both oppressive hierarchies and a distribution of institutional ranks that reinforces oppressive hierarchies. This loop and others make it so that oppression influences patterns of semantic deference.

2.4 Enforcement

This section makes the case that just as corrections and ranks can explain why patterns of semantic deference are as they are, so can patterns or systems of *enforcement*. In Section 2.4.1, I'll appeal to legal terms to make the case that some meanings, extensions, and patterns of deference are best explained by appeal to systems that enforce those meanings, extensions, and patterns of deference. In Section 2.4.2, I'll propose that systems of oppression also enforce meanings, extensions, and patterns of deference. I'll appeal to literature on epistemologies of ignorance, and I'll make the case that when systems of oppression produce ignorance of oppression, they often do so in part by systematically enforcing semantic deference to normative characterizations that obscure oppression. Thus, oppression systematically influences patterns of semantic deference.

2.4.1 Enforcing semantic deference: Legal terms
Let me first make the case that there are terms that (i) are subject to the division of linguistic labor but for which (ii) it's implausible that their meanings and extensions were determined by speakers who elicited assent from other competent speakers in the dialectics Burge describes. Legal terms offer convenient examples. To see that legal terms are subject to the division of linguistic labor, note that they can feature in the sorts of arguments that purport to establish that there's a division of linguistic labor. Indeed, recall that Burge

148   NONIDEAL THEORY AND CONTENT EXTERNALISM

gives one, as we saw above: "contract" (Burge 2007, 109–110). A lawyer's client may have many true beliefs involving the concept expressed by "contract" while also believing, falsely, that "one cannot have a contract with someone unless there has been a written agreement" (ibid. 109). We can imagine that in the actual scenario, the lawyer corrects the client, and this correction is accepted. Then, the thought experiment proceeds as usual:

> In a counterfactual case in which the law enforces both written and unwritten agreements and in which the subject's behavior and so forth are the same, but in which "contract" *means* "legally binding agreement based on a written document," we would not attribute to him [the client] a mistaken belief that a contract requires written agreement. (Ibid. 110)

We can easily produce similar thought experiments for other legal terms, whereby we simply modify the stipulated legal definitions of the terms between the actual and counterfactual scenarios. In each case, competent speakers who are not legal experts (or who are not experts in the relevant parts of law) and who take themselves to be using the legal terms in question will accept correction and give semantic deference to those with relevant expertise.

We can also deploy legal terms in reasoning that mirrors that of Hawthorne and Yli-Vakkuri regarding "sirloin" and "topside." Many competent speakers of English don't know the difference between slander and libel, but their uses of the terms "slander" and "libel" have different meanings and extensions and express different concepts. Suppose that Putnam is such a speaker and he accuses someone of slander; his accusation is different than it would be were he to accuse someone of libel. If a lawyer were to correct Putnam's use—"You mean 'libel,' not 'slander': slander is a defamatory statement that's oral; libel is written"—he would presumably accept it and stand corrected. With regard to the meanings and extensions of at least some legal terms, those who are less competent in the term's use and less knowledgeable about the part(s) of the world to which it refers defer to and accept correction from those who are more competent with regard to the term's use and more knowledgeable about the part(s) of the world to which it refers (see Engelhardt 2019b, 1859–1860).

So I take it that at least some legal terms are subject to the division of linguistic labor. In addition, it's implausible for many legal terms that their meanings and extensions were determined by speakers who elicited assent from other competent speakers in the dialectics Burge describes. Many legal terms have their definitions stipulated by those with the legal authority to make such stipulations (lawmakers or judges, for example); such stipulations determine meanings and extensions no matter whether they are persuasive to others or not, and such legal authorities are seldom (if ever) the *most* competent with regard to the terms for which they stipulate meanings and extensions.

Take the U.S. legal term "fruit." "Fruit" is often used in the context of import/export taxes to pick out a *legal kind*—a kind constituted by social-legal-institutional practices of articulating, passing, and enforcing laws. In this case, the relevant laws involve taxation on imports and exports: in many places, the tax on importing members of the legal (rather than botanical) kind *fruit* is different from the tax on importing members of the legal kind *vegetable*.

There is also a botanical term associated with the word form "fruit," and this term is also subject to the division of linguistic labor. This term may have had its meaning and extension determined in something like the way Burge describes. Through explicit discussions of the term's appropriate applications and explications, people with expertise in botany earned deference from others and developed the sorts of normative characterizations we now find in botany texts: "A fruit, botanically speaking, is any ovary and its accessory parts that has developed and matured. It also usually contains seeds" (Bidlack & Jansky 2010, 130). As the text notes, the extension of the botanical term includes eggplants, tomatoes, avocados, and almonds.

The legal term has a different extension. It's a somewhat famous bit of trivia that there's a U.S. Supreme Court decision according to which tomatoes are *not* legal fruits in the United States; they're vegetables (*Nix v. Hedden*, 1893). Thus, while the botanical term has tomatoes in its extension, the U.S. legal term does not. The legal and botanical terms thus have different extensions, and thus I take it that they have different meanings.

Presumably, the meaning and extension of the botanical term is determined by botanists, and perhaps that's because botanists have elicited assent from all others in a Burgean dialectic. Indeed, it's plausible that botanists are the most competent speakers with regard to botanical terms, and their competence has enabled them to earn semantic deference for "fruit" and other botanical terms by eliciting assent from other competent speakers.

Can we say the same about the U.S. legal term? It's implausible on its face. We know who determined the meaning and extension of the legal term such that it excludes tomatoes. It was the U.S. Supreme Court, not botanists.

150 NONIDEAL THEORY AND CONTENT EXTERNALISM

And we know why it was the Supreme Court decision that determined the term's meaning and extension. It wasn't because the members of the court exhibited the greatest competence regarding the appropriate applications and explications of the term. Although the members of the court might have had the greatest competence regarding the term, we know that *that* isn't what put them in the position to determine the term's meaning and extension. It was their membership on the Supreme Court at the time the case was heard and the court's position in the legal system. The members of the court determined the term's meaning and extension thanks to the power vested in them by the legal system, including practices of enforcing that power and the court's decisions. Relatedly, we know why the court's decision established a norm for appropriate applications and explications of the term. It wasn't because the decision was persuasive—in Burge's strict sense—to other competent speakers and thus elicited their assent. Although the decision might have been persuasive to others, that's not why it established norms governing the uses of the U.S. legal term. It was thanks to the practices of enforcement and the court's powers in the legal system.

I submit that in the legal system, semantic deference is often *enforced* rather than merely elicited. Prima facie, John Nix (the plaintiff in *Nix v. Hedden*, 1893) took himself to be using "fruit," "vegetable," and "tomato" in the normal ways that the English terms are used when he claimed that tomatoes are fruits, not vegetables, and thus shouldn't be taxed as vegetables. Indeed, we might say, with Burge, that since he was willing to "submit his statement and belief to the arbitration of an authority"—the Supreme Court—this "suggests willingness to have his word taken in the normal way" (Burge 2007, 131). Prima facie, then, Nix entered into the case willing to stand corrected with regard to the appropriate applications and explications of the terms at issue. He had—or, anyway, let's suppose that he had—the dispositions appropriate for engaging in the Burgean dialectic regarding the terms' meanings and extensions. If so, then as Burge describes things, when the dialectic led Nix to give semantic deference to the court's decision, this would most likely have been because Nix found the decision persuasive in the strict sense and assented to it. If Nix had not been persuaded and had not assented to the decision, then—on the idealized account of the dialectic—Nix would not have given semantic deference to the court's decision. It's Nix's assent and the court's persuasiveness that are supposed to ground the former's giving semantic deference to the latter. And if Nix were unpersuaded, he could have continued on drawing distinctions, producing precisifications, using linguistic resources, and so on, in attempts to elicit assent from the court, from Edward L. Hedden (collector of the Port of New York), and from other competent speakers. If he weren't persuaded, then Nix wouldn't have to defer to the court's decision regarding the extension and meaning of the legal term "fruit."

But it's not true that if Nix were unpersuaded, then he wouldn't have needed to have given deference to the court for uses of the legal terms "fruit" and "vegetable." This isn't to say that Nix always had to use the legal terms when speaking. He might well have made it a point to use the botanical term "fruit" when speaking to friends and colleagues, and he might have done the same outside of legal contexts. He might even have continued to insist that the legal term should be identical to the botanical term or that botanists should determine the extension of the legal term, not legal authorities. But if he had tried to exclude tomatoes from the items to be taxed as vegetables in official documentation for the tax collector, in his tax payments, or in other cases in which legal and/or institutional context made it so that it was permissible to use only the U.S. legal terms, then he would have come up against legal and institutional efforts to enforce the official legal terms. He would not have been permitted to use the terms otherwise than as they had been determined by the official ruling. Whether he assented to the court's characterizations of the relevant terms or not, institutional and legal structures would have enforced them.

Above, we saw that when a speaker's proposal for a term's meaning and/ or extension is accepted in a conversation, then the conversation evolves to include an s-rule making it appropriate to give semantic deference to that speaker for that term. As we see in the case of the U.S. legal term "fruit," various aspects of the legal system and the U.S. court system make it so that when the U.S. Supreme Court determines a term's meaning and/or extension, many speakers have no reasonable choice but to accept it. Applying or explicating a legal term in official contexts in ways that conflict with the official definition will result either in a failed attempt to make a conversational move or, in some cases, legal sanction. When speakers are in certain official legal contexts in the United States, the Supreme Court's proposals for terms' meanings and/or extensions must be accepted. Since their proposals must be accepted, the conversation that includes all participants in official legal contexts in the United States evolves to include a rule making it appropriate to give semantic deference to the court for the relevant terms. Since this conversation is ongoing and continues throughout the legal system, the rule holds systematically. That is, it's a g-rule, not an s-rule. Thus, legally enforced acceptance of the Supreme Court's official characterizations of legal terms' meanings and extensions suffices to enact g-rules that call for semantic deference to the Supreme Court for the relevant terms.

I take it, then, that at least some patterns of semantic deference are better explained by institutions, practices, systems, and laws that enforce semantic deference than by strict Burgean persuasion that elicits assent in the dialectics. This is helpful for us because it gives us another way to identify patterns of semantic deference. Because corrections and ranks can explain why patterns of semantic deference are as they are, they can help us identify patterns of semantic deference. Where there are systematic patterns in corrections or ranks, patterns of semantic deference will plausibly reflect these patterns. So too for systems of enforcement: where semantic deference is systematically enforced, patterns of semantic deference will be shaped by the enforcing system. In the next section, we'll see that oppression often produces systems that enforce semantic deference. When it does, oppression will thereby systematically influence semantic deference.

2.4.2 Enforcing semantic deference: Dominant terms

The point that oppression often produces systems that enforce semantic deference can be developed by appeal to philosophical work on *invested ignorance*. Cynthia Townley uses the term "invested ignorance" to refer to ignorance that is "systematically produced and sustained to misrepresent reality in ways that not coincidentally sustain patterns of . . . privilege" (Townley 2011, x). Where there is invested ignorance, there are systems that produce false beliefs and/or prevent the dissemination of true beliefs. I'll say that in producing false beliefs, these systems tend to enforce semantic deference to those who advance the relevant false beliefs, and in preventing the dissemination of true beliefs, they tend to enforce norms that prevent semantic deference from going to those who tell the relevant truths.

One paradigm of invested ignorance is what Charles Mills calls "White ignorance": ignorance of racial oppression that is systematically produced and sustained in ways that non-coincidentally sustain White supremacy. White ignorance is a consequence of what Mills calls "the Racial Contract," a contract analogous to the social contract in political theories; the Racial Contract is a contract among Whites that illuminates White supremacy (Mills 1997, 7, 20–21). This contract, according to Mills, requires Whites to adopt White ignorance *in order to be Whites*.

The Racial Contract prescribes for its signatories an inverted epistemology, an epistemology of ignorance, a particular pattern of localized and global cognitive dysfunctions (which are psychologically and socially functional), producing the ironic outcome that whites will in general be unable to understand the world they themselves have made. Part of what it means to be constructed as "white[,]" . . . part of what is required to achieve Whiteness, successfully to become a white person . . . , is a cognitive model that precludes self-transparency and genuine understanding of social realities. (Ibid. 18)

Meanwhile, non-Whites must be made to conform to the worldview of White ignorance using "the two traditional weapons of coercion: physical violence and ideological conditioning" (ibid. 83). If Mills is right, then prima facie, the White-supremacist political system pressures Whites and non-Whites to adopt White ignorance. White ignorance is systematically produced and sustained.

As Rebecca Mason points out, one of the ways in which White ignorance is systematically produced and sustained is by systematically pressuring speakers to use terms and concepts that obscure and/or justify racial oppression (Mason 2011, 302; see Engelhardt 2019a, 12). Adapting usage from Mason, I'll use "dominant terms" to refer to terms that serve these obscuring and/or justifying purposes. Take the term "racism" as an example. Robin DiAngelo has pointed out that there is a "dominant conceptualization of racism," according to which the term is appropriately applied only to "individual acts of cruelty," such that "only terrible people who consciously don't like people of color can enact racism" (DiAngelo 2018, 124). This obviously differs from how the term is used in this book and in scholarship on racial oppression generally. Let me use "racism-D" to mark that I'm referring to the term that's used as DiAngelo describes. Notice that if the rules governing the term "racism-D" are such that it's inappropriate to apply it to systems, institutions, and norms, then following those rules will make it harder to recognize that racism is systemic, institutional, and normalized. That is, following the dominant rules for the term's use would help obscure systemic racism, institutional racism, and individual acts that that might not seem cruel but that reinforce racist systems, racist institutions, or racist norms (see Engelhardt 2019a, 14).

"Racism-D" is a dominant term, and there are many others. Mills discusses "savage" and "civilization," "men" and "equality" (as applying appropriately only to Whites), "empty" and "discovered" (as appropriately applied to lands populated by non-Whites; Mills 2007, 24–28). In the case of racial oppression in the English language community, dominant terms obscure racial oppression or justify a White-supremacist ideology, but dominant terms can serve dominant ideology in other systems of oppression too—patriarchy, classism, imperialism, colonialism, ableism, and so on. Dominant rules for using "flirting," for instance, often help obscure sexual harassment and other sexual abuses—especially of women—while dominant rules for applying "seduction" can obscure date rape (Fricker 2007, 153; Mills 1998, 28; see Engelhardt 2019a, 15). We saw in the previous chapter that uses of race and gender terms developed by 19th-century comparative anatomists often served to obscure or justify race- and gender-based oppression; they made it, for instance, so that non-Whites were excluded from the extensions of "man" and "woman," reinforcing both the European gender binary among Whites and the White-supremacist racial hierarchy. Similar points can be made about terms associated with sexual orientations, nonbinary genders, and non-monogamous relationships: many have dominant uses that exclude non-Whites and/or non-Westerners, thereby obscuring cultures and peoples that have suffered colonization, genocide, and exploitation by European imperial powers. This plausibly reinforces the dominant ideology that such cultures and peoples aren't as 'progressive,' 'civilized,' or 'evolved' as Europeans—and so nothing of value is lost by targeting them for colonization, genocide, and exploitation (Logie & Rwigema 2014; see also Clarke 2019, 911; Morgensen 2010; Park 2017; Engelhardt 2022).

Many dominant terms are homonymous with other terms. Call these "doubled dominant terms." Some of the 'other terms' that are homonymous with dominant terms don't seem very politically charged—"empty" and "discovered," for instance. Others, like "racism" and "equality," could be used to help expose or resist oppression. Of course, "racism" as it's used in scholarship on racial oppression and elsewhere could help reveal oppression, while the dominant term "racism-D" helps obscure what the former term would reveal. The dominance of "racism-D" in the language community primes speakers to suppose that institutions, systems, and so on, cannot be racist, and it makes it more difficult to use the language to refer to racist institutions, systems, and so on.[17] It may be that this sort of 'doubling' occurs

---

[17] We can understand how this works by appealing to Arianna Falbo's account of how dominant concepts can "crowd out, defeat, or preempt the application of an available and more accurate concept" (Falbo 2022, 354).

systematically as speakers who are systematically ignorant of oppression have more power to influence the meanings and extensions of our terms. I won't argue for this claim here. I'll just note that, elsewhere, Sarah Campbell and I have proposed that at least one influential speaker routinely introduced doubled dominant terms. In a study of Rush Limbaugh's radio show—which averaged over 13 million unique listeners each week in 2016—we found that he introduced doubles for all these terms in a just a few months in 2016 and 2017: "race," "racism," "feminism," "equality," "intersectionality," and "diversity" (Engelhardt & Campbell 2019).

In what follows, I'll focus on doubled dominant terms generally (not only those that are homonymous with a term that would reveal oppression). The idea is that to enforce acceptance of doubled dominant terms is to enforce conformity to some normative characterizations—some rules for applying or explicating a word form—rather than others, where the normative characterizations that are enforced help obscure and/or justify oppression. As we saw, where normative characterizations are enforced, the enforcement influences semantic deference. Thus, by systematically enforcing normative characterizations that obscure oppression, oppression systematically influences patterns of semantic deference and the meanings and extensions of relevant terms.

Dominant terms are components of White ignorance in that they help obscure and/or justify racial oppression. As components of White ignorance, they are subject to the pressures described in the discussion of the Racial Contract above: (i) Whites must use dominant terms *in order to be White*, while (ii) non-Whites are compelled—using physical violence and ideological conditioning—to conform their usage to the rules governing dominant terms (Mills 1997, 18, 83; see Engelhardt 2019a, 12–18). For doubled dominant terms, use of the dominant terms is enforced by pressuring speakers to adopt the rules of application and explication associated with the dominant term (not its homonym). With regard to the doubled dominant term "racism-D," for instance, DiAngelo argues that if one uses the word form "racism" in a way that conflicts with the rules for the dominant term, then Whites who hear it very often exhibit behaviors that DiAngelo associates with what she calls "white fragility." These behaviors are, DiAngelo says, a form of sanction or punishment. We might take such punishments as enforcing use of the doubled dominant term "racism-D" as a component of White ignorance. If so, then we should expect that when the speaker being punished is White, then the grounds for punishment are that the speaker has violated one of the

156 NONIDEAL THEORY AND CONTENT EXTERNALISM

requirements on Whiteness. When the speaker is a person of color, meanwhile, the punishment is meant to compel the speaker to conform to the rules governing the dominant term—perhaps, then, the punishment will be harsher. Indeed, according to DiAngelo, this is how it goes:

> White fragility punishes the person giving feedback and presses them back into silence. It also maintains white solidarity—the tacit agreement that we will protect white privilege and not hold each other accountable for our racism. When the individual giving the feedback is a person of color, the charge is "playing the race card," and the consequences of white fragility are much more penalizing.... White fragility functions as a form of bullying: "I am going to make it so miserable for you to confront me—no matter how diplomatically you try to do so—that you will simply back off, give up, and never raise the issue again." (DiAngelo 2018, 125, 112)

Prima facie, White fragility gives us reason to believe that doubled dominant terms are enforced in ways that resemble the enforcement of White ignorance generally. If White fragility is applied systematically to those who use the word form "racism" in ways that conflict with the rules for "racism-D," then use of the doubled dominant term is systematically enforced. If Mills's account of White ignorance is right, then dominant terms in general are systematically enforced.

White fragility is a mechanism that operates at the interpersonal level of oppression; there are also many ways in which pressure to use doubled dominant terms issues from the legal and institutional levels of oppression. We saw in the previous chapter that there are widespread legal and institutional efforts to challenge, undermine, or delegitimize social construction accounts of race or gender. These efforts often also serve to enforce dominant uses of "racism" and other terms related to systemic oppression and/ or to prevent uses of those terms that would challenge dominant ideology. Efforts involving 'critical race theory' in schools are especially interesting in this context. In relevant scholarship, the term "critical race theory" refers to a broad, interdisciplinary intellectual tradition that, among other things, tends to take race to be socially constructed and tends to reveal ways in which laws and institutions can contribute to racial oppression. But in the context of popular and political discussions of education, the term refers, as I said in Chapter 2, to "any educational frameworks that concern institutional racism, the 1619 Project, White privilege, antiracism, or other facets of systemic racial oppression." So understood, it's plausible that political and institutional attempts to prohibit schools from teaching 'critical race theory' serve, in part, to prevent challenges to traditional, individualist uses and understandings of "racism." That is, they use legal and institutional means to enforce the dominant term "racism-D." As noted in the previous chapter, in 2021 alone at least 36 U.S. states adopted or introduced laws or policies that restrict the teaching of "critical race theory," institutional racism, White privilege, or other topics related to systemic racial oppression. Plausibly, these same efforts also enforce dominant racist ideology with regard to other terms that come up in primary and secondary education: as noted above, "savage"· and "civilization" in North American colonization, "men" and "equality" (as applying appropriately only to Whites in the Declaration of Independence), "empty" and "discovered" (as appropriately applied to lands populated by non-Whites prior to European colonization; Mills 2007, 24–28). Legal and institutional efforts surrounding 'critical race theory' are just one example in which legal and institutional processes are marshaled to help enforce dominant terms.

One thing that makes these efforts noteworthy in this context is that they also introduce a doubled dominant term. As a term that refers to a scholarly tradition that reveals systemic, institutional, and legal oppression, "critical race theory" could be useful for revealing oppression. But the aforementioned widespread efforts to discredit this tradition and to enforce dominant terms in education have introduced and tried to popularize another set of rules for using the term. One news source that often reinforces oppressive ideology, Fox News, used the term "critical race theory" only 132 times in 2020 and then used it over 1,800 times from January to July 2021, according to Critical Mention, a media monitoring service (cited in Barr 2021). In typical segments, the news outlet's hosts and their guests warn viewers that 'critical race theory' teaches school students that "America is an oppressive regime that is based on whiteness. And that if you are born with white skin, that you need to be humiliated and ostracized and punished" (Media Matters 2021). On November 3, 2021, after almost a year of using the term this way, Fox News host Tucker Carlson and Brit Hume, Fox's senior political analyst, engaged in a brief discussion of what "critical race theory" refers to—perhaps a modest Burgean dialectic. Hume initially concedes that "technically," critical race theory isn't being taught in schools in the sense that "it's not been handed out as a textbook." But then Hume adds, "But its influence and its tenets are in those schools." Carlson then jokes, "I have never figured out what critical race theory is, to be totally honest, after a year of talking about it." But with a question raised about what the term refers to, Carlson and Hume provide answers. Carlson says, "They're teaching that some races are morally superior to others. That some are inherently sinful, and some are inherently saintly." Hume adds, "It [critical race theory] rests on this idea that racism and racial discrimination permeates the experiences of the citizens of America, that we are inherently and almost incurably racist" (Gillespie 2021). As used on Fox News and elsewhere, the g-rules for applying and explicating the term "critical race theory" are different from those circumscribing the term's scholarly uses. The normative characterizations that elicit assent in the former contexts both reinforce the individualist conception of racism and discredit attempts to reveal systemic and institutional racism. Plausibly, "critical race theory" was introduced as a doubled dominant term partly to help enforce—partly via ideological conditioning in schools—uses of other doubled dominant terms.

There are many other cases and many ways in which use of dominant or oppression-obscuring terms is enforced. Take two examples from the previous chapter. We saw that legal race terms were often stipulated so as to obscure and/or justify oppression. Since the uses of legal terms are enforced in official contexts, official uses of these oppression-obscuring terms was systematically enforced. Similarly, we saw that medical and medical insurance institutions stipulated meanings for terms related to gender dysphoria and gender-affirming care that reinforce binary gender norms and obscure oppression faced by nonbinary persons. These institutions enforced the oppression-obscuring uses of the terms by controlling access to gender-affirming medical care.

How do systems that enforce use of dominant terms enforce semantic deference? To enforce the use of dominant terms is to enforce usage that accords with certain rules regarding a term's appropriate applications and/ or explications. To enforce use of the dominant term "racism-D," for instance, is to enforce a rule that makes it inappropriate to apply the term to institutions, legal systems, or ideologies—to anything other than individuals who harbor animosity toward people by virtue of their race. It enforces a rule that makes it appropriate to explicate the term as appropriately applying to individuals and inappropriately applying to systems, structures, institutions, and so on. These are rules that determine the term's meaning and extension. The systems that enforce the use of dominant terms thus enforce acceptance of s- and g-rules that determine the meanings and extensions of the relevant terms. We saw above that to accept an s- or g-rule governing a term is also to give semantic deference to whoever enacted and/or proposed the rule. Thus, by enforcing the use of dominant terms, White ignorance and other systems shape patterns of semantic deference.

If Mills is right about White ignorance, then racial oppression makes it so that legal, institutional, and interpersonal factors combine to systematically enforce semantic deference to normative characterizations—which determine meanings and extensions—that obscure and/or justify racial oppression. And we saw reasons to think that indeed such semantic deference is systematically enforced for terms that obscure racial oppression, patriarchy, and gender-based oppression. And we saw reasons to think that semantic deference for these terms is systematically enforced at various levels of oppression: legal, institutional, and interpersonal.

This section surveyed three broad ways in which oppression influences patterns of semantic deference: Oppression systematically influences conversational corrections and ranks, and it systematically enforces certain norms of semantic deference. We saw that patterns of semantic deference are influenced by every level of oppression—ideological, legal, institutional, and interpersonal—and we saw reason to think that the influences from some levels are themselves systematic. I propose that these data are best explained by accepting that oppression systematically influences patterns of semantic deference.

3. The de-idealized theory improves upon its predecessor

We saw above that social externalism has two main explanatory goals. (1) It aims to tell us how empirically applicable terms have their meanings and extensions determined; (2) it aims to tell us the meanings and extensions of specific terms. It achieves its aims by appealing to patterns of semantic deference—established in dialectics over meanings and extensions—that lead ultimately to speakers who can elicit assent from all others about (i) what a term picks out in the world and (ii) how best to articulate a term's meaning. In providing their account of (i), these speakers give the term's extension; in providing their account of (ii), they give the term's conventional linguistic meaning. On the idealized account of social externalism, it may be that patterns of semantic deference are influenced by oppression, but it's not necessary to consider it. Presumably, the idea is that such influences are exceptions to the norm, not systematic.

The foregoing section shows otherwise. It says that oppression's influences on semantic deference are systematic. If that's true, then the idealized theory fails to recognize a systematic influence on the social facts that, according to social externalism, determine the meanings and extensions of empirically applicable terms. We should modify the theory. Section 3.1 introduces the needed modifications to account for the influences of oppression. Section 3.2 makes the case that because of this difference, the de-idealized version better serves each of social externalism's main goals. It also considers how the two theories compare with regard to revealing and/or obscuring oppression.

3.1 Ideal and nonideal dialectics

Like objective type externalism, social externalism adopts an idealized social ontology, an idealized cognitive sphere, and an idealized conception of institutions. It assumes that the dialectics that determine meanings and extensions will typically be such that (i) speakers receive semantic deference because they are persuasive in the strict sense and (ii) speakers who determine terms' meanings and extensions will exhibit the greatest competence. With these assumptions, the theory takes it that there is no need to consider or model how oppression might affect the dialectics. It supposes either that oppression doesn't influence the dialectics at all or that its influences are mere deviations from the norm, not systematic. As such, it adopts an idealized social ontology, ignoring how oppressive hierarchies affect semantic deference and normative characterizations. It idealizes institutions, ignoring how laws and institutions shaped by oppression give greater power in the dialectics to people with privilege, enforce normative characterizations that support oppressive ideologies, and reinforce oppressive hierarchies. And it idealizes the cognitive sphere, failing to acknowledge that oppressive influences on semantic deference are rampant and that because oppressive ideology obscures oppression, it makes it more likely that normative characterizations that obscure oppression will be accepted.

In order to de-idealize the theory, we should jettison these two assumptions about the dialectics, (i) and (ii) above. We can still say that the normative characterizations that fix a term's meaning and extension are set by whoever stands at the end of chains of semantic deference regarding the term. We just give up the idea that these speakers will usually be the most competent, and we reject the assumption that they receive semantic deference because they've been persuasive in the strict sense. If it helps to replace these assumptions, we can say that (i) speakers receive semantic deference because they are persuasive in *the broadest sense* and (ii) speakers who determine terms' meanings and extensions *exercise the greatest influence* with regard to the term.

These aren't very substantive claims, but I hope they help orient us toward the empirical matters that will determine who actually receives semantic deference in a given case. On the de-idealized account, for any person that receives semantic deference in the dialectics, it's an empirical question *why* and *how* that person received semantic deference. It could be thanks to persuasion in the strict sense, but we shouldn't assume it. We saw reasons above to think that oppressive influences are often part of the story too, especially when it comes to social kind terms. We can think of *persuasion in the broadest sense* as including one's facility in wielding dominant ideologies, Machiavellian strategizing 'behind the scenes,' being funded by mega-corporations, and anything else that in fact explains why some speaker receives semantic deference.

Similarly, for any person who gives the normative characterizations that fix a term's meaning and extension, it's an empirical question why it's that speaker who's in a position to determine the term's meaning. We shouldn't assume that it's because she exhibits the greatest competence. Instead, we can say simply (and perhaps redundantly) that she exercises the greatest influence with regard to the term. This doesn't offer much explanation for why a speaker determines the term's meaning/extension, though, and that's by design. There are a number of reasons why a speaker might stand at the end of chains of semantic deference for a term, from their relevant expertise to their popularity on social media to their ability to manipulate political figures. If we want to know what these reasons are, we have to look to the circumstances in which the chains of semantic deference were established.

What we've seen in this chapter is that when we look at these circumstances as they concern social kind terms, they're systematically influenced by oppression. Accordingly, we might posit default positions that recognize this. We might say that semantic deference is systematically influenced by oppression, so for any instance in which a person receives semantic deference for a social kind term, it was likely influenced by oppression.

162 NONIDEAL THEORY AND CONTENT EXTERNALISM

As we saw with the de-idealized objective type account, however, this assumption isn't very helpful either. Oppression can influence semantic deference and normative characterizations in manifold ways. If we want to understand what oppression has done to distort patterns of semantic deference and/or normative characterizations for a term, it's nowhere near enough to say simply that one or the other was influenced by oppression. We should try to identify the specific influences, and we should try to say just what their effects on the term's meaning/extension are.

How do we do this? Section 2 demonstrated several unrefined strategies for identifying influences on semantic deference. We can consider what systematic patterns there are in the corrections given and accepted regarding the term's use. Do most people accept corrections from doctors and medical experts regarding the term's applications and explication? That's an empirical question; if the answer is yes, it's a decent indication that doctors and medical experts receive semantic deference for the term. We can ask whether there are some normative characterizations that are more likely to be accepted than others. If so, and if the factors that make those normative characterizations more likely to be accepted hold widely, systematically, or for the most part, that's a defeasible reason to suppose that those normative characterizations give the term's meaning and extension. We can ask whether there are some normative characterizations or patterns of semantic deference that are enforced by systems, institutions, or the law. And so on. These methods can likely be refined and made much more sophisticated— although it's probable that even very sophisticated attempts to identify patterns of semantic deference will deliver only educated guesses. Still, this is better than assuming wrongly that semantic deference just goes to the experts.

Note, however, that deploying these strategies will be little help in correcting the idealized theory if those who deploy them work under the influence of White ignorance or any other systematically produced ignorance of oppression. As noted when discussing de-idealized objective type externalism, a de-idealized theory must be informed by the extensive scholarly literatures on White supremacy, patriarchy, colonialism, hetero-patriarchy, imperialism, misandrogyny, and so on. Thus, social externalists must take steps to disabuse themselves of systematically produced ignorance of oppression. They should become acquainted and keep up with the literatures on systemic oppression.

3.2 The de-idealized theory is superior

If the idealized theory fails to account for a systematic influence on how empirically applicable terms have their meanings and extensions determined, then that theory is inadequate with regard to satisfying its first goal: telling us how empirically applicable terms have their meanings and extensions determined.

Section 2 makes the case that oppression systematically influences semantic deference; since social externalism says that patterns of semantic deference determine what terms' meanings and extensions are determined to be, it should be that oppression systematically influences meanings and extensions on the social externalist view. The idealized theory fails to account for this influence. So it fails to account for a systematic influence on how empirically applicable terms have their meanings and extensions determined, and it is inadequate in satisfying its first goal. It is systematically inaccurate. The de-idealized theory, by contrast, corrects this systematic inaccuracy. If all else is equal, then, the de-idealized theory should serve the first goal better than its idealized counterpart does. Since the only difference between the two theories is that one accounts for the influences of oppression and the other doesn't, all else *is* equal, and we should accept that the de-idealized theory serves the first theoretical goal better than the idealized theory.

Take doubled dominant terms, for instance. We saw that (i) their normative characterizations help obscure oppression, and (ii) deference to their normative characterizations is systematically enforced thanks to oppression. If we adopt the idealized theory for understanding the wide array of doubled dominant terms, then we would fail to recognize systematic influences on the patterns of semantic deference that lead to those who determine their normative characterizations. We would be led to believe that the normative characterizations that obscure and/or justify oppression are accepted because the speakers who offer them are most persuasive on matters of fact, because they can offer precisifications, counterexamples, and so on. We would entirely miss the systematic contributions that oppression makes to the dialectics regarding these terms. That is, the account of how these empirically applicable terms have their meanings and extensions determined would be systematically inaccurate and misleading. Since the de-idealized theory instead enables us to account for these systematic influences, it improves upon its idealized predecessor.

Doubled dominant terms also illustrate how the de-idealized theory better serves social externalism's second goal—namely, to tell us the meanings and extensions of specific terms. For doubled dominant terms, the idealized theory will say that the experts—presumably relevant scholars—on racism, colonialism, patriarchy, and so on, determine their meanings and extensions. While this may be true for *some* uses of terms like "racism" and "flirting," this chapter has shown that it's implausible for the dominant uses. Thus, the idealized theory gives systematically inaccurate accounts of the meanings and extensions of dominant terms and any other terms influenced by systematic oppression. The de-idealized theory corrects these inaccuracies.

We should also consider how the two versions of the theory fare with regard to revealing oppression and its operations. I take it that, all else being equal, a theory that fails to reveal the ways in which oppression influences our terms is less help to us in undermining oppression than is a theory that helps reveal them. We saw above that there are indeed many ways in which oppression influences our terms and the processes that determine their meanings and extensions. The idealized theory fails to reveal these influences, while the de-idealized theory recognizes them by design. Since all else is equal between the idealized and de-idealized theory, but the de-idealized theory helps reveal oppression's influences and the idealized theory doesn't, we should conclude that the de-idealized theory is an improvement on this score.

In addition, by failing to recognize the influences of oppression, the idealized theory plausibly contributes to systematic ignorance of oppression. The idealized theory presents to us a division of linguistic labor that is untouched by oppression, or if there is any oppression, it's an exception to the norm. It thus reflects and serves to entrench the view that our language community is basically just and fair, and any injustices to be found are mere anomalies—anomalies our theories can idealize away without considerable loss.

4. Conclusion

De-idealizing social externalism produces a theory that better serves its goals than the idealized theory does. We saw that systems of oppression influence the processes that, according to social externalism, determine the extensions and meanings of empirically applicable terms. These influences come from various 'levels' of systems of oppression: ideological, legal, institutional, interpersonal, and more. Granted that there are systems of race, gender, and class discrimination in our language community, and given the widespread and multilevel influence that the foregoing has shown them to have on our terms, it's plausible to infer that oppression systematically influences the division of linguistic labor and the meanings and extensions it determines. By idealizing or simplifying away from oppression and its effects, the idealized version of social externalism fails to recognize systematic influences on the meanings and extensions it aims to explain, and it obscures some aspects of systems of oppression.

4

Applications

0. Introduction

Chapter 1 made the case that Western philosophical theories of mind and language have tended to adopt false assumptions about social behavior, interactions, and structure. In particular, the theories idealize away from systemic oppression and its effects. In at least some cases, this idealization makes a theory's descriptions, explanations, and predictions systematically false. In order to address these inaccuracies, we should de-idealize the relevant theories. To de-idealize a theory is to replace its model of society as free of oppression with a model that represents systemic oppression and its effects. Since the systematic inaccuracies in the relevant cases result from inaccurate social models, replacing those models should help correct the inaccurate descriptions, explanations, and predictions.

Chapters 2 and 3 illustrated these points with two versions of content externalism. I made the case that each account is systematically inaccurate because it idealizes away from systemic oppression and its effects, and each theory's purposes would be better served by the de-idealized theory. This chapter sketches some other ways in which these particular de-idealizations might be philosophically useful.

Most obviously, the de-idealized theories can be used to identify the meanings and extensions of terms. The modifications that distinguish the de-idealized externalist theories from their idealized predecessors enable us to account for oppression's influences on the processes that (according to externalists) determine meanings, extensions, and so on. Accordingly, the theories are useful for identifying meanings, extensions, and so on, that have been influenced by oppression. When we appeal to the de-idealized theories, then, we don't assume that our terms have their meanings and extensions determined by reference magnets, by the best empirical research, or by the speakers who are most knowledgeable about relevant parts of the world. Rather, the de-idealized theories draw on scholarship relevant to oppression and enable us to recognize that some terms have their meanings and

Nonideal Theory and Content Externalism. Jeff Engelhardt, Oxford University Press. © Oxford University Press 2024.
DOI: 10.1093/oso/9780197754191.003.0004

extensions determined by social processes that have been influenced by oppression and serve to reinforce it. For those terms, the idealized theories are likely to give us inaccurate accounts of their meanings and extensions, while the de-idealized theories are more accurate. I've suggested that this is true for race and gender terms, terms relating to labor and socioeconomic classes, legal terms, and terms relating to various kinds of oppression, among others. Other works that appeal to content externalism to identify the meaning(s) and/or extension(s) of some term(s) ought to appeal to the de-idealized theories. This requires looking to actual empirical facts about, for example, how ordinary linguistic usage has or hasn't been influenced by relevant empirical research, how relevant research might be influenced by oppression, who receives semantic deference for the term, how oppression might influence patterns of deference for the term, and so on. In addition to correctly identifying the meanings and extensions that are actually determined by externalist processes, works that use the de-idealized theories can also excavate how oppression has influenced the relevant terms.

In the following sections, I'll discuss two further ways in which the de-idealizations developed here might be helpful. First, I'll consider what they might contribute to literature on epistemic injustice and oppression, focusing on hermeneutical injustice. Roughly, hermeneutical injustice is "the injustice of having some significant area of one's social experience obscured from collective understanding" thanks to how oppression has influenced possibilities for collective understanding in one's community (Fricker 2007, 154). I propose that (i) the foregoing de-idealizations give us reason to adopt an expansive conception of hermeneutical injustice, and (ii) if we adopt such an expansive conception, then the arguments in this book should establish that hermeneutical injustice occurs systematically.

Second, I propose that the arguments for the de-idealized theories raise new questions relevant to work on conceptual engineering. "Conceptual engineering" refers to philosophical projects that critically evaluate and propose alterations to the meanings and extensions of a language community's terms.[1] In some works, for instance, Sally Haslanger has proposed that whatever the meaning and extension of the term "woman" actually is, the term *ought* to refer to (roughly) persons who are subordinated on the basis of their

---

[1] As some have noted, it may be that "conceptual engineering" has little to do with concepts (Cappelen 2018, 3–4; Pinder 2021, 144).

168 NONIDEAL THEORY AND CONTENT EXTERNALISM

perceived female role in reproduction (see Haslanger 2000, 39, 42).[2] The proposal is to 'engineer' the term "woman" so that it comes to have the meaning and extension that Haslanger characterizes. Although most conceptual engineers adopt externalism, many have also raised concerns about whether it's plausible that any individuals or groups *could* engineer meanings/extensions if those meanings/extensions are determined in the ways externalism claims they are (Cappelen 2018, 61–71; Koch 2021, 329–332; Pinder 2021). In Section 2, I'll make the case that conceptual engineering is possible for the externalist theories—both idealized and de-idealized—considered in Chapters 2 and 3. For each theory, we have what Steffen Koch calls "collective long-range control" over the processes that determine extensions. Given this sort of control, and given the foregoing arguments that systemic oppression influences what we do with that control, I suggest that several new questions arise in the context of conceptual engineering. For example: Can we engineer meaning-determining processes too? If so, *should* we? If so, how, and what ideals should guide us? I'll motivate these questions and sketch some possible answers before concluding.

1. Epistemic injustice

In arguing that oppression systematically influences the processes that determine externalist meanings and extensions, I've drawn partly from the philosophical literature on epistemic injustice and oppression. At this point, one might ask whether the conclusions of the earlier chapters shed any light on that literature—whether the arguments or conclusions of those chapters tell us anything helpful about epistemic injustice or oppression. Presumably, if oppression systematically influences a community's meanings, extensions, and meaning-determining processes, this would in turn influence epistemic agents in the community and their interrelations. It would be helpful to spell out some of these influences.

Hermeneutical injustice seems particularly apposite here. One way to track how distorted meanings and meaning-making processes affect epistemic agents is to focus on hermeneutical resources. Hermeneutical resources are the various components of a community's practices of interpreting the

---

[2] In Chapter 2, I discuss Haslanger's related argument that when we appeal to externalism, it is revealed that in fact this is what the term "woman" *does* refer to.

world together (Fricker 1999, 206). They include terms, meanings, concepts, theories, standards for evaluating evidence, myths, stereotypes, and more; they include any resources we draw on to interpret the world together. Prima facie, since Chapters 2 and 3 argue that oppression systematically affects terms and their meanings, they show that oppression systematically influences hermeneutical resources.

As developed by Miranda Fricker, hermeneutical injustice occurs when (i) oppression influences the processes that determine hermeneutical resources in a particular way, and then (ii) this influence results in particular wrongs to oppressed epistemic agents. The particular oppressive influence that concerns Fricker is persistent and wide-ranging *hermeneutical marginalization*. A group suffers hermeneutical marginalization when its members are disadvantaged in contributing to hermeneutical resources available for making sense of some significant area of social experience. The particular wrongs occur when oppressed speakers have some significant area of social experience obscured from collective understanding. Thus, hermeneutical injustice is "the injustice of having some significant area of one's social experience obscured from collective understanding owing to persistent and wide-ranging hermeneutical marginalization" (Fricker 2007, 154).

Fricker's lead example of hermeneutical injustice focuses on the hermeneutical resource "sexual harassment."[3] There was a time in the 1970s when the term "sexual harassment" had not yet been developed, and the term's absence from our hermeneutical resources was thanks to women's hermeneutical marginalization. That is, women at the time were marginalized from whatever activities led to the development of hermeneutical resources for making sense of workplace interactions, and this marginalization at least partly explains why those activities didn't produce a term like "sexual harassment." Prima facie, had women been equally included in the activities that develop terms relevant to workplace interactions, their experiences of sexual harassment would have prompted the development of a term that could adequately communicate those experiences. Without the term, however, women were inhibited in their attempts to make experiences of sexual harassment intelligible. Women had a significant area of social experience obscured from collective understanding owing to persistent and wide-ranging hermeneutical marginalization. Women suffered hermeneutical injustice.

---

[3] See Berenstain (2020) for criticism of Fricker's focus on sexual harassment in the context of upper-middle-class White women.

170   NONIDEAL THEORY AND CONTENT EXTERNALISM

In this example, hermeneutical injustice results from a 'gap' or 'lacuna' in collective hermeneutical resources: there is a 'gap' where the resource expressed by "sexual harassment" should be. And, in her initial discussion of hermeneutical injustice, Fricker focuses mostly (but not exclusively) on such 'gaps' in hermeneutical resources (ibid. 150–161). Perhaps for this reason, it is sometimes supposed that on Fricker's view, hermeneutical injustice occurs *only if* (a) a group's hermeneutical marginalization is persistent and wide ranging, (b) this marginalization results in the absence of a hermeneutical resource, and (c) owing to this absence, some member of the marginalized group has a significant area of her social experience obscured from collective understanding. If this is how we think of hermeneutical injustice, then it in fact doesn't seem as though the arguments of Chapters 2 and 3 establish that hermeneutical injustice occurs systematically.

If it were true that hermeneutical injustice occurs only if there are gaps in hermeneutical resources, then an argument for its systematic occurrence should show that such gaps occur systematically.[4] The arguments of Chapters 2 and 3 don't show that, at least not explicitly. They focus on how terms have their paradigmatic applications determined while being developed, how they're refined in scientific research or Burgean dialectics, and how they're taken up by the language community; they don't explicitly show that oppression creates gaps in hermeneutical resources or that it prevents some terms from being developed.

But many scholars have made the case that our conception of hermeneutical injustice shouldn't be limited to cases in which some needed hermeneutical resource is *absent*. Indeed, Fricker herself gives an example in which an agent suffers hermeneutical injustice not because hermeneutical resources are absent but because they're *distorted*: for Edmund White, significant experiences with same-sex attraction are obscured from collective understanding because hermeneutical resources related to homosexuality are distorted by homophobia and heteronormativity (ibid. 163–168). Kristie Dotson and Gaile Pohlhaus Jr. have pointed out that even when a needed hermeneutical resource is available and undistorted by oppression, oppressed speakers can still have their experiences obscured from collective

---

[4] Fricker has motivated the idea that this sort of hermeneutical injustice occurs systematically (Fricker 1999, 208–209). We might follow Arianna Falbo in calling this "negative hermeneutical injustice." In what follows, I'll be concerned with what Falbo calls "positive hermeneutical injustice," in which the presence of hermeneutical resources, not their absence, brings about epistemic wrongs (Falbo 2022, 354). I'll appeal to the earlier chapters in this book to make the case that *positive* hermeneutical injustice occurs systematically.

understanding because when the needed hermeneutical resources are used, those uses are dismissed or silenced (Dotson 2012a, 31; Pohlhaus 2012, 732). Similarly, Rebecca Mason points out that needed hermeneutical resources can be suppressed, especially when they challenge dominant ideology. Katharine Jenkins and Arianna Falbo have both made versions of the case that needed hermeneutical resources can be preempted by resources that obscure oppression (Jenkins 2017; Falbo 2022; see Engelhardt 2019a). These points give us reason to expand our conception of hermeneutical injustice so that it recognizes the many ways in which social experiences can be obscured from collective understanding. That is, we should take it that hermeneutical injustice occurs not only when hermeneutical resources are absent but also when they're preempted, distorted, suppressed, and so on—in any case in which hermeneutical marginalization brings it about that oppressed groups have significant areas of social experience obscured from collective understanding. Since Chapters 2 and 3 show that meanings and extensions are systematically distorted in ways that obscure experiences of oppression, they plausibly show that hermeneutical injustice occurs systematically.

But it must be noted that those arguments don't focus exclusively on hermeneutical marginalization as a cause of distorted hermeneutical resources. For instance, they also point to the influences of oppressive ideology and its institutional, legal, and social enforcement. Perhaps this is a consequence of hermeneutical marginalization, but that's not given or obvious. Thus, if we're to accept that the arguments of the foregoing chapters show that hermeneutical injustice occurs systematically, then we should also expand our conception of what can *bring about* hermeneutical injustice. Our conception should allow that hermeneutical injustice occurs not only thanks to hermeneutical marginalization but also thanks to the influences of oppressive ideology and its enforcement. Indeed, I think we should accept that hermeneutical injustice can result from any cases in which oppression systematically affects hermeneutical resources or the processes that determine them.

This 'expansion' in our conception can be motivated by appealing to Fricker's original discussion of hermeneutical marginalization and injustice. There, Fricker traces hermeneutical injustice to hermeneutical marginalization in order to "find the deeper source of the intuition that there is an epistemic injustice at stake" in her examples. The deeper source of this intuition, she says, is to be found in "the background social conditions that were conducive to the relevant hermeneutical lacuna" (Fricker 2007, 152). What she aims to find is something that makes hermeneutical gaps not only harmful

172 NONIDEAL THEORY AND CONTENT EXTERNALISM

but *wrongful* to those who are epistemically inhibited by them. They could be wrongful, she says, because they're discriminatory or unfair (ibid. 151). She thus appeals to hermeneutical marginalization in the background social conditions that produce relevant hermeneutical gaps because it reveals "the discriminatory nature of hermeneutical injustice" (ibid. 155). Hermeneutical marginalization distorts a community's hermeneutical resources, making it such that they "tend to issue in interpretations of [the excluded group's] social experiences that are biased" (ibid. 155). In sum, then, Fricker says hermeneutical injustice is a result of hermeneutical marginalization because the latter brings it about that a community's hermeneutical resources are discriminatory—in particular, they are distorted such that they obscure the experiences of the marginalized groups.

The foregoing chapters have argued that various features and effects of oppression can bring it about that a community's hermeneutical resources are discriminatory such that they obscure experiences of oppressed groups. Although women and people of color may seem to participate equally in some meaning-making processes, if they have fewer powers and permissions in those processes, and if oppressive ideology pushes those processes toward results that reinforce oppression, then that too can make hermeneutical resources discriminatory (Chapter 2, §2.1.1; Chapter 3, §§2.2–2.4). We saw that ideological, institutional, legal, and social features of systemic oppression can make the meanings and extensions of terms (i.e., hermeneutical resources) so that they obscure experiences of oppression—experiences had by groups burdened by systemic oppression. Prima facie, this is reason to think that these other features of oppression can also play the role that Fricker assigns to hermeneutical marginalization. That is, they can reveal the discriminatory nature of hermeneutical injustice in the background social conditions that produce distorted hermeneutical resources.

Indeed, we might think of some of these 'other' causes of discriminatory hermeneutical resources as different ways of realizing hermeneutical marginalization. Fricker says a group suffers hermeneutical marginalization when its members are disadvantaged in contributing to the hermeneutical resources available for making sense of some significant area of social experience. If members of oppressed groups have fewer conversational powers and permissions, then that is surely a disadvantage in contributing to hermeneutical resources. Similarly, consider what Fricker says about the case of the hermeneutical gap relevant to sexual harassment: "The whole engine of collective social meaning was effectively geared to keeping these obscured experiences out of sight" (Fricker 2007, 153). If that suffices for hermeneutical marginalization, then perhaps it's also hermeneutical marginalization when White ignorance or some oppressive ideology makes it less likely that empirical research and Burgean dialectics will take seriously the experiences of the oppressed (see Chapter 2, §2.2; Chapter 3, §2.4).

If this is right—or if we accept that hermeneutical injustice can result from any of oppression's systematic influences on hermeneutical resources—then, as noted above, the arguments of Chapters 2 and 3 give us reason to think that hermeneutical injustice occurs systematically. We just need reason to think that the distorted meanings and extensions discussed in Chapters 2 and 3 lead to epistemic wrongs.

I think the case that such distortions lead to epistemic wrongs is straightforward. The epistemic wrong in Fricker's paradigmatic cases of hermeneutical injustice is that a speaker has a significant area of social experience obscured from collective understanding thanks to hermeneutical marginalization. On the expanded conception, we can say that someone suffers an epistemic wrong if she has a significant area of social experience obscured from collective understanding thanks to any feature or effect of oppression that makes collective hermeneutical resources discriminatory. The distortions discussed in Chapters 2 and 3 all result from effects of oppression, and they all render collective resources discriminatory by helping obscure systemic oppression. Presumably, since the distortions help obscure oppression, they thereby also obscure experiences of oppression. Assuming that experiences of systemic oppression are significant areas of social experience, the distortions that obscure oppression will obscure a significant area of social experience. Thus, the distortions discussed in Chapters 2 and 3 lead to hermeneutical injustice. And since those chapters make the case that oppression systematically produces the relevant distortions, we should take the arguments of those chapters to establish that hermeneutical injustice occurs systematically.

Summing up the points of the past few pages: We should accept (i) that hermeneutical injustice can occur whenever oppression systematically affects hermeneutical resources or the processes that determine them, (ii) that the presence of oppression-obscuring hermeneutical resources can lead to epistemic wrongs, and (iii) that if we accept (i) and (ii), the arguments of Chapters 2 and 3 make the case that hermeneutical injustice occurs systematically.

2. Externalism and conceptual engineering

Herman Cappelen proposed in 2020 that "conceptual engineering is now a central topic in contemporary philosophy" (Cappelen 2020, 594). "In my lifetime," he continues, "I have never seen interest in a philosophical topic grow with such explosive intensity" (ibid.). One major focus of this work concerns externalist theories. In Cappelen's influential work on conceptual engineering, *Fixing Language*, he adopts an externalist view of meanings and extensions,[5] takes it that conceptual engineering involves changing a term's reference, and accepts that these positions make conceptual engineering extremely difficult: "It's a process that for the most part is out of our control" (Cappelen 2018, 51). Indeed, Cappelen and others have raised the possibility that externalism and conceptual engineering are incompatible (ibid. 51; Koch 2021; Pinder 2021). In this section, I'll first make the case that the externalist theories considered in this book (both idealized and nonidealized) are compatible with the possibility of conceptual engineering—each theory allows for what Steffen Koch calls "collective long-range control." Given this sort of control, I suggest that the arguments for the de-idealized theories raise normative questions relevant to conceptual engineering that concern more than merely what a term's meaning and/or extension ought to be. We should also ask, for instance, How can we make our meaning-making *processes*—not only our meanings—more just? I'll motivate three such questions and sketch possible answers before concluding the chapter and book.

2.1 Is externalist conceptual engineering possible?

Steffen Koch outlines an argument that clarifies the potential incompatibility between externalism and conceptual engineering. He calls it "the externalist challenge."

---

[5] The view Cappelen adopts, however, isn't the same as either of the views discussed here. Rather, he combines elements of each of these views with other externalist views (see Cappelen 2018, 63). Moreover, he says that on his view, "what people say, think, propose, wish and debate about meanings have very little influence on what words mean" (ibid. 59). This is presumably incompatible with the views I've described. On Burge's social externalist view, people *propose* and *debate* normative characterizations, and these have a great influence on what words mean. Likewise for what researchers propose about meanings on Haslanger's objective type externalism.

(1) SE [semantic externalism] is true about many terms of our language, and in particular about those terms typically in the focus of practitioners of CE [conceptual engineering].

(2) If SE is true about a given term t, then it is not within our control to change the meaning of t.

(3) If it is not within our control to change the meaning of t, CE is not applicable to t.

(4) Therefore, CE is not applicable to many terms of our language, and in particular it is not applicable to those terms typically in the focus of practitioners of CE. (Koch 2021, 330–331)

Point (4) follows from (1) to (3). If we accept (2) and (3), then we should accept that conceptual engineering is *not applicable* to those terms for which externalism holds.[6] That is, it should be that we can't engineer the meanings/extensions of terms that have their meanings/extensions determined in the way externalists say. This would be an unwelcome result for both externalists and conceptual engineers. As Koch notes, many of the terms that conceptual engineers focus on seem to be externally determined, so this result would undermine some of the highest-profile projects in conceptual engineering. For externalists, it would presumably be a strike against the view if it were to rule out the very possibility of a kind of project that many take to be possible.

In order to avoid this conclusion, we should reject at least one of (1) to (3). Prima facie, several options are viable. Anyone who doesn't like externalism anyway can of course happily reject (1). Cappelen rejects (3); he takes it that although conceptual engineering is mostly out of our control, we should still keep trying (Cappelen 2018, 72). For our purposes, though, it is most interesting to consider whether we can reject (2). Is it true for the theories I've sketched that if one or the other is true for a term, then it's not within our control to change its meaning?

In fact, it's quite straightforward to show that on the theories I've discussed, we have what Koch calls "collective long-range control" over meanings and extensions. Thus, the theories discussed here are compatible with conceptual engineering.

---

[6] Koch has intentionally left unspecified what it is for conceptual engineering to be "not applicable" to certain cases so that we can fill in different versions, depending on what we take to be justified: "impossible," "not something we should do," and so on. I'm taking "impossible" for the sake of simplicity.

176 NONIDEAL THEORY AND CONTENT EXTERNALISM

Here's how Koch characterizes collective long-range control:

> A group G has long-range control over some condition c iff there is a (set of) series of potentially interrupted actions, to be performed over a potentially significant period of time, that sufficiently many members of G can take that will, with a sufficient degree of likelihood have c as a consequence. (Koch 2021, 339)

As an example, Koch suggests addressing climate change:

> Significantly lowering the carbon dioxide and methane outputs is nothing that an individual can achieve; neither is it something that a collective can achieve by performing a single uninterrupted action.[7] To reach climate goals, we have to take a course of action and perform it over a significant period of time. (Ibid. 339)

On a smaller scale, whenever a committee plans and holds a conference, it exercises collective long-range control. Collectively and often over months or years, the committee members take a series of interrupted actions that have the conference's taking place as a consequence.

Each of the externalist theories we've discussed allows for collective long-range control over meanings and extensions. For social externalism, we engineer the extension or meaning of an empirically applicable term in two steps. First, we develop a normative characterization that would set the term's meaning and/or extension to what we want it to be. Second, we get competent speakers to defer to that characterization (or to those who offer it) such that patterns of semantic deference lead to it. If the normative characterization identifies the term's appropriate applications, then when patterns of deference lead to that characterization, we have engineered the term's extension. If it identifies the term's appropriate explication, then when we collectively defer to that characterization, we have engineered the term's conventional linguistic meaning. Insofar as we as a language community have collective long-range control over a term's normative characterizations and the relevant patterns of deference, we can engineer the meanings and extensions of empirically applicable terms.

---

[7] Thus, no *individual* has control over carbon dioxide and methane outputs, and no collective has *immediate* control over them. Rather, we have only 'long-range' control, and we have it only *as a collective*.

APPLICATIONS   177

Things are more complicated for the objective type theory, but it's plausible that if the theory were true, we would still have considerable control over meanings and extensions. For instance, it allows us to engineer a type term's extension by determining its paradigmatic applications. If we want the term "woman" to include trans women in its extension, for instance, then we can make it so that applications of "woman" to trans women are paradigmatic applications. This makes it so that the term's extension is the most unified, objective type into which these and other paradigms fall. In effect, we can collectively 'choose' which objective type determines a term's extension by engineering the term's paradigmatic applications. In that way, we have collective long-range control over the extensions of objective type terms.

Maybe some would say that in order to have control over the extensions of type terms, we also have to have control over which objective types there are—we need to be able to engineer the objective types into which a term's paradigmatic applications will fall, not just choose among them. In reply, one might object that that would be to engineer *the world*, not our language, but I think we can say more than this for the terms on which Haslanger and I have focused—social kind terms. After all, social kinds—races, genders, classes, and so on—do seem to be within our collective long-range control. Prima facie, it was and is up to us collectively whether or not to maintain a social world with positions like *octoroon*, *child bride*, and *billionaire*. If races, genders, classes, and social kinds generally exist thanks to social arrangements, then presumably which social kinds exist is within our collective long-range control. If so, then even on this more demanding (perhaps too demanding) understanding of conceptual engineering, we can, according to objective type externalism, engineer the extensions of social kind terms.

2.2 Engineering meaning-making *processes*

It seems to be quite straightforward, then, that even the idealized externalist views I've considered are compatible with conceptual engineering. If so, then what, if anything, do the de-idealizations in this book do to advance our understanding of conceptual engineering and/or the relationship between conceptual engineering and externalism? My view is that they raise new questions relevant to conceptual engineering, especially when we consider conceptual engineering in the context of specific accounts of meaning-making. I'll motivate three interrelated clusters of such questions below and sketch possible answers. Among other things, these questions ask, Can we engineer meaning-determining *processes*, not just meanings? If so, how should we do it? How should we think of *ideal* meaning-determining processes?

2.2.1 Can and should we engineer our meaning-making processes? If so, how?

I've argued that oppression systematically influences our meaning-making processes. Chapters 2 and 3 argued that oppression influences the processes that determine the meanings and extensions of our terms; earlier in this chapter, I made the case that this results in systematic hermeneutical injustice. These arguments make it attractive to ask not only whether or not we can engineer the meanings of words but whether we can engineer the processes that determine those meanings. Indeed, if those processes distort our interpretations, help maintain oppression, and contribute to systematic hermeneutical injustice, then presumably if we can engineer them, we ought to. If we ought to, though, then we should figure out *how* they ought to be engineered.

First, *can we* engineer our meaning-making processes? Is it possible? Considerations here are similar to those that arise when asking the analogous question about engineering concepts. Just as the answer about concepts depends on what concepts are, so the answer here depends on just how meanings are determined—it depends on which processes determine meanings and extensions. If terms have their meanings and extensions determined by reference magnetism, there doesn't seem to be much we can do to engineer that process, depending on how, exactly, it works. If just how reference magnetism determines a term's extension is out of our hands—even if *which* reference magnet attracts a term's extension *is* in our control—then it would seem that there's no engineering that meaning-making process. On the externalist processes described here, however, we do seem to have collective long-range control over our meaning-making processes.

For objective type externalism, various important features of its meaning-determining processes are within our collective control over the long-term: who participates in those processes, how empirical research is conducted, and what influences how ordinary speakers respond to that research. Because these processes are complicated and the phases that together determine meanings and extensions can themselves be drawn out over years, decades, or longer, there are complex further questions about which aspects we have control over, which kinds of control we have, and so on. But I take it to be prima facie plausible that we do have collective long-range control over them. Although they're presently influenced by dominant ideology and oppressive hierarchies, and although they produce meanings that obscure oppression, it's within our power to change them.

Similarly for social externalism. Who participates in the dialectics, which practices and ideologies influence them, which patterns of semantic deference they establish, and which speakers and normative characterizations they give deference to are within our collective control. We can collectively, over the long-term, make it so that they don't lead to meanings and extensions that obscure oppression, so that the dialectics aren't distorted by oppressive ideology, by oppressive hierarchies, by oppressive institutions, or by other features of oppression. It's of course quite complicated to figure out how to disentangle our dialectics from the influences of oppression, but the point here is that it is within our collective long-range control.

If we can change our meaning-making processes, *should* we? Above, I took it for granted that if our meaning-making processes are systematically influenced by oppression, and if they systematically produce hermeneutical injustice, then if we can engineer them, we should. But maybe this is mistaken. Maybe those processes are in fact so complicated that we can't be sure what will result from efforts to change them. And maybe they're not so bad as they are; they're not good, of course, but maybe they could be far, far worse. And maybe trying ignorantly to change them is likely to make them worse. Maybe in our ignorance, if we try to change them, it will be a matter of chance whether our attempts make them better or worse, and of all the possible ways they can be, although they're not perfect, they're among the better ways they can be, so attempting to change them is more likely to make them worse. It's as if we've rolled a four, and attempting to engineer the processes is rolling the die again, hoping it'll come up a five or a six. It's more likely that the gamble will give us something worse than we started with.

I don't find this convincing. I think we can identify specific injustices and specific influences of oppression and take steps to address them, and although our efforts might fail or even bring backlash, the odds of making things worse this way aren't even with the odds of improvement. For instance, hermeneutical injustice seems to be rampant and widespread, and there are various proposals about how to address it, from Fricker's account of hermeneutical justice as a virtue of individuals to Elizabeth Anderson's account of

180   NONIDEAL THEORY AND CONTENT EXTERNALISM

structural hermeneutical justice (Fricker 2007; Anderson 2012).[8] It may take time to settle on the best way to address it, and we may never reach complete consensus, but the proposals are all targeted at addressing specific features of meaning-making that lead to hermeneutical injustice, and discussions of the proposals all carefully consider the likely effects. They aren't randomly selected interventions that will simply do *something*, we know not what, to our meaning-making processes. We have good reason to think such targeted efforts will move our processes closer to justice.

If we should change our meaning-making processes, what will it take to make them just? Many possibilities are worth considering. For instance, given that our meaning-making processes have been distorted by oppression for centuries, and given that these distortions have tended to disempower the same groups—women, people of color, colonized peoples, gender-nonbinary persons, poor people—it might be that justice calls for something like semantic reparations. If we somehow stop oppression from influencing our present meaning-making processes and, say, make it so that normative characterizations *really are* determined by the most competent speakers, then that may leave in place the distorting effects of centuries past. It might be that in order to correct the centuries of distortion, we have to adopt a social hierarchy that inverts oppressive social hierarchies, an anti-oppressive ideology, and so on. Or it might be that oppression has so fully influenced our meaning-making processes that any attempts to ameliorate them 'from within' will eventually fail or fall short, and only replacing them with alternative processes can succeed.

One way to make progress on this question, though, is to appeal to Kristie Dotson's distinction between *reducible* and *irreducible* epistemic oppression. Dotson develops several sophisticated ways of distinguishing between the two; I'll focus on one that can be especially useful here.

> Though addressing both forms of epistemic oppression is difficult, I will show that irreducible epistemic oppression is difficult due to features of epistemological systems, [whereas] reducible epistemic oppression is difficult due to socially and historically contingent power relations. *I claim that*

---

[8] Note that although Fricker focuses on hermeneutical justice as an individual virtue, she doesn't claim that cultivating individual virtue will suffice to address hermeneutical injustice. She says, "Shifting the unequal relations of power that create the conditions of hermeneutical injustice (namely, hermeneutical marginalization) takes more than virtuous individual conduct of any kind; it takes group political action for social change" (Fricker 2007, 174). Thanks to an anonymous reviewer for bringing this point and quotation to my attention.

> *a difference between reducible and irreducible epistemic oppression concerns the character of the resistance to change or, in other words, differing causes of inertia.* In reducible epistemic oppression, inertia is primarily caused by social and historically contingent factors, whereas in irreducible epistemic oppression those factors are just the tip of the iceberg. (Dotson 2014, 116–117, original emphasis)

We might put the relevant contrast this way: If a community is beset by *reducible* epistemic oppression, then it can address that epistemic oppression by addressing sociopolitical oppression or injustice in the community. If a community labors under *irreducible* epistemic oppression, then it can't address it merely by addressing sociopolitical oppression or injustice.

Let me give toy examples. Imagine a community in which White men from a certain region are hermeneutically marginalized entirely because and to the extent that they tend to have fewer and worse educational opportunities than White men in other regions do. And suppose that this marginalization leads to systematic gaps in collective hermeneutical resources so that these White men suffer hermeneutical injustice systematically. Here, the relevant White men systematically suffer an epistemic injustice; if we suppose that to suffer an epistemic injustice systematically is to suffer epistemic oppression, then these men are epistemically oppressed (see Fricker 1999, 208). Since the epistemic oppression results entirely from unequal educational opportunities, it can be addressed by addressing that sociopolitical inequality. It may be difficult to address, but if it is, it will be thanks to socially and historically contingent power relations. Those factors won't merely be the tip of the iceberg. In this case, the epistemic oppression suffered is reducible.

However, suppose that poor Black women in the community are also hermeneutically marginalized, and this also leads to systematic hermeneutical injustice, but the causes involved are more complex. The causes might include that poor Black women have fewer and worse educational opportunities, but these are just the tip of the iceberg. There are also pernicious stereotypes of people of color and women that make people dismiss poor Black women as epistemic agents. There are overarching worldviews taught in the schools and represented in popular media that suggest that poor Black women are incapable of having distinctive experiences that, in order to be communicated, might require distinctive hermeneutical resources. Plausibly, the society has built its self-conception—enshrined in its myths, institutions, and laws—partly on such worldviews. As a matter of surviving in a community

182 NONIDEAL THEORY AND CONTENT EXTERNALISM

like this, poor Black women have developed worldviews that clash with the worldviews more popular in the community, but to those who adopt the popular worldviews, this makes it seem as though poor Black women just fail to understand the way the world really is. And so on. In this case, poor Black women systematically suffer an epistemic injustice, and so they are epistemically oppressed. The causes of this epistemic oppression include sociopolitical inequality, but that's not all. It will be difficult to address thanks in part to socially and historically contingent power relations, but those are just some factors among many. The epistemic oppression is irreducible.

Returning to meaning-making processes, we can draw a related distinction. If we use "hermeneutical oppression" to refer to systematic hermeneutical injustice, we can say that the distinction is between reducible and irreducible hermeneutical oppression. One way we might address oppression and/or injustice produced by our meaning-making processes is by addressing sociopolitical features of those meaning-making processes. For instance, suppose it's true that middle- and upper-class White women are systematically excluded from contributing to empirical research that helps determine the extensions of objective type terms mostly because women are excluded from the educational pathways that lead to careers in which empirical research is undertaken. Wealthier White women would thus be systematically excluded from contributing to meaning-making. Prima facie, this results in biased collective hermeneutical resources and hermeneutical oppression in the ways described above. Since, as stipulated, the hermeneutical oppression results mostly from unequal educational opportunities, it can be addressed by addressing that sociopolitical inequality. It may be difficult to address, and if it is, it will be thanks to socially and historically contingent power relations. Those factors won't merely be the tip of the iceberg. Following Dotson's distinction, we might say that the oppression produced by the meaning-making processes in this case is reducible.

Generalizing, we can say that, on the one hand, if oppression produced by meaning-making processes can be addressed mostly by confronting socially and historically contingent power relations that affect *who contributes* to meaning-making and without overhauling meanings or the processes themselves, then the oppression is reducible. On the other hand, if socially and historically contingent power relations that affect who contributes to meaning-making are only the tip of the iceberg and we'll need to overhaul meanings or meaning-making processes themselves, then the oppression is irreducible.

APPLICATIONS 183

In this context, I'll take it that Elizabeth Anderson's proposal for achieving hermeneutical and epistemic justice presumes that hermeneutical oppression is reducible. Anderson says, "The virtue of epistemic justice for institutions is otherwise known as epistemic democracy: universal participation on terms of equality of all inquirers" (Anderson 2012, 172). If this would suffice for hermeneutical justice, then prima facie we can address hermeneutical oppression by integrating our meaning-making processes—that is, by confronting factors relevant to which people have opportunities to contribute to meaning-making. I'll take it that if this strategy were to work, it would have to be that the oppression produced by our meaning-making processes is reducible—it can be ameliorated by addressing who participates in our meaning-making processes.[9]

Anderson motivates her proposal by appeal to her analyses of epistemic injustice. She makes the case that structural epistemic injustice results from the exercise of cognitive biases in contexts of group segregation along the lines of social inequality. If this gets at the fundamental causes of hermeneutical oppression, then epistemic democracy would seem to be an appropriate solution: "If group segregation is the structural ground of the types of epistemic injustice discussed above, then group integration is a structural remedy" (ibid. 171).

Anderson acknowledges that her diagnosis of the causes of structural epistemic injustice is only partial. If the appeal to group segregation goes most of the way to account for oppression in our meaning-making, though, then presumably that oppression is reducible. However, if the diagnosis is partial to the degree that group segregation and other social and historical factors are merely the tip of the iceberg, then we should think that our meaning-making processes produce irreducible oppression.

I won't try to settle the issue here; my goal is just to make the case that when philosophers of language consider engineering concepts, we should also consider whether we can engineer the processes that determine concepts, whether we should, and if so, how that should be done. But let me sketch a reason to think that social and historical factors like group segregation are the tip of the iceberg when it comes to oppressive influences on

[9] Note, however, that this might not be true. It may be that sociopolitical and historical factors are only the tip of the iceberg we need to circumnavigate in order to achieve epistemic democracy in meaning-making processes. If so, then this proposal doesn't presume that we need to address only socially and historically contingent power relations that affect who contributes to meaning-making. Rather, it would take it that the oppression that structures who contributes to meaning-making processes is itself irreducible.

184 NONIDEAL THEORY AND CONTENT EXTERNALISM

our meaning-making processes. If it holds, we should think, pace Anderson, that our meaning-making processes produce irreducible hermeneutical oppression.

You might think that if we don't address the influences of oppressive ideology on our meaning-making processes directly, then it will influence those processes even if they are integrated. We might imagine Burgean dialectics or empirical research into the extensions of type terms with universal, equal epistemic participation, but where the participants nonetheless collectively endorse the sorts of oppression-obscuring meanings described in earlier chapters, where they have developed cognitive habits of blaming and self-blaming victims of structural oppression and ignoring its causes, where few have learned of the community's histories of colonization, genocide, systemic subordination, and so on. If you think integrated meaning-making could be like this, then the following argument might be attractive:

(1) If we achieve epistemic democracy and do nothing else to address oppression produced by our meaning-making processes, the dominant oppressive ideology will still systematically influence those processes.

(2) If the dominant oppressive ideology systematically influences our meaning-making processes, then those processes will systematically produce hermeneutical injustice.

If (1) and (2) are true, then our meaning-making processes will still systematically produce hermeneutical injustice even if we realize epistemic democracy. If epistemic democracy doesn't suffice to address the oppression produced by meaning-making processes, then prima facie that oppression is irreducible.

If our meaning-making processes produce irreducible oppression, then presumably we need to take a more radical approach. Perhaps we need what Nancy Fraser calls a "transformative strategy," a strategy that aims to "correct unjust outcomes precisely by restructuring the underlying generative framework" (Fraser 2003, 74). In this case, the underlying generative framework consists of our meaning-making processes. A transformative strategy would aim to change not only who participates in the meaning-making processes but how they're structured. If they are, as I've argued, systematically influenced by ideological, legal, institutional, and interpersonal levels of oppression, then presumably a transformative strategy would aim to change

APPLICATIONS 185

the underlying framework so as to eradicate or at least minimize those influences.

Michael Doan has developed a transformative strategy for addressing structural epistemic injustice that may suggest a way to address the influences of oppressive ideology noted just above: oppression-obscuring meanings, cognitive habits that ignore structural oppression, and so on. Interestingly, Doan's proposal doesn't seem to involve universal, equal epistemic participation.

Doan proposes that in order to restructure the frameworks that generate structural epistemic injustice, oppressed groups must (i) engage in a collective struggle against the structures that epistemically discredit them and then (ii) create their own terms, values, and conditions for determining credibility (Doan 2018, 15). As I understand it, the struggle serves both to dismantle oppressive structures and to equip the collective with what they'll need to develop epistemically just alternatives. If oppressed groups are 'granted' changes to underlying epistemic structures by prevailing powers—rather than by collective struggle—then the ability to determine how credibility is assessed will "tend to remain in the possession of those in power to bestow on their inferiors in ways they deem appropriate" (Coulthard 2014, 39, cited in Doan 2018, 15). But wresting power through struggle makes it so that "the powerful give something up: in particular, the ability to impose identities on others" (Laden 2007, 278, cited in Doan 2018, 15). Moreover, the struggle to dismantle oppressive structures builds solidarity among the struggling collective as well as intimate, comprehensive knowledge of how oppressive structures disempower, discredit, and so on. These enable the collective to restructure epistemic frameworks in ways that don't reproduce the old oppressions.

Instead of offering an account of what restructured epistemic frameworks would be like, then, Doan tells us who would do the restructuring and why they would be well positioned to do it in ways that correct systematic injustice. On the face of it, this proposal doesn't involve equal epistemic participation: oppressed groups who struggle collectively against injustice play a role in determining the underlying framework and others don't.

As applied to oppression produced by meaning-making processes, this proposal might look like this: In order to restructure the meaning-making processes that generate hermeneutical oppression, oppressed groups must (i) engage in a collective struggle against the processes that oppress them and then (ii) create their own processes for determining terms, meanings, and

186 NONIDEAL THEORY AND CONTENT EXTERNALISM

extensions. If the collective comes out of the struggle with intimate, comprehensive knowledge of how meaning-making processes are affected by and contribute to oppression, then they will presumably know about oppression-obscuring meanings, cognitive habits that ignore structural oppression, and all the other ways that oppression can influence meaning-making process. If the meaning-making processes they create avoid these influences, this would seem to address all or most of the iceberg of hermeneutical oppression, not just the tip.

Although transformative strategies might seem quixotic, there may be some places where they're already being pursued. Doan makes his proposal for an epistemic transformation in the context of efforts to address epistemic injustice relevant to the Detroit and Flint, Michigan, water crises (see Chapter 3, §2.2). Talia Mae Bettcher's accounts of trans activist subcultures in Los Angeles, meanwhile, suggest a struggle to transform meaning-making processes relevant to gender. Bettcher describes the subculture as developing terms, meanings, and meaning-making practices that deliberately conflict with oppressive dominant meanings and meaning-making processes. Dominant meaning-making processes impose identities on trans people, positioning them as "the theorized and researched objects of sexology, psychiatry, and feminist theory" (Bettcher 2009, 98). In the subculture, meaning-making practices make it so that individual trans people are positioned as authoritative not only about which gender terms apply to them but also the *meanings* of any self-applied gender terms (ibid. 109–110; see Bettcher 2012, 247). That is, each person receives semantic deference for any gender terms she applies to herself. Similarly, while dominant meanings marginalize trans people, meanings developed in the subculture center trans experiences. For instance, while the dominant term "woman" doesn't include trans women among its paradigmatic applications, trans women are paradigms for the term used in the subculture. This makes it so that the term used in the subculture has a different extension from the dominant term:

> We end up with an extension of 'woman' [the term in the subculture] different from the [dominant term] that refers to only non-trans women (and to trans women who have just enough features to be argued into the category). (Bettcher 2012, 241)

These altered meanings and restructured meaning-making processes are accompanied by differences in practice and ideology, so that between

APPLICATIONS 187

dominant culture and the subculture, there are "competing visions of gender," different "cultural practices of gender[, and different] relations of these practices to the interpretation of the body and self-presentation" (ibid. 242). Plausibly, what Bettcher describes is a collective that is at once struggling against oppressive meaning-making structures and trying to create replacements. If Doan is right, then this struggle is also deepening the collective's knowledge of how prevailing structures disempower, discredit, and so on, and it's preparing the collective's members to build replacement structures that will be hermeneutically just. Plausibly, they're addressing irreducible hermeneutical oppression.

But this isn't meant to be a fully developed position, and I don't wish to pretend that I've given a fully compelling argument against the epistemic democracy approach. The point is that when we consider conceptual engineering, especially in the context of specific accounts of meaning-making, we should also consider whether the posited meaning-making processes can be engineered, whether they should be, and if so, how. I've given reasons to think that when we do this, the answers aren't obvious, and there are interesting positions to stake out.

2.2.2 What would ideal meaning-making processes be like?

If we can and should engineer our meaning-making processes, it may help to have a model to emulate; it may help to know what *ideal* meaning-making processes would be like. Of course, ideal models of meaning-making will differ depending on what actual meaning-making processes are. If you think that our meaning-making processes involve Burgean dialectics and semantic deference, then the model will involve ideal dialectics and ideal patterns of semantic deference; if you think meanings and extensions are determined by empirical research and public uptake, then the model will have ideal research and uptake. So the specifics of ideal models for meaning-making will vary widely depending on which theory of meaning-making one adopts. And, accordingly, one will face different questions when developing different ideal models for different theories. For instance, the social externalist developing an ideal model might ask whether all conversations among competent speakers should play an equal role in establishing patterns of deference or whether, say, conversations among experts should matter more than others do. This question won't arise for many other theories.

But there are also questions that should be answered when developing any ideal model of meaning-making. For instance, anyone developing such an ideal model will have to make a decision about which ideals to be guided by. What are the ideals that ideal meaning-making processes would realize? Perhaps the traditional, idealized externalist accounts can be thought to realize epistemic ideals (and only epistemic ideals): the best empirical research determines the extensions of objective type terms, and the most competent speakers determine the meanings and extensions of empirically applicable terms. If we're going to consider how our meaning-making processes should be, however, it's worth asking whether there are other ideals we should aim to realize.

In light of the considerations raised in this book, it's particularly worth asking whether our meaning-making processes should aim to realize justice, fairness, equity, or other prima facie non-epistemic ideals. We've seen that epistemic oppression harms persons *qua knowers* and that this is wrong and/or unjust. Prima facie, a system of meaning-making that realizes oppression would be unjust, but it's unclear whether it would thereby fail to satisfy epistemic ideals. If there can be epistemically ideal meaning-making processes that are unjust, unfair, or inequitable, then we do need to decide which ideals should guide us. Should we aim to make our meaning-making processes epistemically ideal, setting aside non-epistemic considerations? Should we strive for just or fair meaning-making processes, perhaps settling for processes that aren't epistemically ideal? Or perhaps one can make the case that realizing just or fair meaning-making processes is necessary for realizing epistemically ideal processes, and so there is no conflict between epistemic and non-epistemic ideals.

As above, I won't try to settle the issue here. Rather, I'll make a brief argument that when developing at least some ideal models of meaning-making, we should be guided in part by non-epistemic ideals. The argument is simple:

[P1] The processes and products of meaning-making can be unjust, unfair, biased, oppressive, and so on.
[P2] If the processes or products of meaning-making can be unjust, unfair, biased, oppressive, and so on, then it is appropriate to evaluate them in light of non-epistemic ideals.
[P3] If it is appropriate to evaluate the processes or products of meaning-making in light of non-epistemic ideals, then, defeasibly, ideal meaning-making processes/products would satisfy non-epistemic ideals.
Therefore:
[C] Ideal meaning-making processes/products would satisfy non-epistemic ideals.

By "the products . . . of meaning-making," I mean the meanings and extensions of terms. As we saw above, a community's collective meanings and extensions can be biased against groups that are hermeneutically marginalized; they can be unjust when they contribute to hermeneutical injustice, and they can be oppressive when they contribute to systematic hermeneutical injustice. So, as P1 says, the products of meaning-making can be biased, unjust, and oppressive. Similarly, meaning-making *processes* can be biased against a group because they exclude its members; they can be unjust because they exclude a group without warrant, and they can be oppressive when they persistently exclude an individual or group and thereby hinder their contributions to meaning-making (see Dotson 2014, 116). P1 strikes me as well established.

I take it that P2 is close to uncontroversial. To say that something is unjust or oppressive is to evaluate it in the light of ideals of justice. To say that something is unfair or biased is to evaluate it in the light of ideals of fairness. If such an evaluation is accurate—that is, if the thing evaluated *is* unjust, oppressive, unfair, or biased—then presumably the evaluation is appropriate. If the evaluation is true, then the burden of proof falls on whoever says that the evaluation, while true, is nonetheless inappropriate. If the processes or products of meaning-making can be unjust, unfair, biased, oppressive, and so on, then it is appropriate to evaluate them in light of ideals of justice and fairness. Prima facie, these are non-epistemic ideals, but I won't argue for this claim. If they are, then P2 is established. But it may well be that epistemically ideal meaning-making processes will necessarily also be just, fair, or unbiased; if so, one might say that these ideals are not fully non-epistemic.

I take it that P3 is also fairly uncontroversial. When we evaluate meaning-making processes and products in light of non-epistemic ideals, we take them as falling short of those ideals to the extent that they fail to realize the ideals. Prima facie, we measure them against models of meaning-making that do realize the non-epistemic ideals. If these evaluations are appropriate, then it's also appropriate that the models (implicitly or explicitly) that are appealed to in the evaluations realize the (non-epistemic) ideals that they do. Since these models realize non-epistemic ideals, then unless there's some conflict with an overriding or defeating ideal, it should be that ideal meaning-making processes/products will satisfy non-epistemic ideals.

This argument is meant to be general, but there's a simpler version that can work for the externalist theories I've discussed in this book. It goes like this: Social processes ought to be just. If social processes ought to be just, then ideal models of social processes ought to model them as just. Meaning-making processes are social processes. Thus, ideal models of meaning-making processes ought to model them as just.

We might try to develop a similar argument for any theory that takes it that social processes determine which terms we have. That is, this argument should apply to any theory that accepts that a community has the terms it does thanks at least in part to social processes—for instance, the processes that made it so that in the 1950s there wasn't yet a well-known English term that referred to what the term "sexual harassment" refers to now. The argument goes like this: Social processes ought to be just. If social processes ought to be just, then ideal models of social processes ought to model them as just. The processes that determine which meanings and extensions a community has (by determining which terms it has) are social processes. Thus, ideal models of processes that determine which meanings and extensions a community has ought to model the processes as just. Models of meaning-making processes are partly constituted by models of processes that determine which meanings and extensions a community has. Thus, ideal models of meaning-making are partly constituted by models that ought to model relevant processes as just. Prima facie, that's enough to say that when we develop ideal models for theories like this, we ought to be at least partly guided by non-epistemic ideals.

If any of these arguments go through, then we should think that when developing at least some ideal models of meaning-making, we should be guided in part by non-epistemic ideals.

But I don't think that this settles things. It could be that realizing ethical ideals is necessary or sufficient for realizing epistemic ideals or vice versa. For instance, one might make the case that epistemic democracy would be both epistemically and ethically optimal. If so, then we could develop ideal models of meaning-making guided only by epistemic ideals, and if we would arrive at epistemic democracy, then we would arrive at an ideal model that realizes relevant non-epistemic ideals.

Moreover, if we must appeal to non-epistemic ideals in developing ideal models of meaning-making, many questions will still remain. If we have to make tradeoffs between epistemic and non-epistemic ideals, how should that be done? Should we aim for epistemic optimality while merely avoiding injustice as best we can? Might the answers to these questions differ for different theories of meaning-making processes?

2.2.3 How should we determine who determines meanings?

The traditional externalist accounts take it that terms have their meanings and extensions determined by the community members who are epistemically best positioned to do so—the best empirical researchers, the most competent speakers. When we accept that our meaning-making processes can be engineered, we seem to accept that we can collectively *decide* who determines meanings and extensions. We can decide who does linguistic labor for which terms. The possibility of making such decisions raises further questions. How should we decide who does linguistic labor for a given term? The considerations of the last section arise again: should we be guided by epistemic or ethical ideals—should we decide on epistemic grounds, on ethical grounds, or in some other way? We can also ask whether we should make the decision on the same grounds for all terms or if it would be better to adopt different guiding ideals for different terms. For instance, maybe we should be guided by epistemic ideals when deciding who determines the extensions of natural kind terms, but when it comes to social and legal terms, we should be guided by ideals of justice. Where these two questions intersect, there are questions about how we should allot linguistic labor for specific terms or specific kinds of term. Should we be guided by epistemic or ethical ideals when deciding who does the linguistic labor for social kind terms? Natural kind terms? Legal terms? This section proposes that some questions of this last type are more difficult than they may first seem.

Start with the intuitive view that for each term, its meaning and extension should be determined by those who are epistemically best positioned with regard to the part(s) of the world picked out by the term's paradigmatic applications (see Hacking 1983, 78; Putnam 1975, 128). Prima facie, chemists are epistemically best positioned with regard to the parts of the world picked out by paradigmatic applications of "water," so chemists should determine the term's meaning and extension. Botanists are epistemically best positioned with regard to the parts of the world picked out by paradigmatic applications of "beech" and "elm," so they should determine the meanings and extensions for those terms. And so on.

What does it look like to apply this approach more broadly? For race and gender terms, we should figure out who is epistemically best positioned with regard to the parts of the world picked out by paradigmatic applications of "woman," "man," "genderqueer," "White," "Asian," "Black," and so on. For "racism," "White supremacy," and "colorism," the meaning and extension should be determined by whoever knows the most about the relevant parts of the world. Similarly for "patriarchy," "sexism," "rape culture," and so on. This strategy is viable so long as (i) there's some part of the world picked out by a term's paradigmatic applications and (ii) some speakers are epistemically best positioned with regard to the relevant part of the world.

There are reasons to worry about this approach. For instance, where a term's paradigms are skewed by oppression, the selection of experts would also be skewed. Take the term "woman." Talia Mae Bettcher says that paradigmatic applications of the term as used in dominant discourse don't include trans women (Bettcher 2012). Prima facie, the term has the paradigmatic applications it does thanks to the influences of dominant gender ideology. Furthermore, many have pointed out that paradigmatic applications of gender terms are influenced by oppressive racial ideology. Angela Davis notes that Black and Indigenous American women were incarcerated in men's prisons in the 19th century, suggesting that White women are more likely to be among the paradigmatic applications of "woman" (Davis 2003, 72). Robin Zheng points out that "Asians as a racialized group are stereotyped as feminine," and "Blacks as a racialized group . . . are stereotyped as masculine," suggesting again that Black women are unlikely to be among the paradigmatic applications of "woman," and that Asian men are unlikely to be among the paradigmatic applications of "man" (Zheng 2016, 405–406). More generally, it's plausible that paradigmatic applications of gender terms tend to pick out middle- or upper-class, young, non-disabled, White, straight, cis people. If these are the paradigms, then if the intuitive approach is to work for "woman," it should be that the people who are epistemically best positioned with regard to middle or upper-class, White, young, non-disabled, straight, cis women are epistemically best positioned with regard to *women* generally. But there's little reason to think that's how it goes—just as there's little reason to think that the people with expertise on tulips are epistemically best positioned with regard to all plants. Similar considerations apply to any terms for which the paradigms have been skewed by oppression. We saw throughout Chapter 2 that this is plausible for a wide variety of terms, including race and gender terms, but also terms related to work, intelligence, and sexual orientation.

Thus, there are reasons to doubt the strategy under consideration for social kind terms. In addition, it's just unworkable for many terms. The problem is that part of what's at issue for some terms is just what their paradigmatic applications are or should be. The strategy for appealing to the epistemically best positioned with regard to the relevant part(s) of the world requires that the term 'already' picks out some determinate part of the world. If we can't appeal to the part of the world picked out by the term's paradigmatic applications because those applications are controversial or unjust, it's unclear how we can identify a determinate part of the world that the term picks out. If we can't do that, we would seem to be unable to identify community members who are epistemically best positioned for the term.

Return to the term "woman." As we saw above, Bettcher proposes that while the *dominant term* "woman" doesn't include trans women in its paradigmatic applications, there's also a term "woman" that's used in trans sub-communities, and the latter term does apply paradigmatically to trans women. Prima facie, this is a kind of community engineering project: the trans sub-community has developed a term that counts trans women as paradigmatic women, thereby ameliorating the influence of transphobia that distorts the dominant term. Now suppose that we as a language community are engineering our meaning-making processes, and we want to decide who should determine the meaning and extension for the term "woman," and suppose that we've committed to the aforementioned intuitive approach: a term's meaning and extension should be determined by those who are epistemically best positioned with regard to the part(s) of the world picked out by the term's paradigmatic applications. But we don't know which part of the world is picked out by the term's paradigmatic applications, and the intuitive approach doesn't give us any way to decide. We could say it's the part picked out by the dominant term or the part picked out by the term engineered in trans sub-communities. Or we could say that there are really two different terms here: each picks out a different part of the world, and each should have its meaning and extension determined by whoever has expertise relevant to the appropriate part of the world. That is, in cases like this, the intuitive approach is inadequate. In order to use it to figure out who should determine the term's meaning and extension, we first have to make a decision that will have a nontrivial effect on the term's meaning and extension.

In addition, we can raise doubts about whether the simple epistemic approach can be adequately supplemented without appeal to non-epistemic considerations. It's doubtful that there are epistemic or empirical grounds for choosing one of the three options described above. The most obvious ways forward, at least, appeal to ethical and political grounds.

Perhaps, then, we can say that the decision about paradigmatic applications in a case like this should itself be made by whoever is

194   NONIDEAL THEORY AND CONTENT EXTERNALISM

epistemically best positioned to make it. Who are they? Maybe it's the people who are experts on *all* the parts of the world that might be picked out by the term "woman"—the people who have expertise with regard to the parts of the world picked out by the dominant term *and* the parts of the world picked out by the term engineered in the trans sub-community. Or maybe it's the people who are experts on *any* of the parts of the world that might be picked out by the term "woman"—the people who have expertise with regard to the parts of the world picked out by the dominant term *or* the parts of the world picked out by the term engineered in the trans sub-community. Or maybe it's people who have expertise in making decisions about terms' paradigmatic applications—conceptual engineers, perhaps? There are many other possibilities besides. Can we decide among *these* possibilities on epistemic grounds? It's doubtful.

I've tried to show that if we're engineering meaning-making processes and we want to decide who should determine a term's meaning and extension, it's not obvious just how we should make the decision or what ideals should guide us. I made the case by appealing to a social kind term "woman." Plausibly, these considerations generalize even to natural kind terms. Recall Joseph LaPorte's discussion of "water," summarized in Chapter 2. Upon the discovery of deuterium oxide, D_2O, in 1931, researchers faced a decision about whether or not to include it in the extension of the term "water." Deuterium is an isotope of hydrogen: while most hydrogen on Earth has only a proton in its nucleus, deuterium has a proton and a neutron. Molecules of D_2O, like molecules of H_2O, have an oxygen atom and two atoms of an element with a single proton in its nucleus. If paradigmatic applications of "water" pick out molecules with an oxygen atom and two atoms of an element with a single proton in its nucleus, then the term is paradigmatically applied to D_2O. If the paradigmatic applications pick out only H_2O, then D_2O isn't among the paradigms. It's possible that the set of experts on H_2O is not identical to the set of experts on both H_2O and D_2O. If the two sets differ, then we would face the difficulties described above even in deciding who should determine the meaning and extension of the term "water."

It seems, then, that at least for many terms, we can't simply appeal to the intuitive epistemic strategy. For some terms, the paradigms are controversial, and perhaps part of what we want 'experts' to do is to decide which are the term's paradigmatic applications. For these terms, we can't decide who the relevant experts are by identifying the people who know the most about the relevant parts of the world. We don't yet know which parts of the world are relevant! There are presumably ways to navigate the difficulties described, but the point of my discussion is just that there are difficulties, and questions about who should perform linguistic labor are more difficult than they may first seem.

The point of the foregoing three sections is that when we consider engineering not just meanings but also the processes that determine them, there arise interesting, distinctive possibilities and substantive questions without obvious answers. There's room for substantive disagreement among those who adopt the same theory of meaning-making processes, and there may be novel insights to be gleaned from discussion among those who adopt different theories. The questions concern justice, the nature and extent of our control over meaning-making processes, and the nature of meaning-making processes themselves. They deserve further consideration.

3. Conclusion

In this chapter, I've illustrated two ways in which the de-idealizations in this book can advance philosophical discussion that isn't solely concerned with the content externalist theories. First, I made the case that the de-idealizations (i) motivate an expanded conception of hermeneutical injustice and (ii) supply an argument for the claim that hermeneutical injustice occurs systematically. Second, I proposed that the arguments for the de-idealized theories raise new questions relevant to work on conceptual engineering— namely, questions about how we might engineer the processes that determine concepts, not just concepts themselves.

In addition to these helpful consequences, the de-idealized theories in Chapters 2 and 3 give us superior alternatives to the traditional content externalist theories. The de-idealized theories deliver more accurate accounts of how meanings and extensions are determined, more accurate accounts of individual meanings and extensions, and better resources for revealing oppression and its effects.

Most generally, the general discussion of de-idealization in Chapter 1 and the examples of de-idealized theories in Chapters 2 and 3 can offer guidance on developing other de-idealized theories. Wherever a theory—in any field—has adopted a social model that ignores systemic oppression, it's plausible (but not guaranteed) that de-idealizing the theory will deliver a theory that is systematically more accurate than its predecessor is.

Bibliography

Abramson, Kate. (2014). Turning up the lights on gaslighting. *Philosophical Perspectives, Ethics, 28*(1): 1–30.

ACLU of Florida. (n.d.). *HB 1557/SB 1834: Harming LGBTQ+ Youth and censoring discussions related to sexual orientation and gender identity in schools.* https://www.acl ufl.org/en/legislation/hb-1557-sb-1834-harming-lgbtq-youth-and-censoring-discussi ons-related-sexual-orientation

Adkins, Karen. C. (2019). Gaslighting by crowd. *Health, Well-Being, and Society, 35*: 75–87.

Alcoff, Linda Martín. (2003). Latino/as, Asian Americans, and the Black-White binary. *Journal of Ethics, 7*(1): 5–27.

Anderson, Elizabeth. (1995). Feminist epistemology: An interpretation and a defense. *Hypatia, 10*(3): 50–84.

Anderson, Elizabeth. (2012). Epistemic justice as a virtue of social institutions. *Social Epistemology, 26*(2): 163–173. http://doi.org/10.1080/02691728.2011.652211

Appiah, K. A., & Gutmann, A. (1996). Race, culture, identity: Misunderstood connections. In *Color conscious: The political morality of race* (pp. 30–105). Princeton, NJ: Princeton University Press.

Austin, J. L. (1962). *How to do things with words.* Oxford: Oxford University Press.

Barnes, Elizabeth. (2020). Gender and gender terms. *Nous, 54*(3): 704–730.

Barr, Jeremy. (2021, June 24). Critical race theory is the hottest topic on Fox News: And it's only getting hotter. *The Washington Post.* https://www.washingtonpost.com/media/ 2021/06/24/critical-race-theory-fox-news

Bartelt, D. W. (2010). Redlining. In R. Hutchison (Ed.), *Encyclopedia of urban studies* (p. 643). Thousand Oaks, CA: Sage.

Beaver, David, & Stanley, Jason. (2019). Toward a non-ideal philosophy of language. *Graduate Faculty Philosophy Journal, 39*(2): 503–547.

Berenstain, Nora. (2020). White feminist gaslighting. *Hypatia, 35*(4): 733–753. https:// doi.org/10.1017/hyp.2020.31

Bettcher, Talia Mae. (2007). Evil deceivers and make-believers: Transphobic violence and the politics of illusion." *Hypatia: A Journal of Feminist Philosophy, 22*(3): 43–65.

Bettcher, Talia Mae. (2009). Trans identities and first-person authority. In Laurie Shrage (Ed.), *You've changed: Sex reassignment and personal identity* (pp. 98–120). Oxford University Press.

Bettcher, Talia Mae. (2012). Trans women and the meaning of "woman." In Nicholas Power, Raja Halwani, & Alan Soble (Eds.), *The philosophy of sex: Contemporary readings* (6th ed.) (pp. 233–250). New York: Rowman & Littlefield.

Bidlack, J., & Jansky, S. (2010). *Stern's introductory plant biology* (12th ed.). New York: McGraw Hill Education.

Blake, John. (2019, February 17). *Stop "Whitesplaining" racism to me.* CNN. https://www. cnn.com/2019/02/17/us/whitesplaining-racism-blake-analysis/index.html

198 BIBLIOGRAPHY

Brownstein, Michael, & Saul, Jennifer (Eds.). (2016). *Implicit bias and philosophy* (Vols. 1–2). Oxford: Oxford University Press.

Burge, T. (1979). Individualism and the mental. In French, P., Euhling, T., & Wettstein, H. (Eds.), *Studies in epistemology: Vol. 4. Midwest studies in philosophy* (pp. 73–121). Minneapolis: University of Minnesota Press.

Burge, T. (1982). Other bodies. In A. Woodfield (Ed.), *Thought and object: Essays on Intentionality* (pp. 97–120). London: Oxford University Press.

Burge, T. (2007). Intellectual norms and the foundations of mind. In *Foundations of Mind: Philosophical Essays* (Vol. 2) (pp. 254–274). Oxford: Clarendon Press.

Burge, T. (1986b). Individualism and psychology. *Philosophical Review, 95*(1): 3–45.

Burge, T. (2007). *Foundations of mind: Philosophical essays* (Vol. 2). Oxford: Clarendon Press.

Cabrera, Cristian Gonzalez. (2020, May). *Supreme court strikes down bigotry in Brazil's schools.* Human Rights Watch. https://www.hrw.org/news/2020/05/19/supreme-court-strikes-down-bigotry-brazils-schools

Campbell, Sue. (2003). *Relational remembering: Rethinking the memory wars.* New York: Rowman & Littlefield.

Cappelen, Herman. (2018). *Fixing language: An essay on the foundations of conceptual engineering.* Oxford: Oxford University Press.

Cappelen, Herman. (2020). Conceptual engineering, topics, metasemantics, and lack of control. *Canadian Journal of Philosophy, 50*(5): 594–605.

Cappelen, Herman, & Dever, Joshua. (2021). On the uselessness of the distinction between ideal and non-ideal theory (at least in the philosophy of language). In Justin Khoo & Rachel Katharine Sterken (Eds.), *The Routledge handbook of social and political philosophy of language* (pp. 91–105). New York: Routledge.

Carbado, Devon W. (2009) Yellow by law. *California Law Review, 3*: 633–692.

Collins, Patricia Hill. (1990). *Black feminist thought: Knowledge, consciousness, and the politics of empowerment.* Boston: Unwin Hyman.

Collins, Patricia Hill. (2015). Intersectionality's definitional dilemmas. *Annual Review of Sociology, 41*: 1–20.

Coulthard, Glen Sean. (2014). *Red skin, White masks: Rejecting the colonial politics of recognition.* Minneapolis: University of Minnesota Press.

Clarke, J. A. (2019). They, them, and theirs. *Harvard Law Review, 132*(3): 894–991.

Davis, A. (2003). *Are prisons obsolete?* New York: Seven Stories Press.

DiAngelo, Robin. (2018). *White fragility.* Boston: Beacon Press.

Diaz-Leon, Esa. (2016). Woman as a politically significant term: A solution to the puzzle. *Hypatia, 31*(2): 245–258.

Doan, Michael. (2017). Epistemic injustice and epistemic redlining. *Ethics and Social Welfare, 11*(2): 177–190.

Doan, Michael. (2018). Resisting structural epistemic injustice. *Feminist Philosophy Quarterly, 4*(4), https://doi.org/10.5206/fpq/2018.4.6230

Doan, Michael, Harbin, Ami, & Howell, Sharon. (2019). Detroit to Flint and back again: Solidarity forever. *Critical Sociology, 45*(1): 63–83.

Dotson, Kristie. (2011). Tracking epistemic violence, tracking practices of silencing. *Hypatia, 26*(2): 236–257.

Dotson, Kristie. (2014). Conceptualizing epistemic oppression. *Social Epistemology, 28*(2): 115–138.

Engelhardt, Jeff. (2019a). Rules, resources, and oppression. *Hypatia, 34*(4): 619–643.

BIBLIOGRAPHY 199

Engelhardt, Jeff. (2019b). Linguistic labor and its division. *Philosophical Studies, 176*(7): 1855–1871.

Engelhardt, Jeff. (2019c). Ideal DoLLs as ideology [Special issue]. *Studia philosophica Estonica, 12*: 44–63.

Engelhardt, Jeff. (2021, December 27). *Misandrogyny and cis gender discomfort. Blog of the APA.* https://blog.apaonline.org/2021/12/27/misandrogyny-and-cisgender-dis comfort/

Engelhardt, Jeff. (2022). The logic of misandrogyny. *Philosophers' Imprint, 22*: 10. https://doi.org/10.3998/phimp.556

Engelhardt, Jeff. (2023). Some reflections on gaslighting and language games. *Feminist Philosophy Quarterly 9*(3). https://ojs.lib.uwo.ca/index.php/fpq/article/view/15077.

Engelhardt, Jeff, & Campbell, Sarah. (2019). False double consciousness. *Journal of Applied Philosophy, 36*(2): 298–312.

Engelhardt, Jeff, & Moran, Molly. (forthcoming). Using the ideal/nonideal distinction in philosophy of language (and elsewhere). *Australasian Journal of Philosophy.*

Falbo, Arianna. (2022). Hermeneutical injustice: Distortion and conceptual aptness. *Hypatia, 37*: 343–363.

Farkas, Katalin. (2003). What is externalism? *Philosophical Studies 112*(3): 187–208.

Ford, Donna Y. (2005). *Intelligence testing and cultural diversity: Pitfalls and promises.* National Research Center on the Gifted and Talented. https://nrcgt.uconn.edu/news letters/winter052/#

Fraser, Nancy. (2003). Social justice in the age of identity politics: Redistribution, recognition, and participation. In *Redistribution or recognition? A political-philosophical exchange* (pp. 7–109). New York: Verso.

Fraser, Nancy, & Honneth, Axel. (2003). *Redistribution or recognition? A political-philosophical exchange.* New York: Verso.

Frasier, M. M., García, J. H., & Passow, A. H. (1995). *A review of assessment issues in gifted education and their implications for identifying gifted minority students* (research monograph 95204) (ED388024). ERIC. https://files.eric.ed.gov/fulltext/ED388024.pdf

Fricker, Miranda. (1999). Epistemic oppression and epistemic privilege. *Canadian Journal of Philosophy, 29*(1, Supplement): 191–210.

Fricker, Miranda. (2007). *Epistemic injustice: Power and the ethics of knowing.* Oxford: Oxford University Press.

Frye, Marilyn. (2000). Oppression. In Lorraine Code (Ed.), *Encyclopedia of feminist theories* (p. 370). New York: Routledge.

Gendler, Tamar Szabó. (2008a). Alief in action (and reaction). *Mind and Language, 23*(5): 552–585.

Gendler, Tamar Szabó. (2008b). Alief and belief [Special issue]. *Journal of Philosophy, 105*(10): 634–663.

Gillespie, B. (2021, November 4). *Brit Hume rips media, left-wing pundits for denying CRT is taught in Virginia schools: "Baloney."* Fox News. https://www.foxnews.com/media/brit-hume-rips-left-pundits-denial-critical-race-theory-virginia-schools

Greenberg, Susan H. (2022, March). *Wyoming senate votes to defund gender and women's studies.* Inside Higher Ed. https://www.insidehighered.com/quicktakes/2022/03/01/wyoming-senate-votes-to-defund-gender-and-women%E2%80%99s-studies

Hacking, Ian. (1983). *Representing and intervening: Introductory topics in the philosophy of natural science.* Cambridge, MA: Cambridge University Press.

200 BIBLIOGRAPHY

Hancock, Ange-Marie. (2007). When multiplication doesn't equal quick addition: Examining intersectionality as a research paradigm. *Perspectives on Politics, 5*(1): 63–79.

Harmon, D. (2002). They won't teach me: The voices of gifted African American inner-city students. *Roeper Review, 24*: 68–75.

Haslanger, Sally. (2000). Gender and race: (What) are they? (What) do we want them to be? *Noûs, 34*(1): 31–55.

Haslanger, Sally. (2005). What are we talking about? The semantics and politics of social kinds. *Hypatia, 20*(4): 10–26.

Haslanger, Sally. (2006). What good are our intuitions: Philosophical analysis and social kinds. *Aristotelian Society Supplementary Volume, 80*(1): 89–118.

Haslanger, Sally. (2008). A social constructionist analysis of race. In Barbara A. Koenig, Sandra Soo-Jin Lee, & Sarah S. Richardson (Eds.), *Revisiting race in a genomic age* (pp. 56–69). New Brunswick, NJ: Rutgers University Press.

Haslanger, Sally. (2012). *Resisting reality: Social construction and social critique.* Oxford: Oxford University Press.

Haslanger, Sally. (2020a). Going on, not in the same way. In Alexis Burgess, Herman Cappelen, & David Plunkett (Eds.), *Conceptual ethics and conceptual engineering* (pp. 230–260). Oxford: Oxford University Press.

Haslanger, Sally. (2020b). How not to change the subject. In Teresa Marques & Asa Wikforss (Eds.), *Shifting concepts: The philosophy and psychology of conceptual variability* (pp. 235–259). Oxford: Oxford University Press.

Huasman, Bernice L. (1995). *Changing sex: Transsexualism, technology, and the idea of gender.* Durham, NC: Duke University Press.

Hornsby, Jennifer. (1993). Speech acts and pornography. *Women's Philosophy Review, 10*: 38–45.

Hornsby, Jennifer. (1995). Disempowered speech. *Philosophical Topics, 23*(2): 127–147.

Hornsby, Jennifer. (2000). Feminism in philosophy of language: communicative speech acts. In M. Fricker & J. Hornsby (Eds.), *The Cambridge companion to feminism in philosophy* (pp. 87–106). Cambridge: Cambridge University Press.

Jacobsen, Anja Skaar. (2006). Review of David Philip Miller, *Discovering water: James Watt, Henry Cavendish and the nineteenth century "water controversy." Minerva, 44*(4): 459–462.

Jenkins, Katharine. (2017). Rape myths and domestic abuse myths as hermeneutical injustices. *Journal of Applied Philosophy, 34*(2): 191–205.

Joyce, James. (1986). *Ulysses.* New York: Random House, Inc.

Keiser, Jessica. (2023). *Non-ideal foundations of language.* New York: Routledge.

Khoo, Justin, & Sterken, Rachel Katharine (Eds.). (2021). *The Routledge handbook of social and political philosophy of language.* New York: Routledge.

Koch, Steffen. (2021). The externalist challenge to conceptual engineering. *Synthese, 198*(1): 327–348.

Koggel, Christine. (2014). Relational remembering and oppression. *Hypatia, 29*(2): 493–508.

Kukla, Quill. (2014). Performative force, convention, and discursive injustice. *Hypatia, 29*(2): 440–457.

Laden, Anthony S. (2007). Reasonable deliberation, constructive power, and the struggle for recognition. In Bert van den Brink & David Owen (Eds.), *Recognition and power: Axel Honneth and the tradition of critical social theory* (pp. 270–289). New York: Cambridge University Press.

Ladd, H. F. (1998). Evidence on discrimination in mortgage lending. *The Journal of Economic Perspectives, 12*(2): 41–62. doi: 10.1257/jep.12.2.41

LaPorte, Joseph. (2004). *Natural kinds and conceptual change.* Cambridge: Cambridge University Press.

Langton, Rae. (1993). Speech acts and unspeakable acts. *Philosophy and Public Affairs, 22*(4): 293–330.

Langton, Rae. (2010). [Review of the book *Epistemic injustice: Power and the ethics of knowing,* by Miranda Fricker]. *Hypatia, 25*(2): 459–464.

Lewis, David. (1979). Scorekeeping in a language game. *Journal of Philosophical Logic, 8*: 339–359.

Logie, C. H., & Rwigema, M.-J. (M2014). "The normative idea of queer is a white person": Understanding perceptions of White privilege among lesbian, bisexual, and queer women of color in Toronto, Canada. *Journal of Lesbian Studies, 18*(2): 174–191.

Manne, Kate. (2019). *Down girl: The logic of misogyny.* Oxford: Oxford University Press.

Martin, Annette. (2021). What is White ignorance? *The Philosophical Quarterly, 71*(4): 864–885.

Martschenko, Daphne O. (2017). *The IQ test wars: Why screening for intelligence is still so controversial.* The Conversation. https://theconversation.com/the-iq-test-wars-why-screening-for-intelligence-is-still-so-controversial-81428

Mason, Rebecca. (2011). Two kinds of unknowing. *Hypatia, 26*(2): 294–307.

May, V. (2015). *Pursuing intersectionality, unsettling dominant imaginaries.* New York: Routledge.

McGowan, Mary Kate. (2004). Conversational exercitives: Something else we do with our words. *Linguistics and Philosophy, 27*(1): 93–111.

McGowan, Mary Kate. (2009). Oppressive speech. *Australasian Journal of Philosophy, 87*(3): 389–407.

McGowan, Mary Kate. (2019). *Just words: On speech and hidden harm.* Oxford: Oxford University Press.

McWeeny, Jennifer. (2016). Varieties of consciousness under oppression: False consciousness, bad faith, double consciousness, and *se faire objet.* In S. West Gurley & Geoff Pfeifer (Eds.), *Phenomenology and the political* (pp. 149–163). Palgrave Macmillan.

McWeeny, Jennifer. (2017). The second sex of consciousness: A new temporality and ontology for Beauvoir's "Becoming a woman." In Bonnie Mann & Martina Ferrari (Eds.), *"On ne naît pas femme: On le deviant . . . "; the life of a sentence* (pp. 231–273). New York: Oxford University Press.

McWeeny, Jennifer. (2021). Feminist philosophy of mind. In Kim Q. Hall & Ásta Sveinsdóttir (Eds.), *Oxford handbook of feminist philosophy* (pp. 169–183). New York: Oxford University Press.

Media Matters. (2021, April 22). Fox contributor: Critical race theory is a "Marxist concept" that will "warp the minds of American children." https://www.mediamatters.org/fox-news/fox-contributor-critical-race-theory-marxist-concept-will-warp-minds-american-children

Medina, Jose. (2012). *The epistemology of resistance.* Oxford: Oxford University Press.

Mills, C. (1997). *The racial contract.* Ithaca, NY: Cornell University Press.

Mills, C. (1998). *Blackness visible.* Ithaca, NY: Cornell University Press.

202 BIBLIOGRAPHY

Mills, C. (2005). Ideal theory as ideology. *Hypatia, 20*(3): 165–184.

Mills, C. (2007). White ignorance. In N. Tuana & S. Sullivan (Eds.), *Race and epistemologies of ignorance* (pp. 11–38). Albany, NY: SUNY Press.

Morgensen, S. L. (2010). Settler homonationalism: Theorizing settler colonialism within queer modernities. *GLQ: A Journal of Lesbian and Gay Studies, 16*(1–2): 105–131.

Mühlebach, Deborah. (2022). Non-ideal philosophy of language. *Inquiry.* DOI: 10.1080/0020174X.2022.2074884.

Park, Shelley. (2017). Polyamory is to polygamy as queer is to barbaric? *Radical Philosophy Review, 20*(2): 297–328.

Perlman, Merrill. (2019, February 18). *"Mansplaining" and its offspring.* Columbia Journalism Review. https://www.cjr.org/language_corner/mansplaining.php

Pinder, Mark. (2021). Conceptual engineering, metasemantic externalism, and speaker-meaning. *Mind, 130*(517): 141–163.

Pohlhaus Jr., Gaile. (2012). "Relational knowing and epistemic injustice: Toward a theory of *willful hermeneutical ignorance.*" *Hypatia, 27*(4): 715–735.

Pohlhaus Jr., Gaile. (2020). Gaslighting and echoing, or why collective epistemic resistance is not a "witch hunt." *Hypatia, 35*(4): 674–686.

Putnam, H. (1975). The Meaning of "meaning." In K. Gunderson (Ed.), *Minnesota studies in the philosophy of science: Vol. 7. Language, mind, and knowledge* (pp. 131–193). Minneapolis: University of Minnesota Press.

Quaranto, A., & Stanley, J. (2021). Propaganda. In Justin Khoo & Rachel Katharine Sterken (Eds.), *The Routledge handbook of social and political philosophy of language* (pp. 125–146). New York: Routledge.

Redden, Elizabeth. (2018, December 4). *Global attack on gender studies.* Inside Higher Ed. https://www.insidehighered.com/news/2018/12/05/gender-studies-scholars-say-field-coming-under-attack-many-countries-around-globe

Rietveld C. A., Esko, T., Davies, G., Pers, T. H., Turley, P., Benyamin, B., Chabris, C. F., Emilsson, V., Johnson, Andrew D., Lee, James J., Leeuw, C. d., Marioni, R. E., Medland, S. E., Miller, Michael B., Rostapshova, Olga, van der Lee, S. J., Vinkhuyzen, A. A. E., Amin, N., Conley, D., Derringer, J. . . . Koellinger, P. D. (2014). Common genetic variants associated with cognitive performance identified using the proxy-phenotype method. *Proceedings of the National Academy of Sciences USA, 111*(38): 13790–13794.

Ruiz, Elena Flores. (2014). "Spectral phenomenologies: Dwelling poetically in professional philosophy." *Hypatia, 29*(1): 196–204.

Saul, Jennifer Mather. (2006). Philosophy analysis and social kinds: Gender and race. *Proceedings of the Aristotelian Society, 80*(1): 119–143.

Schuller, Kyla. (2018). *The biopolitics of feeling: Race, sex, and science in the nineteenth century.* Durham, NC: Duke University Press.

Solnit, Rebecca. (2014). *Men explain things to me.* Chicago: Haymarket Books.

Somerville, Siobhan B. (2000). *Queering the color line: Race and the invention of homosexuality in American culture.* Durham, NC: Duke University Press.

Spade, D. (2006). Mutilating gender. In Susan Stryker & Stephen Whittle (Eds.), *The transgender studies reader* (pp. 315–332). New York: Routledge.

Spelman, Elizabeth. (1988). *Inessential woman.* Boston: Beacon Press.

Stanley, Jason. (2015). *How propaganda works.* Princeton, NJ: Princeton University Press.

Stark, Cynthia A. (2019). Gaslighting, misogyny, and psychological oppression. *Monist, 102*(2): 221–235.

BIBLIOGRAPHY 203

Stoljar, Natalie. (1995). Essence, identity and the concept of woman. *Philosophical Topics*, 23: 261–293.

Stone, Sandy. (1987). The empire strikes back: A posttranssexual manifesto. In Susan Stryker & Stephen Whittle (Eds.), *The transgender studies reader* (pp. 221–235). New York: Routledge.

Tirrell, Lynne. (2012). Genocidal language games. In Ishani Maitra & Mary Kate McGowan (Eds.), *Speech and harm: Controversies over free speech* (pp. 174–221). Oxford University Press.

Tirrell, Lynne. (2018a). Authority and gender: Flipping the F-switch. *Feminist Philosophy Quarterly*, 4(3). https://doi.org/10.5206/fpq/2018.3.5772

Tirrell, Lynne. (2018b). Toxic speech: Inoculations and antidotes. *Southern Journal of Philosophy*, 56(1, Supplement): 116–144.

Townley, Cynthia. (2011). *A defense of ignorance: Its value for knowers and roles in feminist and social epistemologies*. Lanham MD: Rowman & Littlefield.

Ture, Kwame (writing as Stokely Carmichael). (1966, Autumn). Toward black liberation. *Massachusetts Review*, 7(4): 639–651.

Ward, Fred, & Ward, Charlotte. 1996. *Jade*. Bethesda, MD: Gem.

Watson, L. (2020). Gender policing: Comments on *Down girl*. *Philosophy and Phenomenological Research*, 101: 236–241.

Yli-Vakkuri, Juhani, & Hawthorne, John. (2018). *Narrow content*. Oxford: Oxford University Press.

Zheng, R. (2016). Why yellow fever isn't flattering: A case against racial fetishes. *Journal of the American Philosophical Association*, 2(3): 400–419.

Index

For the benefit of digital users, indexed terms that span two pages (e.g., 52–53) may, on occasion, appear on only one of those pages.

assent-eliciting, 108, 109–10, 111, 113, 114–16, 120–21, 122–24, 125–26, 127, 138–39, 147–51, 152, 157–58, 159–60
assent-enforcing, 4–5, 127–28, 150–52, 155
Austinian Exercitives, 118

biological kind terms, 56–57, 87
    See also natural kind terms
Black/White binary, 68–69, 70
Burgean dialectic, 138–39, 149–51, 152, 157–58, 159–61, 170, 172–73, 179, 184, 187
Burgean normative characterizations, 58n.18, 109, 110–11, 112, 125, 127–28, 138–39, 143, 147, 149–50, 155, 157–58, 159, 160–62, 163, 174n.5, 176, 179, 180

Charles Mills, 2, 6–10, 12–13, 14, 16–17, 18–20, 22–23, 27–28, 29–31, 127–28, 133, 152–54, 156, 159
cognitive value, 112–13
collective long-range control, 114–79
comparative anatomy, 74–75, 76, 78, 81–82, 153–54
conceptual engineering, 2, 167–68, 174–75, 176–78, 179, 183–84, 187, 191, 193–95
content externalism
    natural kind externalism, 32–33, 34, 38, 84, 92, 105
    objective type externalism, 32–33, 38, 54, 55, 56–58, 59–60, 61–62, 65, 68, 76–77, 78, 82–84, 87–88, 91, 93–94, 95–96, 99–100, 113, 160, 174n.5, 177, 178–79
    social externalism, 34–36, 100, 101–2, 105, 109, 113–16, 159–60, 163, 164–65, 174n.5, 176, 179, 187
conventional linguistic meaning, 110, 112–13, 114–15, 127, 159–60, 176
conversational challenges, 142–43
    See also conversational corrections

conversational corrections, 127–30, 134, 138–39, 143, 144, 147, 148, 152, 159, 162
    patterns of corrections, 117, 127–29, 141–42, 143, 144, 152, 162
    semantic correction, 130–32, 140–41
conversational moves, 117–18, 119–20, 123, 127–29, 130–32, 140–41, 151–52
    covert exercitives, 117–18, 120
    g-rules, 117–18, 121–22, 121n.8, 124–26, 128–29, 132–33, 134, 144, 151–52, 157–59
    s-rules, 117–18, 120–25, 126, 127, 129–32, 151–52, 158–59
    See also language games
conversational powers, 3–4, 14–15, 21, 95–96, 139–40, 141, 142, 143, 144, 146–47, 172–73
conversational ranks, 117, 126, 139–42, 143, 147, 152, 159
conversational score, 119–20, 121–22, 127–28
critical race theory, 1–2, 89–90, 156–58

de-idealized semantics, 12
division of linguistic labor, 34, 77, 105–6, 115–17, 121–22, 126, 127, 141–42, 143, 147–49, 164–65, 191, 194 95
dominant terms, 90, 153–59, 186, 193–94
    doubled dominant terms, 154–58, 163–64

epistemic deference, 132–33, 134, 138, 144
epistemic injustice, 2, 92, 167–68, 171–72, 181–82, 183, 185–86
epistemology of ignorance, 6–8, 10, 147, 153
    white ignorance, 6–9, 29–30, 152–53, 155–56, 158–59, 162, 172–73

gaslighting, 14–15
gender dysphoria, 65–66, 67, 98, 158
gender identity disorder, 65–66, 67
    binary gender ideology, 65–67, 75–77, 78, 81–82, 87–88, 98, 153–54, 158, 192
    See also gender dysphoria

206 INDEX

heavy water, 47–49, 51, 53–54, 194
Herman Cappelen, 24–26, 27–30, 174, 175
hermeneutical gaps, 170, 171–73, 181
hermeneutical injustice, 167, 168–73, 178, 179–80, 181–83, 184, 189, 195
hermeneutical marginalization, 169–73, 181–82, 189
hermeneutical resources, 168–73, 181–82

ideal theory, 2, 5, 10, 12–14, 29, 31, 93–94
  idealized capacities, 10
  idealized cognitive sphere, 11, 29, 92, 160
  idealized exemplars, 20–22, 23–24, 27–28
  idealized simplifications, 17–20, 23, 95
  idealized social institutions, 11, 29, 92, 160
  idealized social ontology, 10, 11–12, 29, 30–31, 92, 160
impressibility, 80–81
institutional ranks, 143–47, 152
intelligence quotient, 72–74, 98
invested ignorance, 152
irreducible epistemic oppression, 180–82, 183, 184–85

language games, 1–2, 3–4, 19, 21–22, 30–31, 95–96, 141, 142
  entrance transitions, 21, 30–31, 95–96, 141–42, 146–47
legal kinds, 149
linguistic conventions, 1–2, 4–5, 113

manifest concept, 55–56, 61, 82
morphological features, 41–42, 81

natural kind terms, 34, 37–40, 42–43, 46–47, 49, 56, 102–3, 104–5, 109, 191, 194
nonideal theory, 10, 12–14, 15

operative concept, 55–57, 60, 61–63, 64–66, 67–68, 70, 82, 88, 98
oppressive social hierarchies, 2, 10, 42, 60–61, 85, 92–93, 95–96, 115–16, 126, 128–29, 130–32, 133, 143–47, 160, 178–79, 180

race and gender kind terms, 1, 39n.8, 40–41, 42, 49–50, 54–55n.16, 55–57, 59–61, 74, 76–77, 78–79, 81–83, 87–88, 90–91, 92, 97, 98–99, 113–14, 123–24, 153–54, 158, 166–67, 186, 191–92
Racial Contract, 152–53, 155–56
redlining, 135, 138
  epistemic redlining, 135, 136, 138–39
reducible epistemic oppression, 180–81, 182–83
  See also irreducible epistemic oppression

reference magnet, 40–42, 43, 48–49, 71, 84, 97, 166–67, 178
rigid designators, 28
rules of accommodation, 119–20, 121–23, 129–30

Sally Haslanger, 24, 38–42, 49–51, 55–57, 60–61, 83–84, 92, 113–14, 167–68
semantic deference, 35, 85, 106–8, 109–10, 112, 114–18, 120–27, 128–33, 134, 138–39, 140, 143, 144–45, 146, 148, 149–52, 155, 158–62, 163, 166–67, 179, 186, 187
  patterns of deference, 108, 109–10, 114–15, 117, 124–26, 127, 132, 134, 138–39, 141–42, 144–45, 147, 152, 158–60, 163, 166–67, 176, 179, 187
semantic enforcement, 126, 147, 150–52, 155–59
semantic reparations, 180
sentimentalism, 79–82
sexual ambiguity, 74–78, 82
silencing, 12, 128–29, 170–71
social constructionism, 46–47, 49–50, 61, 88–90, 156–57
social kind terms, 32–33, 40–42, 49–50, 54, 55, 56–58, 59–60, 62, 64–65, 70, 71–72, 86, 91–92, 93–94, 95–97, 98–100, 101–2, 105, 113, 161, 177, 191, 194
socioeconomic status, 62–63, 98, 166–67
sociolinguistic state, 34–35, 105, 106, 108
speech act, 22, 30–31, 118
'Splaining, 131n.11, 132n.12
  mansplaining, 128–32, 132n.12
  Whitesplaining, 128–29, 130–32, 132n.12, 133
strong de-idealization, 93–94
systematic subordination, 41–42, 54, 114, 184

tharthritis, 35–36, 102, 103–5, 107–8, 140
transformative strategy, 184–85, 186
transsexual narrative, 65–67
Twin Earth, 34, 35–38, 39–40, 48, 105
  See also natural kind externalism; natural kind terms
Tyler Burge, 35–36, 102–3, 104–5, 108–13, 114, 115–16, 120–21, 122–23, 126, 140, 147–51
type terms, 38–39, 40–41, 42–43, 52, 55, 57, 58–59, 60, 83–85, 92, 177, 182, 184, 187–88
  Floam, 39–41, 42

weak de-idealization, 93–94
white fragility, 155–57

yü, 44–46, 49, 51, 84